Management for Quality Improvement

The Seven New QC Tools

Management for Quality Improvement

THE SEVEN NEW QC TOOLS

Edited by

Shigeru Mizuno

Foreword by Norman Bodek, President
Productivity, Inc.

Productivity Press

Cambridge, Massachusetts and Norwalk, Connecticut

Productivity Press
P.O. Box 3007
Cambridge, MA 02140
(617) 497-5146

Library of Congress Catalog Card Number: 88-042625
ISBN: 0-915299-29-1

Cover design: Bill Stanton
Typeset by Publication Services, Boston, MA
Printed and bound by Maple-Vail Book Manufacturing Group
Printed in the United States of America

Library of Congress Cataloging-in-Publication Data

Management for quality improvement.

Translation of: Kanrisha to sutaffu no shin QC nanatsu-dōgu.
Includes index.
1. Production management — Quality control.
I. Mizuno, Shigeru, 1910- . II. Title.
TS156.K35413   1988   658.5′62   88-42625
ISBN 0-915299-29-1

89 90 91 10 9 8 7 6 5 4 3 2

Contents

Publisher's Foreword

Productivity Press is pleased to present *Management for Quality Improvement: The Seven New QC Tools*. This book introduces the latest advances in tools for quality management—tools that promote a new, more creative and effective approach to quality planning and project management. *The Seven New QC Tools* are used by top executives for strategic planning as well as at all levels of management for planning, goal-setting, and problem-solving.

Most of us are familiar with the original seven tools used in statistical quality control: the cause-and-effect diagram, pareto chart, histogram, check sheet, control chart, bar graph, and scatter diagram. These are used in data-gathering and analysis to solve specific QC problems while total quality control (TQC), as the name implies, involves problem-solving companywide. TQC marshals the skills, information, and efforts of many people—across different departments and over extended periods of time—to address quality problems that go beyond manufacturing into such areas as design, delivery, and service. Total quality control demands that we build quality into our products; the seven new QC tools were designed to help us build quality into every single management decision.

How can we assure quality in planning and management?

Lately, we have been hearing more and more about the hidden "software" of the Japanese — the management techniques that permit the most productive companies to plan and successfully implement wide-ranging and detailed TQC objectives. *The Seven New QC Tools* are at the heart of this management "program for success." Look at almost any Japanese book published in the last ten years on achieving manufacturing excellence: You don't have to understand Japanese to see that these new graphic QC management tools are essential to the Japanese quality improvement effort. Over and over, we see them used both to analyze information and to communicate it graphically and effectively.

For example, the affinity and relations diagrams introduced in this book are widely used during the planning stage to identify problems by organizing diverse forms of verbal data and clarifying complex causal relationships. Once problems are identified, the systematic diagram and the matrix diagram methods facilitate the search for appropriate solutions and organize the steps toward achievement of quality objectives. Finally, the arrow diagram (used in PERT) and the process decision program chart (PDPC) assist in planning and controlling actual implementation.

Our mission at Productivity Press is to make available the ideas and tools that have revolutionized manufacturing in Japan. We are especially proud to introduce the first book dealing with this important new approach to total quality management.

We extend our special thanks to Mrs. Haruko Mitsuaki, Managing Director of JUSE Press, Ltd. (Japanese Union of Scientists and Engineers) for her help and cooperation in bringing this book to America. Thanks also to Connie Dyer who supervised the project and to the staff of Editorial Services of New England, Inc., who helped produce the book.

Norman Bodek

Preface

The meetings of the Society of QC Technique Development, part of the quality control basic course sponsored by the Japanese Federation of Science and Technology, served as the birthplace of this book. The Society's first meeting was held on April 26, 1972. Now, nearly seven years later, it gives us great pleasure to observe the publication of this book. The authors would like to take this opportunity to briefly note the main points of *Seven New QC Tools*.

The general consensus remains that the main objective of company-wide promotion of quality control is achieving the company's business goals through basic reform in the following five areas:

1. *Distinguishing potential future development projects.* Merely finding out what sells and then trying to produce it less expensively than competitors is not enough. Instead, development of technology and systems capable of competing in the world market must be found. It is necessary to transform potential market needs into future development projects.

2. *Planning seriously for the future.* Simply "putting out the fire" once trouble has begun is not sufficient. Anticipating likely trouble spots before problems occur is much more important.

3. *Paying strict attention to processes.* Increased profit is not always an indicator that systems are functioning well. If that were the only criterion, recessions would indicate a poorly operating system. Processes need to be continually evaluated to facilitate needed improvements.

4. *Prioritizing and focusing attention on problems.* Efforts should be made to achieve business objectives within set resource and expense limits. From all the problems a company faces, being able to distinguish those which must be dealt with first is necessary in order to meet the corporate goals.

5. *Focusing attention on the corporate system.* Individuals working alone, even though they are doing their best, cannot compete with a company in which members cooperate in a closely interrelated system.

In order to promote these basic reforms, every employee of a business should be thoroughly familiar with the philosophy of "thinking quality management." The need for managers and staff to "think quality management" has increased dramatically in recent years as a result of the continually changing social and economic atmosphere.

The tools used in the past for quality management include the former seven tools, various statistical methods, experimental design methods, etc. These tools have been used effectively in all fields of company-wide quality control by managers and QC circle members. But now, to meet the demands that social change requires, managers and staff must supplement the traditional tools of quality control with new techniques. This served as the motivating factor when the Society for QC Technique Development was originally organized.

Managers and staff who promote company-wide quality control should not place heavy emphasis only on data collection and analysis. More appropriately, their duty lies in identifying problems, establishing plans, and supporting interdepartmental coordination. Managers and staff must assimilate diverse verbal as well as technical information and develop it into specific plans with innovative flair. The tools they need are those which can be most useful now. Some of these new techniques have already been used in various ways by QC "pioneers" with considerable success. Hoping to promote these new methods, the Society for QC Technique Development presents *Seven New QC Tools*.

Since April of 1972, the Society for QC Technique Development has held monthly study meetings for the purpose of putting together the seven new tools. The Society's activities consisted of identifying and evaluating various management-control techniques used in areas such as operations research (OR) and value engineering (VE), diverse creativity techniques, and other company-wide QC techniques, looking for those which have proven most effective. Each technique was investigated through applications and outcome. In addition, each technique was also tested in companies not affiliated with Society members. *Seven New QC Tools* is based on the cumulative results of these investigations and other experimental trials.

The proposed seven new tools are as follows:

1. Relations diagram
2. KJ method (affinity diagram)
3. Systematic diagram
4. Matrix diagram
5. Matrix data analysis
6. Process decision program chart (PDPC)
7. Arrow diagram

The rationale for designating these techniques as the seven new tools is based on the collective experience of Society members that an outcome is assured and success is heightened when the techniques are applied to all aspects of company-wide quality control in a closely coordinated manner. It is further believed that these techniques in no way contradict or detract from earlier QC techniques; they actually complement each other, thus contributing to the promotion of total quality control.

The Society for QC Technique Development finished its research late in 1976. Starting in January of 1977, the Society devoted itself to the refinement and promotion of its ideas through lectures, conferences, seminars, and symposia. In 1978, the Society invited Mizuno Shigeru, professor at the Tokyo Industrial University and Kondo Yoshio, professor at Kyoto University to act as advisors. For nine months, monthly meetings were held under the name the Research Society for the Seven New QC Tools. These meetings contributed enormously to the development of a conceptual framework and techniques for the *Seven New QC Tools*. At the same time, a large number of applications of these principles began to pour in from various companies.

As our promotional activities progressed, we received many requests from different people in diverse fields asking us to teach more about the theory, use, and application of the seven new tools. In addition, many people whose opinions we value advised us to make this material on the seven new tools more widely available. In response to these demands and this advice, we have compiled the present book.

The book consists of two parts. Part I describes the background and rationale behind the seven new tools, provides an outline of each technique, examines the relationship of each tool to other QC techniques, and discusses the graphic and linguistic basis of the new tools. We also introduce examples of systematic application in policy management, hoping that the reader will be able to grasp fairly quickly not only the main features, but also a few of the different types of applications.

Part II provides a detailed discussion of the conception, construction, and use of each one of the seven new tools. A variety of examples to which these methods can be applied is given so readers will be able to modify and apply the tools to their respective companies and situations. We hope our readers will apply these techniques and inform us of their experiences in order for us to improve on any weak points that might surface.

We gratefully acknowledge the guidance and advice of Professors Mizuno and Kondo. In spite of his busy schedule, Dr. Mizuno agreed to take on the role of editor-in-chief and has written a gracious foreword. He has also been my lifelong mentor, for which I am extremely thankful.

We are indebted to Chizumi Shizuo, professor at Keio University, who provided guidance on relations diagrams to the committee members of the Society, and to the numerous executives and managers of various companies for their encouragement and assistance. Unfortunately, space will not allow all of them to be mentioned here.

Messrs. Aima and Tanaka of the Osaka Office of the Japanese Federation of Science and Technology have made personal sacrifices in supervising the Society for QC Technique Development since its inception in 1977, and they have provided continuing assistance to us. We would like to express our extreme gratitude to them.

Finally, we are indebted to Mr. Tahara and his colleagues at JUSE Press, Ltd. for helping us with the graphs and other complicated tasks inherent in publishing this type of book. It would be impossible to imagine this book ever being completed without the assistance and guidance of these people. We are indeed fortunate to have had their assistance, and accordingly, we are very much indebted to them.

Nayatani Yoshinobu
President
Society for QC Technique Development
April 1979

Contributors (in alphabetical order)

Futami Yoshiji (Osaka Electro-Communication College)

Kato Shoichi (Nippon Paint Co.)

Kurabayashi Mikihiko (Mitsubishi Electric Co.)

Nayatani Yoshinobu (Osaka Electro-Communication College)

Sano Motohiko (Sekisui Chemical Co.)

Yagi Juichi (Mitsubishi Electric Co.)

Introduction

It probably goes without saying that the quality of Japanese products, such as automobiles, home appliances, and cameras, is far above the quality of similar foreign-made products. These products were originally designed and manufactured overseas, but the recent superior quality level of Japanese products has resulted in massive exports, giving rise to a growing chorus of objections to the further expansion of Japanese manufacturing, which supposedly deprives workers in foreign markets of their jobs. Japan's future options appear limited to either manufacturing at foreign plants that draw from the local work force, manufacturing products that do not compete with foreign products, or developing creative new products that meet the needs of foreign markets.

As Dr. Juran pointed out at the International Conference on Quality Control held in October of 1978 in Tokyo, the quality of Japanese products in the 1950s was so poor that it seemed that Japanese industry would not survive unless it could improve its products enough to be able to export to foreign markets. Since that time, Japanese industry's efforts for improved quality control, fueled by survival instincts, have brought about splendid results, and now Japan faces the new challenge of searching in new directions for the future. Even prior to Dr. Juran's comments, the Japanese business sector had been expanding the application of quality control (QC) from traditional areas such as manufacturing to planning, development, and design and even extending it to include postmanufacturing areas such as sales and service. In other words, the scope of quality control had been expanded companywide. As part of these promotion activities, efforts were made to improve the fundamental company culture, for example, through companywide participation in quality control activities from top management to the basic quality control circles.

There are seven traditional tools of quality control, including the well-known pareto chart, the cause-and-effect diagram, and the control chart. These tools have been used as an effective means of analysis and control, and they have contributed significantly to quality improvement. The seven tools have been the favorites of QC staff as well as of QC circle members, largely because the tools are easy to understand. No one doubts that these tools will continue to be used extensively. Quality control has entered a new era of development, however, and there is no room for complacency with the present tools. A new era demands new tools.

In this new era of quality control, the boundaries for QC involvement are limitless: Activities of managers and staff are expanding to include resolving major quality problems, developing products with new levels of quality, and setting up and managing the systems necessary for attaining goals such as these.

Management for Quality Improvement: The Seven New QC Tools is designed to meet the needs of this new QC era. This book is the result of the tireless efforts of Dr. Nayatani and his colleagues with the Kansai QC Leadership Group. Although designation as the "seven new tools" runs the risk of creating what may become a passing fad in facing the new era, and although the designation may impart the impression that the seven new tools are better than the original tools, the seven new tools are new techniques not intended to replace the original tools, but to aid in coping with the problems that the new era poses.

In varying degrees, these tools have been used in other fields; however, they have almost never been used for quality control. It is significant that recognizing the need for these tools in quality control, the Kansai group has named them the seven *new* tools.

Although an editor-in-chief might typically be involved in all the details of a book's production, my role was limited to offering suggestions I felt might be useful based on my experience. I wish to emphasize the limited nature of my contribution, lest I be given any undue credit simply because of the title editor-in-chief.

Management for Quality Improvement presents tools that lend themselves to an approach that is forward-looking. This is worthy of special note. In this sense the new tools may provide momentum for new directions in this new era. The practical examples enhance this potential. The many examples reflect actual applications that were of major importance to the companies involved and which, in fact, were candidates for the respective company's President's award. For reasons of privacy and to prevent premature disclosure, some information and a few names had to be changed. Nonetheless, these tools have great promise and potential for immediate results.

I sincerely hope that the seven new tools will be adopted by managers and staff and will contribute to the establishment of a new era for quality control.

Mizuno Shigeru

A Note on Japanese Names

In Japan, the family name appears first. Thus, the famed inventor of the Toyota production system is known in Japan as Ohno Taiichi, and not Taiichi Ohno as usually written in the West.

In Productivity Press books we try to follow the Japanese practice of placing the surname first, in part, to make the representation of Japanese names uniform but primarily out of common courtesy. The reader therefore will find contributors and authors referred to surname first in the text and notes.

Management for Quality Improvement

The Seven New QC Tools

An Overview of the Seven New Tools for Quality Control

1

Total Quality Control and the Seven New QC Tools

Expanding the promotion of total quality control

The basic objective of total quality control (TQC) consists of bringing about company reforms in the following areas: (1) distinguishing potential future development projects, (2) planning seriously for the future, (3) paying strict attention to processes, (4) prioritizing and focusing attention on problems, and (5) focusing attention on the corporate system. Concerted efforts to improve in these areas make it possible to expect progress in fulfilling corporate duties to society as well as to develop better management systems.

In order to promote and fulfill the basic objectives of total quality control, the following four elements are extremely important:

1. Ideals and viewpoints concerning quality control. What are the company's management goals? What are the company's viewpoints concerning the promotion of total quality control? What is the

company's long-range plan for the promotion of total quality control? What are the social responsibilities connected with the business?

2. Specifying and attaining policy directives. What needs to be done to attain corporate ideals? Are the goals stated clearly? Are expected levels of achievement clearly defined?

3. Establishing management systems. Are the quality assurance system, cost-control system, and other necessary systems in place? Are the systems functioning effectively?

4. Tools for quality control. Are the seven tools for quality control and other statistical methods being utilized? Are new ideals, goals, policies, systems, and QC tools being researched?

Because these four things are interrelated and complement each other, if a company is willing to attempt to implement them effectively, then that company can expect the practical results from their application to soar. Essentially, then, the true purpose in desiring reform in the five areas listed in the first paragraph is for all employees of a company, including managers and staff, to develop the talent of "better thinking." This is exactly the expectation of every business manager and the goal of TQC human-resource development. A wise manager once commented that he wished his employees would bring their minds to work, not just their bodies. From this perspective, the adoption of "thinking total quality control" and "thinking quality management" is necessary for expanding the promotion of total quality control.

The seven new QC tools are presented with the conviction that they are the QC techniques that offer the best methods for the stimulation of thinking.

Background behind "thinking total quality control"

In the past several years, dramatic changes in TQC thinking and promotion have taken place. The major social and economic factors that have helped bring about these changes can be summarized as follows:

Continuation of stable economic growth

Even though an era of stable economic growth started in Japan at the end of the 1973 oil crisis, it is unlikely that a growth rate equivalent to the Jinmu-Iwato boom* will ever be experienced again. It is now necessary to reinforce the business systems that must be adopted in order to maintain stable economic growth.

Shift to multiple economic indicators

In the past, countries were concerned merely with their own economic welfare, but recently, the interrelationships among countries in terms of the world economy have become increasingly evident. Countries have realized that GNP alone does not suffice as an adequate economic indicator. A comprehensive evaluation of industrial activities and economic prosperity must now be made on the basis of a variety of indicators such as business trends within other countries, financial market trends, relative trade balances among countries, and the trade of specific products. Many nations need to reevaluate policies designed to simply boost their own GNP.

When only one indicator was used, the obvious goal was to maximize that indicator's value. Presently, however, with the use of multiple indicators to measure an economy, it is neither feasible nor permissible to obtain the highest values for every indicator. A careful, balanced selection of individual indicator levels must be made in terms of overall merits and demerits. This is an era of searching.

Conservation of energy and resources

After surviving the confusion of the oil crisis, the worldwide availability of energy has stabilized. However, many observers forecast a shortage of oil resources again in the 1980s. Although alternate energy plans, such as the "sunshine plan," the "moonlight plan," and nuclear fusion research geared toward the twenty-first century have

---

*The Jinmu-Iwato boom was a post-World War II period of extreme economic growth for Japan in the 1950s.

been promoted, the prospects for a practical substitute for petroleum
are not bright.

While exhaustion of the world oil supply during this generation
may not be realistic, our obligation to future generations to pass on
all the natural resources possible remains. These considerations
highlight the task of businesses to conserve resources in product
design and production.

Environmental and public hazards

Viewed from the standpoint of improving the quality of life and
respecting human dignity, protecting the environment and avoiding situations that might prove hazardous to the public become
increasingly important. Systems for the production, delivery, circu-
lation, use, and disposal of products must be evaluated to confirm
that they have no adverse effects on the environment. These are
important constraints that relate to all business activities.

Product liability

Judging from recent trends in the United States and the rising
awareness of human rights in Japan, the importance of product
liability will continue to increase. This also will act as a large industrial constraint, along with the environmental and public concerns
just mentioned.

Awareness of customer needs

Despite the various constraints under which businesses must operate, consumers are demanding increasingly sophisticated and ad-
vanced products that complement their diverse lifestyles and values. Businesses that want to remain competitive both nationally and
internationally, must research and develop products that will maintain
a certain level of exportability despite the reduced export competitive-
ness of Japan caused by the present yen-dollar exchange rate.

Reduced prospects for technology import

Postwar economic development of Japan was based on the import of new technologies from foreign countries. The present situation is drastically different from the 1940s: New and radical technologies are emerging constantly. Fewer technological "seeds" can be developed into giant industries, the foreign ideas that might become these "seeds" are next to impossible to import. The advancement of developing countries has narrowed the technological gap in a number of industries and products. These technological constraints further emphasize the need to promote total quality control for the development and refinement of new products.

A new era for quality

The "new era for quality"[1] proposed by Professor Mizuno could have been anticipated if thoughtful consideration had been given to the economic and social factors discussed above. The first requirement of the new era for quality is the creation of an "added value" over and above consumer needs. It is necessary to first uncover latent customer needs and then, in response, not only meet those needs, but also to discover an added value that will surpass them. The new era for quality expects the generation of new ideas.

The second requirement inherent in the new era for quality is the ability to cope with varying limitations, hopefully without missing any necessary items: In other words, the key is to prevent failure in meeting customer needs. The constraints businesses must work around are numerous: environmental pollution, product liability, efficient use of resources, cost, and productivity, just to mention a few. In the future, business activities will undoubtedly be subject to additional constraints and limitations. In this sense, as Professor Kigure proposed, the major task facing businesses is to shift "from defensive QC to offensive QC."[2] It is important to solidify defenses against constraining factors while at the same time emphasizing an aggressive posture toward new product development.

The book *Quality Deployment*, edited by Professors Mizuno and Akao, represents an outstanding achievement as a quality system for new product development, responding to the needs of the new era.[3] Hopefully, a wide adoption of this system in industry will help businesses to march through this new era for quality.

This is the true objective of the *Seven New QC Tools*.

Highlights of "thinking total quality control"

Based on the background presented earlier, when the four elements of total quality control are applied company-wide in a comprehensive manner, the roles of managers and staff increase dramatically in company reform. In order to promote "thinking total quality control," seven items that highlight this way of thinking are listed and explained below.[4]

Conducting multidimensional evaluations

Managers and staff should always keep multidimensional characteristics and their evaluation in mind, even when pursuing a single objective. In the early stages of importing total quality control, concern frequently centered on reducing the rate of defective products or reducing costs. Now, however, desired outcomes would be difficult to obtain if quality is pursued as a single issue. Disruptions in other related functions often accompany any improvement in quality. Simply put, improvement in one function must be carried out while at the same time considering the constraints it might place on other functions and characteristics.

Thinking that "cost is cost and quality is quality" is no longer sufficient; these concepts are not exclusive of each other. An awareness of functional interrelationships is necessary: "Does the lowered cost bring about irregularities in quality?" "Is there a firm basis to back up the guarantee for product longevity?" Unless one is fully prepared to answer related questions, there will be unexpected claims later. The pressures associated with lowering costs have often created unexpected accidents after shipping that ultimately brought near disasters to businesses. Thus multidimensional evaluation refers to looking at a problem in its context and totality.

Eliminating the phrase "recurrence prevention"

An important point in the current promotion of total quality control is forbidding the use of the phrase "recurrence prevention." Promotion should proceed with the firm conviction that failure is unacceptable from the beginning. Previously, the phrase "recurrence prevention" was used frequently, and it was sometimes said that "in quality control, the first mistake is acceptable, although its recurrence is not." However, this is an era in which even an initial failure or mistake in the design or development of a new product is simply not permissible. It is crucial to deliver a product to the market as planned and therefore to ring up sales as planned.

Such failures as lower profit because of higher production costs and unanticipated claims after shipment cannot be afforded. When faced with the problem of environmental pollution or product liability, it is totally inconceivable for anyone to maintain the naive posture that "It was a design mistake. Quality control now only has to prevent it from recurring."

In this era, failure is unacceptable from the very beginning. Merely "putting out the fire once it has started" is not sufficient. In the promotion of total quality control, preventing mistakes is necessary. Moreover, to prevent mistakes and errors during the promotion of total quality control, it is important to list all the correlated items.

Consider this issue from the standpoint of problem solving. A current problem causing a malfunction must be corrected as soon as possible. A secondary problem, however, is a situation which, left unattended, has the potential to create malfunctions in the future: It is necessary to be able to predict such malfunctions and introduce corrective measures now. The former type of problem is sometimes called an "emergent" problem; the latter is known as a "prognostic/predictive" problem.[5] Stating that recurrence prevention is not a permissible approach to quality control reflects an emphasis on the predictive type of problem.

Specifying a desirable condition

Understanding the statement "Specify a desirable condition and move toward achieving it" is easier than actually dealing with a situation within the framework of a predicted problem. There are several reasons for this. First, after talking with someone, a person may admit that there is a problem and strive toward a desirable condition. Second, in improving predictive ability, experience shows that thinking in terms of striving for a more desirable condition is more likely to produce interesting and creative ideas than talking only in terms of the problem.

In striving for a "desirable condition," it is important to note that desirable conditions, products, and systems all vary from one type of business to another. Even within a specific type of business, desirable conditions may differ depending on the size and scope of the business. To illustrate this point, consider that some taxis in metropolitan areas are painted yellow or orange, while others have sober colors such as black. Both companies believe they have the right color.

Further, an interview was held with the executive officer of a small taxi company that uses a bright color for its taxis. This company prefers a bright color because it is easier to detect from a distance. Since it changed from black to a brighter color, revenues have increased. Because there is a greater ability to identify the company, the drivers are less likely to refuse customers, and this has resulted in a reduction of complaints. As secondary effects, job stability among drivers is up and their attitudes toward customers have improved as well. The executive concluded that choosing the bright color has been very beneficial. There are some drawbacks, however. For example, the bright-colored taxis cannot be used for funeral services.

Another larger company prefers black because its cars are often hired by large corporate customers and the sober color is more fitting to their tastes and status. Owing to the large number of cars in operation, there is a high risk of minor accidents. In cases of minor accidents, the sober color makes the taxis indistinguishable from private automobiles, which is to the company's advantage. However, the sober color shows dust and dirt easily. For these reasons, these cars are probably not as suitable for operating as taxis.

Although the preceding example is mundane, it illustrates the importance of "thinking total quality control." In other words, this is an era in which simply copying other companies' quality control will not suffice. Each business must establish its own "desirable condition."

As is clear from the preceding example, a "desirable condition" may not be the best one for every evaluative dimension. Both advantages (merits) and disadvantages (demerits) must be considered, various means of achieving the objectives must be compared, and the solution that maximizes merits over demerits must be selected. This is similar to the importance of multidimensional evaluation explained earlier.

Making a truly prioritized effort

As described earlier, total quality control entails the task of prioritizing efforts. Probably foremost in prioritizing efforts is the allocation of resources. This refers to allocating the limited resources of a nation or a business (i.e., human, material, and financial resources, as well as facilities) to those objectives with the most merits. It is particularly important to place emphasis on investment in research and development.

Although the phrase "prioritized effort" has long been emphasized in the field of quality control, the reality of TQC promotion in the business world reveals that the principle of overall harmony, a typical Japanese trait, prevails. In order to determine the relative importance of suggestions made by the subordinates, it is critical for the manager to be decisive and able to distinguish the important from the unimportant.

The second task of the prioritized effort is to assign relative importance to the various steps and processes in promoting reform. Generally speaking, a single project is comprised of many tasks that have to be implemented. In evaluating a project after the passage of a certain amount of time, to cite an extreme example, one may find that 95 percent of the tasks have been completed, but that the overall result is nil. Upon closer examination of such a case, the remaining 5 percent of tasks frequently are discovered to be technically quite difficult. There is a natural human tendency to start with easy tasks and postpone difficult ones. Although the number of tasks to be implemented may be large, usually it is only a small portion that poses any real difficulty. Yet without executing the difficult tasks, the desired objective can never be obtained. In executing long-range plans, an efficient manager identifies the difficult tasks at the beginning and works gradually toward completing them.

For this reason, it is necessary at the inception of a project to list all items or tasks that need execution and to assess the level of ease or difficulty of each by attaching as much technical detail as possible.

Encouraging system-wide promotion

The system-wide promotion of total quality control requires that every member of a company or team cooperate fully. A system functions like a human body. The entire organization of a business should act in organic harmony. For this purpose, it is essential that the function of information transmission, like the brain function in the human body, be performed faithfully. Professor Oba proposed a method called the "theory of QC hearing"[6] which articulates the need for each project director to develop and maintain a close relationship with other project directors or counterparts. It is an excellent idea that attempts to get everyone who is involved in a project to the same level of awareness and knowledge.

In addition to transmitting simple information, it is necessary to study information pertaining to other fields or projects, including their complex language, so that information can be transmitted accurately. For example, suppose that a business planning department's top directive is to "secure x new users." Under such circumstances, those in charge of field operations would naturally endeavor to secure the designated number of new users. In the process of securing new users, however, it often happens that old users are lost to competitors. Unknown to the directive's audience, though, the idea of securing a designated number of users presumed certain unstated preconditions. Among these, for example, may be that the existing users be retained or that limits be set on the types of orders received, the suggested price, or the quantity per customer. Directives usually do not spell out such details, but managers and staff are expected to grasp the underlying presumptions, as well as how they relate to other departments or projects, rather than simply to carry out the directives blindly and literally.

In the example just described, the desired result can be obtained only when there is system-wide cooperation among the planning department, the plant, and the field office. In gaining the cooperation of other departments, it is not sufficient to resort only to official channels. It is nothing more than an excuse if one has to say, "We have talked to them, but they just wouldn't do it." It is clear that unless the related sectors are mobilized, any system-wide reform is hard to achieve. What is important here is to think of ways that encourage one's counterparts to *want* to work. Helpful in this connection are ideas that motivate one's counterparts and provide incentives.

The education of subordinates emerges as an important problem in executing system-wide management. Managers and staff need to meet with subordinates at least once a month to share thoughts, perspectives, and progress. In other words, it is necessary to lead one's subordinates with words and theory and at the same time let them possess the same information. Here the problem of transmitting complex information in a way that is simple to understand is encountered.

Actively making changes

One of the important ideas permeating the present concept of total quality control is that of change. In order to create products with "added value" and to avoid not meeting consumers' needs, previous methods will undoubtedly have to be changed somewhat. Basically, change is the essence of reform. No one could reasonably suggest that drastic reductions in a product's fraction defective rate or a significant lowering of cost could occur if, as in the past, the same employees in the same organization use the same system with the same equipment and the same methods. At any rate, change is critical. It would not be overstating the point to say that managers and staff need only to think of "What should we change?"

Change is important not only in terms of results, but it is also necessary in terms of avoiding becoming entrenched in routines: Through change, people are able to avoid job stagnation. People often tend to become invigorated when they join a new company, change job locations, or get promoted. Managers and staff should constantly introduce changes in their TQC activities to prevent the organization from becoming lifeless and stale.

Looking at the other side, however, failures also tend to occur at the time of change. Trouble might occur when systems change or operators change as a result of personnel transfers, yet without constant change, improvement and reform are hopeless. This is a time when companies cannot afford not to change. In this new era for quality, one of the prime responsibilities of managers and staff is to actively promote change based on a balanced grasp of the various merits and demerits entailed in that change.

Anticipating and predicting the future

As an idea about adjusting to the new era for quality, one last comment is necessary: A smooth and quick rotation through the PDCA (plan, do, check, act) cycle is invaluable. Stated another way, it is better not to waste time rotating through PDCA cycles that will be useless. Therefore, it is important to try to anticipate and predict the expected outcomes. In the future promotion of total quality control, managers and staff will be required to be able to predict and be prepared for future events.

Concerning the problem of prediction, even QC specialists have voiced their concern about whether it is possible to "predict what has not yet happened." However, such predictions are made unconsciously every day. When people play "Go" or chess, they anticipate what their opponents will do during the next two or three moves. Players will at least predict what their opponents will do in response to this move or that move. Professional players can think through various contingency outcomes for a number of moves ahead. QC personnel are professionals in design, production, research, development, business operations, and sales. Unlike the situation when amateurs play "Go" or chess, QC personnel should be able to consider a multitude of factors and contingencies and take action with a certain degree of seasoned prediction. This opinion probably results from the belief that predictive potential has not been fully utilized.

In order to be able to predict, one must be able to assimilate the relationships between potentials, such as verbal information and likely outcome.

QC techniques designed to encourage thinking

As discussed in the preceding section, riding through the new era for quality requires the promotion of total quality control with a new frame of mind and a new perspective. Therefore, it is necessary to introduce new QC techniques which are appropriate to the demands of the new era.

The seven well-known tools of quality control[7] are as follows:

- Cause-and-effect diagram
- Pareto chart
- Checksheet
- Histogram
- Scatter diagram
- Control chart
- Various graphs

These constitute fields of company-wide QC activities. Results from using these tools have proven to be most effective when they are used comprehensively throughout companies, from managers to TQC circle members. However, managers and staff need special techniques in order to utilize the tools mentioned here and elsewhere.

In addition to the seven tools listed above, the tools used in quality control include a number of statistical methods, experimental design methods, and multivariate analysis methods. These tools, however, are used for obtaining data and analyzing available data after the objectives of the investigation have been decided. Although statistical quality control is based on these methods, as a practical matter, not all managers and staff can become proficient enough with statistics to use these tools.

Hopefully, managers and staff will consider the complex relationships among technical details and between departments and then organize and systematize this information as they initiate the phases of their QC activities. In order to accomplish this, managers and staff need new tools to help sort the confusing elements, uncover the underlying problems, and devise a measure of the extent of implementation. This need has long been recognized by authorities in the field of quality control, and the development of a partial solution has been advocated for some time now (see the first section of Chap. 3). It is important to think about how to treat previous problems rather than to simply gather more data. Of the original seven tools, only the cause-and-effect diagram appears to accommodate this need. However, expectations for the seven new tools run high.

Basically, there are seven desirable prerequisites for any tools or methods designed to be of use in the new era. The following subsections illustrate these prerequisites.

The ability to process verbal information

In general, the problems confronting managers and staff involve more verbal data. This is usually data involving both in-house and out-of-house matters, i.e., dealing with technological as well as market information. Managers and staff have a high-level ability to make use of this information. In the promotion of total quality control, it is important to transform language data into either graphs or some other quantitative form so that everyone in the company has equal access to it.

In other words it is hoped that any new techniques will be useful in helping managers and staff consolidate complex and varied verbal information. Such new techniques do not necessarily have to be quantitative or computational. In fact, if possible, computational techniques should be avoided. Rather, techniques that develop and express complex phenomena in terms of graphs and diagrams and uncover underlying problems clearly are sought. An appropriate new technique would be able to identify and adjust problematic elements when quantitative data do not exist, and it would specify the types of quantitative data needed for future analyses.

The ability to generate ideas

In the future, no one could contest the need to consistently promote total quality control using new ideas (see preceding section). New techniques should generate new ideas. Therefore, with this in mind, two needs surface.

The first is that any new technique should make managers and staff feel that they are utilizing their intellectual capabilities. The generation of ideas starts with the use of brainpower. In addition to this "thinking" process, thoughts and ideas need to be expressed in clear statements and diagrams. Through repetition of this process, ideas are transformed into sentences and diagrams that can serve as the starting point for ensuing rounds in the thinking process.

Methods of generating ideas also vary greatly from person to person. New techniques also should be capable of yielding results in proportion to the user's ability. In addition, new techniques should have some positive effects by virtue of having been utilized. For example, anyone can construct a cause-and-effect diagram, brainstorming and listing ideas to be sorted according to their relative importance. However, frequently it is merely the drawing of this cause-and-effect diagram that contributes to a better articulation of problems.

The second need for new techniques in terms of the generation of ideas is that there should be an orderly procedure for the construction and use of cause-and-effect diagrams, while at the same time leaving room for improvement. Because there are numerous ways of drawing these diagrams, any method should be flexible enough to accommodate new ways to utilize these diagrams.

The ability to complete tasks

When a directive is received to proceed with or complete a certain task, one should take into consideration the directive's relationship with other tasks. Any new technique brought to bear should incorporate ways to dissect tasks and assist in forming a step-by-step work schedule.

One of the important aspects of completing a task closely relates to the problem of prediction (see the preceding section). For example,

QC activities in research and development aim at completing constantly changing themes and objectives. An important element here is the establishment of a hypothesis designed for problem resolution based on various kinds of verbal and technical information. QC methods in research and development quickly and thoroughly test such hypotheses. Such hypotheses are evaluated from a theoretical perspective and examined for potential value; then a detailed test is designed based on the resulting predictions. It is commonly believed that the quality of plans cannot be evaluated. In specific instances, this is probably due to the fact that there has not been sufficient appreciation of either the problem-solving hypothesis or its predicted outcome.

This situation is not restricted to research and development applications. Since the new era for quality aims to improve conditions across the board in industry, this concept deserves serious consideration in all departments, including the QC activities for high-level products. Hopefully, new techniques will be responsive to these requirements.

The ability to eliminate failure

When quality improvement is suggested in a department and, accordingly, reform plans are implemented, complex problems surface relating to cost, payment period, and facilities. Reform plans can rarely be implemented at the upper levels of management alone; they have to be coordinated with the production process, outside clients, supervisors, and subordinates. It is necessary to promote improvement and consolidate efforts on all fronts while at the same time working to prevent failures or eliminate slippage that might occur during the transition period. New techniques should be useful here as well.

The ability to assist in the exchange of information

As explained earlier, research, design, and development in total quality control, along with QC development in such new fields as atomic power plants, shipbuilding, and building construction, require a higher degree of information sharing between the departments concerned. In order to achieve this, several things are required: Information should be made accessible to everyone involved. Departmental relationships should be well-defined. Each manager or supervisor should list all the tasks for which they are responsible, as well as the specific tasks inherent to their project. Efforts should be made to merge company-wide technical forces. Presumably, new techniques should be responsive to these needs.

The ability to disseminate information to concerned parties

Since TQC activities are aimed at merging company-wide intellectual power, new techniques should provide a process whereby individuals' ideas can be clearly communicated to others who could benefit from that information. As long as reform is a group activity, ideas and thoughts need to be expressed in an easy to understand manner. The essential aim of this prerequisite, then, is for all the information contained in the group to become the possession of the entire group, and this, in turn, leads to the generation of new ideas.

The ability to use "unfiltered expression"

Quality control materials often suggest "resorting to unfiltered expression," in other words, saying things as they are. This is the equivalent of encouraging an uncensored, unfiltered, lively expression of successful results, the troubles endured during the process of some improvement, or the birth or death of a new idea.

Essentially, "unfiltered expression" correlates closely with another well-known saying in quality control: "Evaluation of the process is more important than the outcome." When one listens to the history of quality improvement in another department in one's company, it is very helpful if the changes in deficiency rate and values of characteristics have been recorded over the years. However, people rarely go so far as to record implementation details over the course of several years of reform. Practically speaking, however, it is hopeless to expect to rouse the interest of the younger generation of employees by sharing with them only tales of trials and hardships.

Preferably, new techniques should encourage an unfiltered, lively, and truthful expression of the promotion process, as well as presenting the information obtained in a manner that is accessible to succeeding generations.

As an attempt to fulfill these prerequisites, seven new QC tools are advocated and promoted here. Details of these tools are provided generally in Chapter 2 and more specifically in Part II. At this point, let us just list the seven tools briefly:

1. Relations diagram method
2. KJ method (affinity diagram method)
3. Systematic diagram method
4. Matrix diagram method
5. Matrix data-analysis method
6. PDPC (process decision program chart) method
7. Arrow diagram method

These methods have all been used in other fields, but an attempt has been made to avoid simply importing these techniques. Each method was assessed in terms of its potential effectiveness in quality control or in terms of previous experience with the techniques in QC applications, especially in areas that pose QC problems. These new methods do not have to be newly invented ideas; if they were techniques that had not previously existed, their utility would be rather suspect.

These seven new tools are being promoted in the belief that they can be used most efficiently when they are combined in an interrelated manner. It also needs to be made clear that the seven new QC tools do in no way contradict or replace the existing tools; the new tools are simply meant to supplement and complement the previous tools (see the second section of Chap. 2).

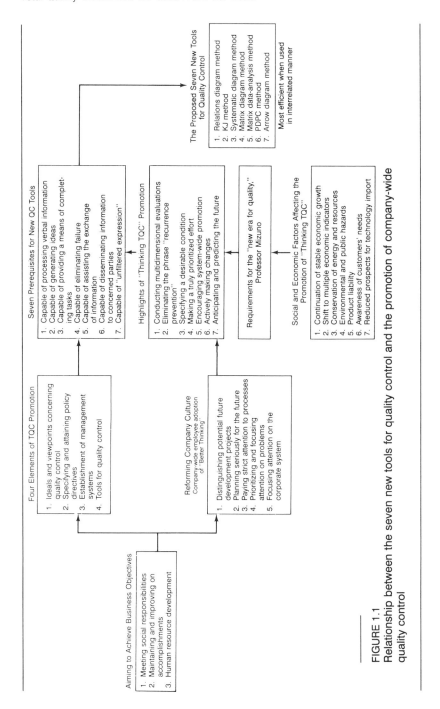

FIGURE 1.1
Relationship between the seven new tools for quality control and the promotion of company-wide quality control

Notes

1. Mizuno Shigeru and Akao Yoji, *Hinshitsu Kino Tenkai* (JUSE Press, Ltd., 1978). See Chapter 1 by Dr. Mizuno; he coined the phrase "new era for quality" at the 1972 Quality Control Convention.

2. Kigure Masao, "Quality Control in an Era of Reduced Quantity," *Hinshitsu Kanri (Quality Control)*, vol. 29 (July 1978), p. 44.

3. Mizuno Shigeru and Akao Yoji (Eds.), *Hinshitsu Kino Tenkai (Quality Deployment)* (Nikka Giren Publishing Co., 1978).

4. This section benefits from the following sources, and the writer gratefully acknowledges them: Asayoshi T., "Strengthening of Company Culture in TQC," *Standardization and Quality Control* (Sept. 1978); Asayoshi T., "Suggestions to Managers — Coping with a Low-Growth Stable Economy," *Monthly Quality Text*, vol. 78 (1975); and Ishikawa T., "Riding Through Turbulent Periods with Quality Control," *Monthly Quality Text*, vol. 71 (1974).

5. Sato Mitsuichi, "How to Structure and Solve a Problem," *Diamond Harvard Business*, vol. 3, no. 3 (May–June 1978), p. 49.

6. Oba Koichi, "Problems in Introducing and Planning QC — A Few Examples and Practical Advice," *Hinshitsu Kanri, (Quality Control)*, vol. 20, Supplement (November 1969), p. 5–8.

7. There is no fixed or definitive theory regarding the seven tools of quality control. This section relies on *Techniques for On-Site Improvements* by Imazumi. In other lists of the seven tools, control charts are replaced by stratification.

2

Seven New QC Tools

Overview of the seven methods

This section will introduce only the fundamentals of each method; detailed explanations will be presented in Part II.

ⓙ The relations diagram method

This is a technique developed to clarify intertwined causal relationships in a complex problem or situation in order to find an appropriate solution.

The method

In order to analyze problems with a complex network of cause-and-effect relationships, a relations diagram is constructed by indicating the logical relationships that exist between the causal factors (Fig. 2.1). Such a diagram facilitates solutions to problems by allowing the whole problem to be viewed from a broad perspective.

To solve problems using the relations diagram method, a team composed of as many members as necessary should draft diagrams several times. By constructing diagrams in this way, the team generates new ideas that may lead to an effective solution.

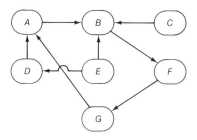

FIGURE 2.1
Abstract relations diagram

Uses

The relations diagram method can be used to

- Determine and develop quality assurance policies
- Establish promotional plans for TQC introduction
- Design steps to counter market complaints
- Improve quality in the manufacturing process (especially in planning to eliminate latent defects)
- Promote quality control in purchased or ordered items
- Provide measures against troubles related to payment and process control
- Effectively promote small group activities
- Reform administrative and business departments

Applications

Example 1. At the first symposium on quality control, a survey was conducted on the major items necessary for the introduction and promotion of total quality control. The items obtained from this study are presented in the relational diagram pictured in Fig. 2.2. This diagram clarifies the important items that companies might consider in their promotion of total quality control.

Example 2. Company U investigated the causes of a chronic deficiency in its assembly line of a certain product by using a relational diagram (Fig. 2.3). As a result of drawing the relational diagram, the staff's preconceptions regarding the causes of the deficiency were corrected and countermeasures were taken that result in a drastic reduction in the defective rate.

2 The KJ method*

This technique clarifies important but unresolved problems by collecting verbal data from disordered and confused situations and analyzing that data by mutual affinity.

The method

The KJ method attempts to clarify the nature, shape, and extent of problems that affect the near and distant future in fields where there is little or no prior knowledge and/or experience. This technique consists of gathering ideas and opinions in the form of verbal data and drawing a complete diagram based on the common relationships and similarities found among the data.

The KJ method is an organizational technique based on "participatory group formation." Problems are solved through the creation of teams that gather the opinions, ideas, and experiences of diverse people and then coordinate and organize those data in terms of mutual affinity.

The KJ method was originally conceived, developed, and promoted by Kawakita Jiro. Mr. Kawakita attempts to solve all problems by cumulatively using the affinity diagram, which is further explained in Chap. 5. Contrasting the KJ method with statistical techniques (Table 2.1 and Fig. 2.4) highlights its effectiveness as one of

---

*The KJ method is a trademark registered by the founder of the Kawayoshida Research Center. The trademark is still held by the center. We gratefully acknowledge the center's permission to use its materials in this chapter.

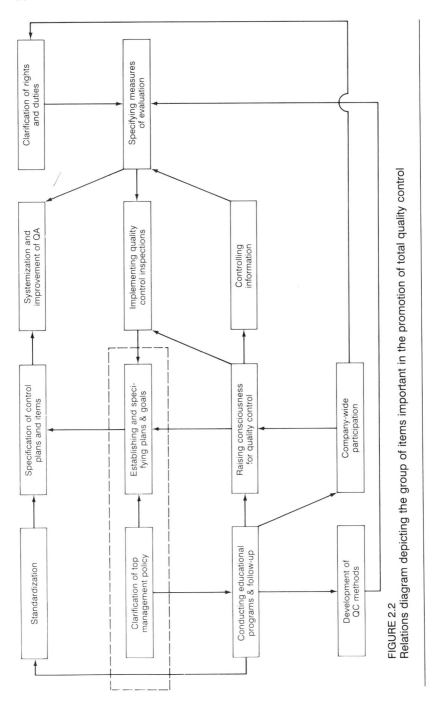

FIGURE 2.2
Relations diagram depicting the group of items important in the promotion of total quality control

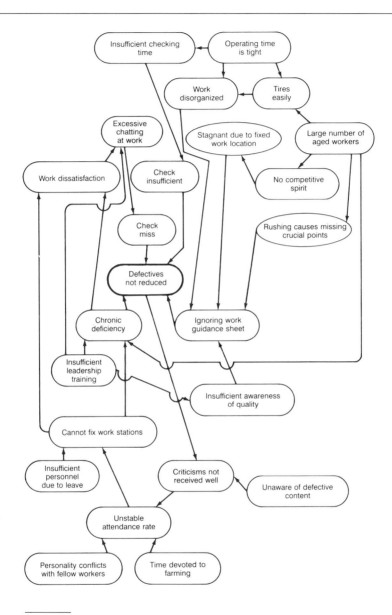

FIGURE 2.3
Relations diagram examining the causes of a deficiency in
assembly-line production

the seven new tools in solving problems in conjunction with other methods.

Uses

The KJ method can be used to

- Establish a QC policy for a new company or a new factory and to implement that plan
- Establish a QC policy concerning new projects, new products, or new technology and to implement that plan
- Conduct quality assurance market surveys when entering a new untested market
- Find a starting point for TQC promotion by creating a consensus among people with varying opinions regarding the problems that arise within each department
- Invigorate project teams and QC circles and promote teamwork within various groups.

Applications

Example 1. Shown in Fig. 2.5 is a portion of the affinity diagram obtained from the second round of cumulative KJ method discussions on the topic of "Where and how should our research and development proceed from here?" This discussion was conducted

TABLE 2.1
KJ method versus statistical techniques

Statistical techniques	The KJ method
1. Oriented for testing hypotheses	1. Oriented for discovering problems
2. Quantifies and transforms an event into numerical data	2. Expresses data in language and symbols without quantifying
3. Capable of analytic understanding; ability to stratify	3. Overall understanding possible; harmonizes heterogeneous elements
4. Can grasp by reasoning	4. Can grasp through feeling
5. Western way of thinking introduced through translation	5. Thinking based on Japanese language (said not to be amenable with language written horizontally)

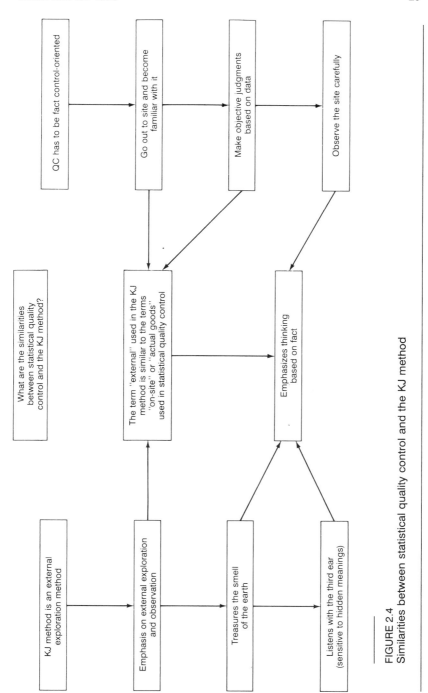

FIGURE 2.4
Similarities between statistical quality control and the KJ method

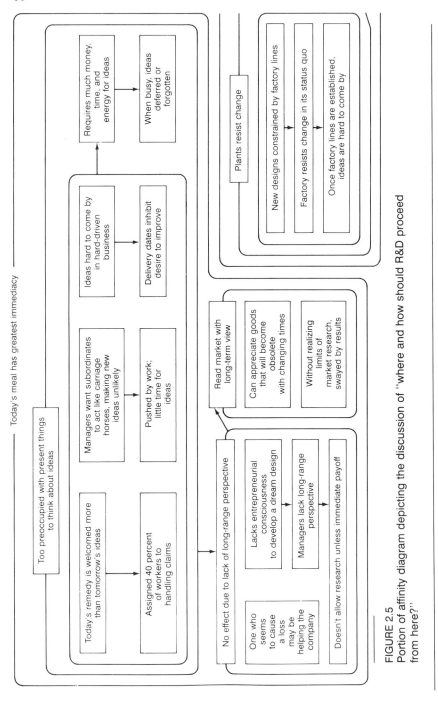

FIGURE 2.5
Portion of affinity diagram depicting the discussion of "where and how should R&D proceed from here?"

by a 10-member team of engineers and research managers from heterogeneous fields. Since the members were from different fields, the synthesis of their opinions led to a conclusion that will have wide applicability.

3 The systematic diagram method

This technique searches for the most appropriate and effective means of accomplishing given objectives.

The method

The systematic diagram method searches for techniques that will be most suitable for attaining established objectives by systematically clarifying important aspects of the problem. Such systematic diagrams enable workers to have an overview of the whole situation at one glance, effectively delineating the means and measures necessary for achieving the desired objectives (Fig. 2.6).

Systematic diagrams can be divided into two types: The *constituent-component-analysis* diagram breaks down the main subject into its basic elements and depicts their relationships to the objectives and means of attaining those objectives. The *plan-development* diagram systematically shows the means and procedures necessary to successfully implement a given plan.

Uses

The systematic diagram method can be used to

- Deploy a design-quality plan in the development of a new product
- Depict the relationship between a QC production process chart and the development of certified levels of quality designed to improve the accuracy of quality assurance activities
- Create a cause-effect diagram
- Develop ideas in order to solve problems dealing with quality, cost, and delivery that arise in new businesses
- Develop objectives, policies, and implementation steps

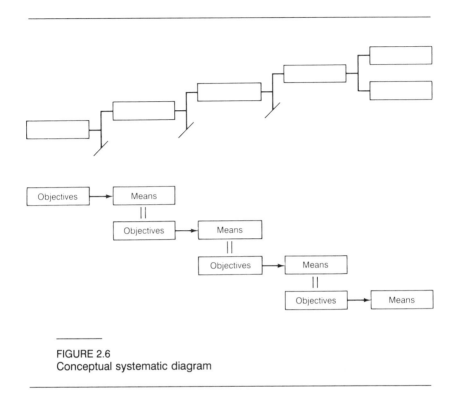

FIGURE 2.6
Conceptual systematic diagram

- Pursue the specification of increased efficiency in parts and control functions

Applications

Example 1. A systematic diagram of the plan-development type is shown in Fig. 2.7. This diagram illustrates the development of design-quality and implementation steps necessary for production of a UHF tuner for a television.

4 The matrix diagram method

This technique clarifies problematic spots through multidimensional thinking.

The method

The matrix diagram method identifies corresponding elements involved in a problem situation or event. These elements are arranged in rows and columns on a chart (Fig. 2.8) that shows the presence or absence of relationships among collected pairs of elements. Hopefully, this method will assist in specifying (with a two-way layout) the nature and/or location of problems, enabling idea conception on the basis of two-dimensional relationships. Effective problem solving is facilitated at the intersection points, also referred to as "idea conception points."

Matrix diagrams are classified on the basis of their pattern into five different groups: (1) the L-type matrix, (2) the T-type matrix, (3) the Y-type matrix, (4) the X-type matrix, and (5) the C-type matrix.

Uses

Matrix diagrams can be used to

- Establish idea conception points for the development and improvement of system products
- Achieve quality deployment in product materials
- Establish and strengthen the quality assurance system by linking certified levels of quality with the various control functions
- Reinforce and improve the efficiency of the quality evaluation system
- Pursue the causes of nonconformities in the manufacturing process
- Establish strategies about the mix of products to send to market by evaluating the relationships between the products and market situations

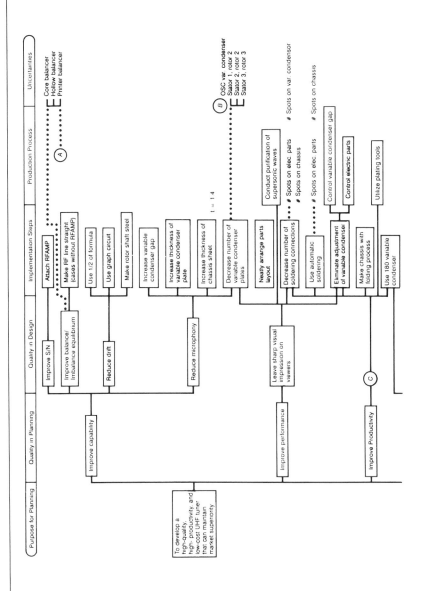

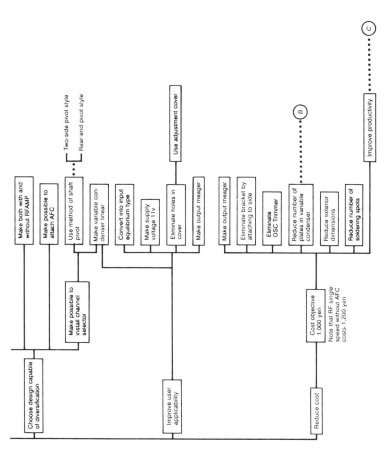

FIGURE 2.7
Systematic diagram for design quality for a television UHF tuner

- Clarify the technical relationships among several projects
- Explore the application potential of currently available technology and raw materials

Applications

As Fig. 2.9 indicates, a T-type matrix was constructed in the investigation of smearing during the production of printed cloth. The matrix helped to clarify the relationships between nonconformities and their causes. Based on the results of this matrix, a list of countermeasures was produced (see Table 7.1), and their implementation considerably reduced smears.

⌒ The matrix data-analysis method

This technique arranges data presented in a matrix diagram so that the large array of numbers can be visualized and comprehended easily.

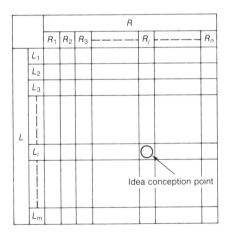

FIGURE 2.8
Conceptual matrix diagram method

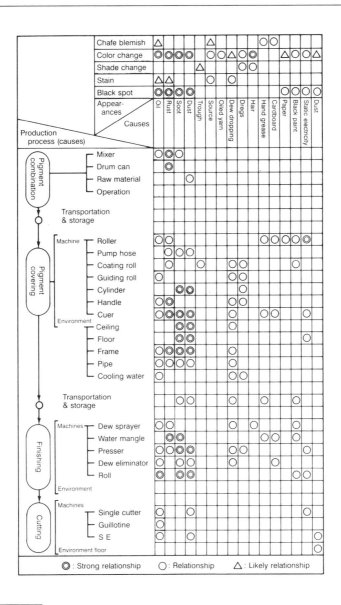

FIGURE 2.9
T-type matrix searching for causes of smears in printing of cloth

The method

The matrix data-analysis method quantifies and arranges matrix di-agram data so that the information is easy to visualize and compre-hend. The relationships between the elements shown in a matrix diagram are quantified by obtaining numerical data for intersection cells.

Of the seven new QC tools, this is the only numerical analysis method. The results of this technique, however, are presented in diagram form. One major technique that this method also utilizes is known as principal-component analysis, one of the multivariate analysis techniques. The matrix data-analysis method has been in-cluded as one of the seven new QC tools so that managers and staff can become more familiar with multivariate analysis techniques.

As an example of how this technique is used, Table 2.2 is pre-sented as a data matrix showing the relationships between 40 uses of cloth and their desired qualities. Suppose that a new material, ma-terial *A*, is developed. The data in Table 2.2 does not readily provide information about the potential uses of material *A*; however, the matrix data-analysis method does offer answers by analyzing the data in Table 2.2.

Uses

The matrix data-analysis method can be used to

- Analyze production processes where factors are complexly intertwined
- Analyze causes of nonconformities that involve a large volume of data
- Grasp the desired quality level indicated by the results of a market survey
- Classify sensory characteristics systematically
- Accomplish complex quality evaluations
- Analyze curvilinear data

TABLE 2.2
Product uses and their desired qualities

Uses	Desirable Qualities	1 Resists Fading	2 Washable	3 Resists perspiration	...	23 Flame retardant	24 Chemical resistant	25 Non-irritating to skin
1. Mens' summer suits		$x_{1\text{-}1}$	$x_{1\text{-}2}$	$x_{1\text{-}3}$	...	$x_{1\text{-}23}$	$x_{1\text{-}24}$	$x_{1\text{-}25}$
2. Mens' all-season suits		$x_{2\text{-}1}$	$x_{2\text{-}2}$	$x_{2\text{-}3}$	...	$x_{2\text{-}23}$	$x_{2\text{-}24}$	$x_{2\text{-}25}$
3. Ladies' summer dresses		$x_{3\text{-}1}$	$x_{3\text{-}2}$	$x_{3\text{-}3}$	...	$x_{3\text{-}23}$	$x_{3\text{-}24}$	$x_{3\text{-}25}$
4. Ladies' all-season dresses		$x_{4\text{-}1}$	$x_{4\text{-}2}$	$x_{4\text{-}3}$	...	$x_{4\text{-}23}$	$x_{4\text{-}24}$	$x_{4\text{-}25}$
5. Skirts		$x_{5\text{-}1}$	$x_{5\text{-}2}$	$x_{5\text{-}3}$	...	$x_{5\text{-}23}$	$x_{5\text{-}24}$	$x_{5\text{-}25}$
6. Trousers		$x_{6\text{-}1}$	$x_{6\text{-}2}$	$x_{6\text{-}3}$	...	$x_{6\text{-}23}$	$x_{6\text{-}24}$	$x_{6\text{-}25}$
7. Overcoats		$x_{7\text{-}1}$	$x_{7\text{-}2}$	$x_{7\text{-}3}$	...	$x_{7\text{-}23}$	$x_{7\text{-}24}$	$x_{7\text{-}25}$
8. Raincoats		$x_{8\text{-}1}$	$x_{8\text{-}2}$	$x_{8\text{-}3}$	...	$x_{8\text{-}23}$	$x_{8\text{-}24}$	$x_{8\text{-}25}$
9. Office wear		$x_{9\text{-}1}$	$x_{9\text{-}2}$	$x_{9\text{-}3}$	...	$x_{9\text{-}23}$	$x_{9\text{-}24}$	$x_{9\text{-}25}$
10. Work clothes		$x_{10\text{-}1}$	$x_{10\text{-}2}$	$x_{10\text{-}3}$	...	$x_{10\text{-}23}$	$x_{10\text{-}24}$	$x_{10\text{-}25}$
11. Sports wear		$x_{11\text{-}1}$	$x_{11\text{-}2}$	$x_{11\text{-}3}$	...	$x_{11\text{-}23}$	$x_{11\text{-}24}$	$x_{11\text{-}25}$
12. Student wear		$x_{12\text{-}1}$	$x_{12\text{-}2}$	$x_{12\text{-}3}$	...	$x_{12\text{-}23}$	$x_{12\text{-}24}$	$x_{12\text{-}25}$
13. Home wear		$x_{13\text{-}1}$	$x_{13\text{-}2}$	$x_{13\text{-}3}$	...	$x_{13\text{-}23}$	$x_{13\text{-}24}$	$x_{13\text{-}25}$
14. Baby wear		$x_{14\text{-}1}$	$x_{14\text{-}2}$	$x_{14\text{-}3}$	...	$x_{14\text{-}23}$	$x_{14\text{-}24}$	$x_{14\text{-}25}$
15. Dress shirts		$x_{15\text{-}1}$	$x_{15\text{-}2}$	$x_{15\text{-}3}$	...	$x_{15\text{-}23}$	$x_{15\text{-}24}$	$x_{15\text{-}25}$
⋮ ⋮		⋮	⋮	⋮	⋮	⋮	⋮	⋮
40. Foot warmer blankets		$x_{40\text{-}1}$	$x_{40\text{-}2}$	$x_{40\text{-}3}$	...	$x_{40\text{-}23}$	$x_{40\text{-}24}$	$x_{40\text{-}25}$
Material A		x_1	x_2	x_3	...	x_{23}	x_{24}	x_{25}

Applications

A principal-component analysis is performed on the matrix data provided in Table 2.2. The resulting first and second principal components are shown graphically in Fig. 2.10. This figure reveals that the new material *A* would probably be better suited for skirts and trousers than for sports wear, work uniforms, or gloves.

6 The PDPC method

This technique helps determine which processes to use to obtain desired results by evaluating the progress of events and the variety of conceivable outcomes.

The method

Implementation plans do not always progress as anticipated. When problems, technical or otherwise, arise, solutions are frequently not apparent.

The PDPC (process decision program chart) method, in response to these kinds of problems, anticipates possible outcomes and prepares countermeasures that will lead to the best possible solutions. By anticipating potential outcomes of events, this technique allows process adjustments in light of actual progress.

If an unanticipated event occurs, then it becomes necessary to rewrite the process decision program chart (PDPC) at once so that adjustive countermeasures can be taken.

The PDPC method[1] is borrowed from the operations research field for use in quality control.

Uses

The PDPC method can be used to

- Establish an implementation plan for management by objectives
- Establish an implementation plan for technology-development themes
- Establish a policy of forecasting and responding in advance to major events predicted in the system

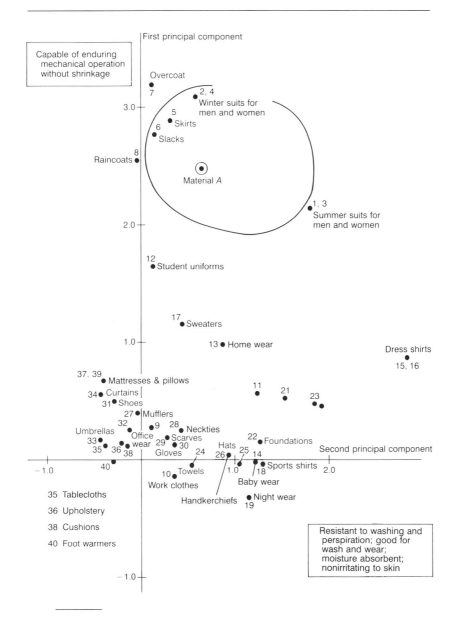

FIGURE 2.10
Searching for uses of new material A

- Implement countermeasures to minimize nonconformities in the manufacturing process
- Set up and select adjustment measures for the negotiating process

Applications

Suppose that a company's objective is to deliver a fragile item to an addressee in a developing country. The company must anticipate various contingencies from shipment time to delivery, and address all the problems that might arise as a result of transportation and landing. The company must then develop countermeasures to avoid possible mishaps. The PDPC method approach to this hypothetical example and the results are shown in Fig. 2.11.

The arrow diagram method

This technique establishes the most suitable daily plan and monitors its progress efficiently.

The method

The arrow diagram method, utilized by PERT and CPM, is a network diagram for daily plans. It illustrates the network of lines that connect all the elements related to plan execution, as shown in Fig. 2.12.

Use of the arrow diagram method in advancing and monitoring daily plans has the following advantages:

1. It establishes a finely tuned plan.
2. It establishes the most suitable daily plan, since changes can be made easily during the early planning stages.
3. It allows one to cope easily with changes that occur in a given situation or during plan execution.
4. It expedites necessary action by quickly providing information on the impact delays in certain subparts will have on the operation as a whole.
5. It is increasingly useful in proportion to the size of the plans.
6. It controls the process efficiently because the progress highlights are easily discernible.

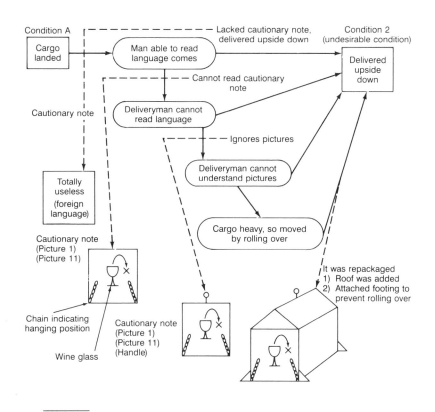

FIGURE 2.11
Delivery of fragile item (pattern II)

The control of daily plans is extremely important in the promotion of QC activities. An efficient method of constructing and utilizing arrow diagrams that employs cards will be introduced mainly to assist staff members.

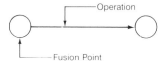

FIGURE 2.12
Elements of an arrow diagram

Uses

The arrow diagram method can be used to

- Implement plans for new product development and its follow-up
- Develop product-improvement plans and follow-up activities
- Establish daily plans for experimental trials and follow-up activities
- Establish daily plans for increases in production and their follow-up
- Synchronize the preceding plans with QC activities
- Develop plans for a facility move and for monitoring follow-up
- Implement a periodic facility maintenance plan and its follow-up
- Analyze a manufacturing process and draw up plans for improved efficiency
- Plan and follow up QC inspections and diagnostic tests
- Plan and follow up QC conferences and QC circle conferences

Applications

In a low-cost project to produce special resistor electrodes used in a starter for an electric motor, value engineering (VE) experimental trials and quality confirmation tests were implemented based on an arrow diagram (Fig. 2.13) of daily plans constructed using the "card method." This diagram made the trials and tests possible.

The role of the seven new QC tools in quality control

The seven new tools proposed fulfill the planning steps often mentioned in the "plan, do, check, act" (PDCA) TQC cycle. Figure 2.14 graphically demonstrates the placement of various QC techniques applied in the *plan* and *do* stages to solve an important problem. If an adequate amount of past quantitative data is available, the traditional seven tools would probably suffice; however, as mentioned in Chap. 1, this is not always the case in TQC problem solving. Therefore, Fig. 2.14 should be viewed as relating to a situation where data are relatively scarce.

The plan stage can be divided into the following three phases:

Plan 1: This phase reviews a confusing event and arranges the information so to clarify the underlying nature of the problem.

Plan 2: This phase searches for various means that might be employed to solve the problem and identifies the relationships between the objectives and the means.

Plan 3: This phase establishes an implementation strategy in a time-order sequence in order to increase the chance for success.

During the plan 1 phase, the relations diagram and the KJ methods are used. During plan 2, the systematic diagram and matrix diagram methods, as well as the cause-and-effect diagram and matrix data-analysis methods are used. The plan 3 phase relies on the arrow diagram and the PDPC methods. The arrow diagram method is most often used when the sequence of steps is relatively fixed and

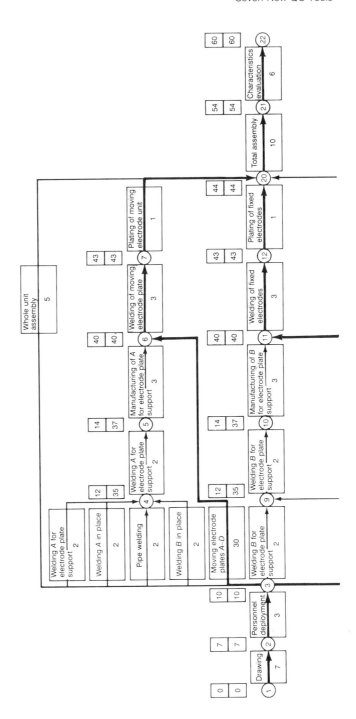

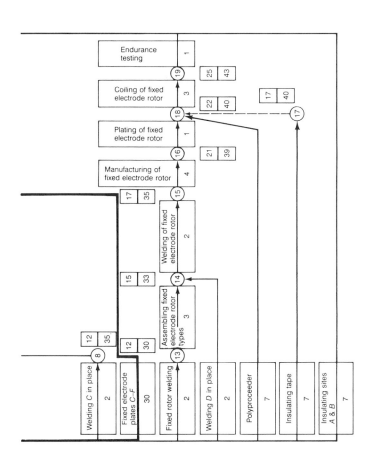

FIGURE 2.13
Experimental trials and quality confirmation plan for VE improvement of special resistor electrodes

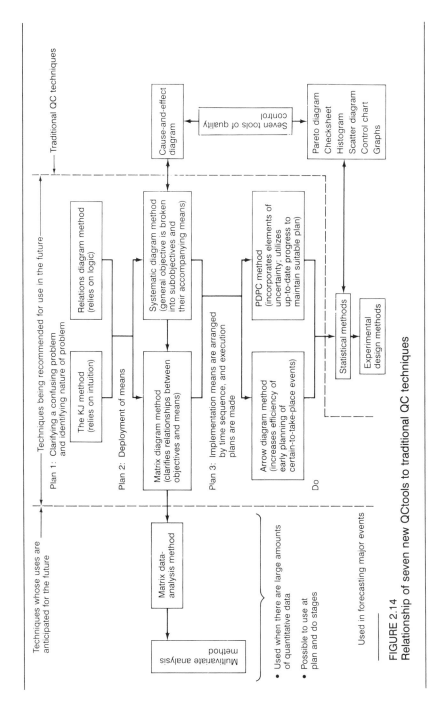

FIGURE 2.14
Relationship of seven new QCtools to traditional QC techniques

predetermined, as in the construction of a building or in shortening the delivery time of a product. However, in QC-related activities, the original readings or plans frequently must be modified because of an unexpected development or occurrence. Whenever there is an unexpected development, information collected up to that point must be analyzed, underlying causes must be understood, and appropriate changes in plans must be made in order to achieve the overall objectives. The PDPC method is an extremely useful technique in such situations, and the PDPC method also can be used to forecast major accidents in such related areas as environmental hazards and product liability.

During the *do* stage, other statistical and experimental design methods are selected from the traditional seven tools depending on the particular circumstances of implementation.

Although the *check* and *act* stages of the PDCA cycle are not shown in Fig. 2.14, they proceed from the outcome of the *do* stage. But in Fig. 2.14 it is clear that the following six of the seven new tools should be used in every stage of TQC promotion in the future:

- Relations diagram method
- KJ method
- Systematic diagram method
- Matrix diagram method
- PDPC method
- Arrow diagram method

The matrix diagram method provides a readily comprehensible graphic representation of complex data when each cell in the matrix is given a numerical value. It corresponds to the principal-component analysis method, one of the multivariate analysis methods. Hopefully, the matrix diagram method will be accepted as a tool that can simplify and bring order to numerical or quantitative confusion.

During product planning and process-improvement activities, situations are frequently encountered in which numerous intertwined causes must be untangled. Keeping pace with the development of computers, many businesses have aggressively introduced this method with good results. Even though this technique should be brought to the attention of managers and staff, it should not necessarily be overused.

To prevent misunderstandings about the origin of the seven new QC tools, five points should be highlighted:

1. The seven methods described here do not necessarily exhaust the list. Selection of these seven tools came after much hesitation and thought. Actually, it is hoped that these techniques enrich QC techniques even further. Even people who use the traditional seven tools use them differently over time. Therefore, some modifications and revisions of the seven new tools in response to future developments are necessary. There is also nothing sacred about the number seven. What is essential is that one's toolbox contain all the useful and necessary tools.

2. Most of the techniques described above are already known and were not recently created as QC methods. This also applies to the traditional seven tools, such as the histogram, pareto chart, scatter diagram, and other statistical methods. Some of these even appear in elementary school textbooks. However, because of their promotion, along with the cause-and-effect diagram, as part of the seven tools for quality control, they have come to be used extensively in QC activities. By christening the preceding methods as the seven new QC tools, it is hoped that they too will receive the attention necessary to allow the development of diverse applications in fields concerned with quality control.

3. There are two important reasons for using the seven new tools as a group. One is that, as previously mentioned, the seven tools act like an organically integrated set; it would be hard to expect excellent results if they were used independently. The seven new tools should be used in combination, as shown in the second section of Chap. 3, for best results in solving problems. The second reason is that the seven new tools are best used when promoted in all facets of operation under the direction of the company or department head. Effects are limited if the tools are used sporadically in isolated divisions or units.

4. The pioneers who promoted quality control deserve our thanks for having introduced various techniques and for having successfully completed the original seven QC tools, the statistical

and experimental design methods for quality control. Unfortunately, however, over the course of the past decade or so, few
innovative proposals similar to the ones promoted by the first-
generation pioneers have been set forth. As the succeeding generation, though, it is important for us to gather all the seedlings
and fruit of the preceding generation, develop them as much as
possible in a systematic fashion, and pass them on to the next
generation.

5. All the techniques described here have been used previously in
   various fields and have demonstrated some level of effectiveness. Although not unique to quality control, the requirements
   for using these tools include a keen awareness of the problem at
   hand, an incessant desire for improvement, and an enhanced
   spirit and thought process. Without these kinds of mental preparation, the tools cannot be used effectively. Anyone who expects a tool to do all the work cannot expect good results and
   cannot really be considered a "user."

The seven new QC tools and the basics of graphics-language theory[2]

As discussed earlier, the seven new tools make considerable use of
graphics. Table 2.3 presents a classification system developed by T.
Kahn[3] that shows the differences between language and graphics as
they apply to manner of recognition and relative ease of understanding. When viewing graphics, we first comprehend the overall
structure (pattern, balance, and trends of dots and lines) and then
reach out for that which is interesting.

Regardless of nationality and race, any person can understand
pictures. Language, however, presupposes an understanding of
pre-existing rules, without which the language is totally incompre-
hensible, for example, when a non-Japanese speaking person tries to
make sense of Japanese characters. The understanding of graphics
and language is analogous to the human developmental process.
Infants start out as "contact beings," whose exchanges of information with others, including their mother, occur through physical

TABLE 2.3
Differences between graphics and language

	Graphics	Language
Manner of recognition:	First, the whole is grasped. Next, elements are analyzed.	First, elements are recognized. Next, whole is constructed.
Ease of understanding:	Understood by almost anybody immediately (pictures).	If rules are not understood, then it is incomprehensible (foreign languages).

contact. These contact beings later grow into "picture beings," who are able to understand information based on pictures, drawings, and graphics of various sorts. Finally, these picture beings turn into "character beings," who are capable of information transmission through written characters. The recent popularity of commercial drawings and comic books may be viewed as an extension of the picture-being stage. In other words, the human capability to understand graphic forms easily seems to be a developmental characteristic. It should be evident that tools anchored in graphics will emerge as powerful techniques in the promotion of company-wide total quality control because of their ready comprehension by all concerned.

Computer graphics theorists distinguish pictures that contain characters, such as the seven new tools, from graphics that contain only drawings by calling them "graphics language." The graphics-language group is further divided into the following four types:

1. Relational system
2. Network system
3. Column-row system
4. Coordinate system

A further explanation of these system types is contained in *Computer Graphics Theory*. However, their names alone suggest their meanings. Of the four types listed, the coordinate system has been in use the longest. Table 2.4 shows the seven new and seven "old" tools classified into the different graphics-language types. Notice that the "old" tools are primarily coordinate-based, while the new tools rely,

TABLE 2.4
The seven new tools and the traditional seven tools classified by
graphics-language systems

Graphics-language system	Seven new tools	Traditional seven tools
Relational system	KJ method	—
Network system	Relations diagram method Systematic diagram method Arrow diagram method PDPC method	Cause-and-effect diagram
Column-row system	Matrix diagram method	Checksheet
Coordinate system	Matrix data-analysis method	Pareto chart Histogram Scatter diagram Control chart Graphs

primarily on the relational or network systems.

Experience has shown that the ease or difficulty involved in constructing graphics for the seven new tools varies from one person to another. The graphics tools used can be divided into two groups:

Soft graphic tools: The KJ method, the relations diagram method, and the PDPC method offer a relatively greater degree of freedom in graphics construction.

Hard graphic tools: The systematic diagram method, the matrix diagram method, and the arrow diagram method have considerably less freedom in graphics construction.

Even though the former may appear to be the easier to people just starting to use the new tools, they are actually more difficult because they allow a greater degree of freedom. Nevertheless, some beginners have produced outstanding graphics.

A necessary step in company-wide QC activities is for all employees to become thoroughly acquainted with pictorial or graphic thinking. This is accomplished by practicing the construction of various graphics and through the cooperation of everyone involved. All employees should be exposed to a wide variety of graphics so they may identify their own weak areas and learn to construct the diagrams properly. Only this kind of total exposure will make the combined use of all the seven new tools feasible.

Notes

1. Kondo Jiro, *Operations Research* (Tokyo: JUSE Press, Ltd., 1973), pp. 128–136.

2. This section relies heavily on information in Chaps. 2 and 3 of *Computer Graphics Theory*, by Yoshikawa Hiroyuki, published by JUSE Press in 1977. Grateful acknowledgment is due.

3. Yoshikawa Hiroyuki, *Computer Graphics Theory* (Tokyo: JUSE Press, Ltd., 1977).

3

Applying the Seven New QC Tools

Fields of application for the seven new QC tools

Each one of the seven new QC tools has been in use for some time now in the field of quality control. A review of the proceedings of quality control conferences held between 1966 and 1978 shows that use of the techniques included in the seven new tools has increased dramatically since the seven new tools were announced in 1977. (See Fig. 3.1.) This increase should continue in the future.

Application of the seven new tools began with the analysis and consolidation of verbal data and is continuing to expand. Diverse applications of the new tools in different fields and for varied purposes have been widely publicized in Japan, which has contributed to a healthy momentum for further promotion. We can expect to see applications in unexpected, heterogeneous fields.

Table 3.1 shows both the publicized and unpublicized applications, indicating the fields where we may expect future use. Although there may have been some unrefined usage, the table will be helpful as a guide to applications of the seven new QC tools in total quality control.

Examples introduced in individual chapters are also listed in Table 3.2 (by technique), so this table serves as a guide to various examples, as well as a way of finding fields of future application.

TABLE 3.1
Listing of fields where applications are expected

Step	Primary implementation	Secondary implementation	Relations Diagram Method	KJ Method	Systematic Diagram Method	Matrix Diagram Method	Matrix Data-Analysis Method	PDPC Method	Arrow Diagram Method
	Policy control	Priority imposed on many implementation items	●	○	○	○			
		Policy transmitted from top down	●		◎				
		Clarify responsibilities for implementation items	○		◎	○			
		Develop a plan with high probability of success for objectives			◎			◎	◎
	Education and training	Training items are prioritized	○	○		○			
		Relate training items with the expected standards	○	○		○			
Overall	Labor and personnel relations	Clarify lines of responsibility by job title		○	○	◎		◎	
		Smooth out interpersonal conflicts	○		○				
	Financial matters and accounting	Comparative diagnosis of one's business culture					◎		○
	Promotion of total quality controls	Smooth out interdepartmental relationships	○	○	○	○	◎		○
	QC circle activities	Invigorate QC circle activities	○	●	○	○			
	Market analysis	Monitor and classify needs		◎	○		●		
		Perform demand forecasts		○			●		
		Analyze competitors				◎	●		
		Explore uses for new products	○	○		○	●		
		Survey circulation routes				○			
		Conduct search for themes	○	○	○	○			
Development of plans	Quality design	Understand quality characteristics			●	○	●		
	Quality assurance	Transform needs into alternative characteristics		●	●	●			
		Relate soft and hard functions	○	○	●	●			
		Relate alternative characteristics to process-control items	○		●	●			
		Develop planning policy into design quality		●	●	○			
		Clarify factors that enhance reliability	○	○	●		◎	○	
		Attempt to complete PLP activities							

Category	Sub-category	Item							
Development of plans	Evaluation and development of test trials	Develop production techniques							
		Clarify relationship between functions and cost		○	◎			○	
		Examine status of research and development					◎		
	Stocking and purchasing	Conduct price negotiations		○		○		○	
		Clarify the reasons for shipment delay		○		○		○	○
		Reduce nonconforming items in received shipments		◎					
	Inventory control	Understand conditions of cargo movement by item		◎		○		○	
	Quality control and improvement	Analyze reasons for nonconforming items and improve production process		●	●	●		●	●
		Relate experimental characteristics and measurement items		●		●		●	
		Analyze and solve claims and improve quality		●	○	○		○	
Production	Productivity control and improvement	Clarify problems and make improvement; increase rate of operation		○		○		●	○
		Analyze obstacles to timely delivery and meet deadlines		●		○	○	●	
		Conduct high-precision quality control		○			◎		◎
	Cost control and reduction	Reduce cost by VE		○		○	○		
	Facilities control and improvement	Execute investment in facilities as planned		○			○		◎
		Adopt measures that require small investment but yield big results						●	
	Safety control	Examine reasons for worker injuries and minor accidents	○	○		○			
		Examine safety measures against major accidents and disasters	○	○		○		●	
	Sales policy and strategy	Adjust relationship between needs and product types	○	○	◎	◎		●	
		Critically compare one's own company against competitors' companies regarding needs	○	○	◎	◎		●	
		Understand regional characteristics of high-volume sales items		○				○	
Sales		Develop sales-promotion measures	◎		◎			○	
	Sales record and profit control	Understand sales by retail stores		○				○	
		Understand sales by product items		○					
	Before service and after service	Acquire more accurate user needs	○	○	◎	○		○	
		Feed information obtained back to design	○	○		○		○	

Note: ● Listed in this text as examples   ◎ Existing examples but not publicly announced   ○ Fields where uses are conceivable.

TABLE 3.2
Applications of the seven new QC tools (mentioned in text)

Techniques	Applications	Titles
Relations diagram method	TQC promotion	Relations diagram for major item clusters in promoting the introduction of TQC
		Relations diagram for substance of TQC implementation
		Relations diagram for administrative improvement in administrative department
	Policy control	Simple examples of relations diagrams made for selection of implementations items
		Relations diagram for policy control
	Quality control and improvement (analysis of the production process)	Relations diagram designed to help identify causes of nonconforming items in assembly line
		Relations diagram for market claims
		Relations diagram for dispersion of characteristic values
		Reduction of nonconforming items among items received
	Production method	Relations diagram for introduction of new production method
	Production control and improvement	Relations diagram for delays in assembly process
KJ method	Development	Direction of future research and development (first and second round)
	TQC promotion and QC circle	How to promote QC circle smoothly
	Quality assurance	What quality assurance will be
Systematic diagram method	Development	Systematic diagram for design quality of television UHF tuner
	Quality assurance	Systematic diagram for quality guarantee of a television VHF tuner
		Systematic diagram for quality guarantee of automobile brakes
	Quality improvement	Systematic diagram for identification of causes regarding dispersion of wall panel thickness
		Systematic diagram for reducing loss due to trunk nonconformities

Contents

TABLE 3.2 continued

Techniques	Applications	Titles
Matrix diagram method	Development	Functional family matrix regarding the weight and combination of granules
	Quality assurance	Substitute characteristics matrix for required properties of water pipe couplings
		Matrix of process-control items for substitute characteristics of water pipe couplings
		Matrix related to guaranteed properties, test items, and test machines for automotive brakes
	Quality improvement	Matrix designed to investigate causes for blemishes in printed cloth
Matrix data-analysis method	Planning and development	Classification of preferences for a variety of food products
		Exploration of the uses for new product, cloth A
		Spectrum analysis of the pleasing fluorescent lamp
		Forecast of the fashion cycle
		Expected automotive style
	Analysis of the manufacturing process	Analysis of nonconformities in automotive parts caused during pressing
		Search for the causes of scars on metal surfaces
		Analysis of the change in the dyeing outcome in the photo industry
PDPC method	Planning and quality assurance	PDPC of useless delivery
	Safety control	PDPC of the Gemini Plan
		Applicability to inspection of PDPC system safety
	Test evaluation (development)	PDPC for research and development

Contents	Page Nos.

TABLE 3.2 continued

Techniques	Applications	Titles
PDPC method	Test evaluation (development)	Examination of techniques and PDPC
	Control and improvement of production volume	PDPC for increased productivity
	Management and improvement of facilities	Ways of reducing NO_2 using PDPC
		Example where solution was found by writing the process of examination in terms of PDPC
Arrow diagram method	Quality design	Experimental run of the VE improvement plan for special resistor electrodes and quality confirmation plan
	Development	Development plan for electronic device model 52 (plan for initial stages; plan for shortening production schedule)
		Development plan for electronic device model 60 (plan for initial stages; plan for shortening production schedule)
		Promotion plan for quality production of model 62
	Quality improvement	Improvement plan for model T-827

Applying the seven new QC tools to policy control

At the first QC symposium, entitled Quality Control: Introduction, Promotion, and Establishment (sponsored by the Japanese Federation of Science and Technology (JUSE), participants completed a questionnaire regarding important items of common interest in introducing and promoting total quality control.[1] These items, shown in Table 3.3, range from setting and clarifying policies and objectives to developing QC techniques. The "Rank" column indicates the ranking given to each item by the participants. The "Frequency" column refers to the number of participants who chose a particular item, and the "Points" column is the sum of the value of each rank. (*Note:* Assign a value of 6 to rank 1, a value of 5 to rank 2, etc., and a

Contents	Page Nos.
In order to solve a problem in the manufacturing technique, mobilize all knowledge and information to generate possible solutions; write and rewrite PDPC three times to arrive at a solution	192
Devise a measure to increase productivity by 20 percent	190
There are five measures for reducing NO_2; examine alternatives and select among them so that the result may be obtained with minimal investment	191
Since an examination of accident-prevention measures was too complicated, a PDPC was written; as a result, what was considered unfeasible in the past analysis emerged as a promising solution; the whole situation was reexamined and appropriate measures were taken	195
Both experimental runs were based on the VE improvement plan for special resistor electrodes used in electric motors, and daily plans for quality confirmation were constructed using cards	34
In making development plans for electronic device, schedule was shortened by reducing number of days required on critical paths	213 215
Schedule was shortened through a modification of arrow diagram introduced by an addition of work	216 217
The daily plan for volume production of a new product was expressed in a time-scale arrow diagram for each participating department	220
The quality-improvement plan was expressed in a time-scale arrow diagram for each participating department	219

value of 1 to rank 6. Multiply the frequency by the value and add up the totals; this results in the sum total of points.) Table 3.3 lists items in order of total points.

According to this table, the establishment (and clarification) of policies, objectives, and plans, which constitutes the theme of this section, occupies the highest rank; it is the most important item in the introduction and promotion of quality control. We frequently consider the question of what steps have the highest priority in the implementation of total quality control. Other related questions we are often asked are how far on the list one should go in selecting implementation measures, whether starting with standardization is a detour, and so on. These questions arise from a misconception that the items listed in Table 3.3 exist in functional isolation from each other. Although Table 3.3 shows the relative importance of the listed

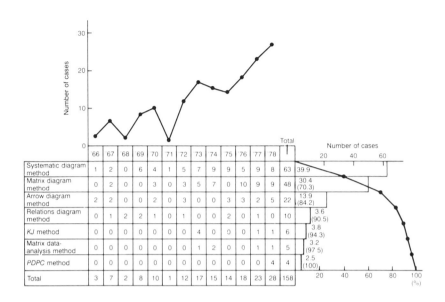

The table in the figure:

	66	67	68	69	70	71	72	73	74	75	76	77	78	Total	
Systematic diagram method	1	2	0	6	4	1	5	7	9	9	5	9	8	63	39.9
Matrix diagram method	0	2	0	0	3	0	3	5	7	0	10	9	9	48	30.4 (70.3)
Arrow diagram method	2	2	0	0	2	0	3	0	0	3	3	2	5	22	13.9 (84.2)
Relations diagram method	0	1	2	2	1	0	1	0	0	2	0	1	0	10	3.6 (90.5)
KJ method	0	0	0	0	0	0	0	4	0	0	0	1	1	6	3.8 (94.3)
Matrix data-analysis method	0	0	0	0	0	0	0	1	2	0	0	1	1	5	3.2 (97.5)
PDPC method	0	0	0	0	0	0	0	0	0	0	0	0	4	4	2.5 (100)
Total	3	7	2	8	10	1	12	17	15	14	18	23	28	158	

FIGURE 3.1
Trends in the applications of the seven new QC tools (based on the
Proceedings of the quality control conferences)

items, as indicated by the participants, it does not show that the
items are interdependent and related to each other, as shown in the
relations diagram in Fig. 2.2.

The establishment and clarification of policies, objectives, and
plans are important, but they presuppose a clearly established policy. Implementation would be troublesome without thorough control and quality consciousness. Furthermore, without effective quality and QC inspection, it would not be possible to anticipate
favorable results either in setting and clarifying policies, objectives,
and plans or in the PDCA (plan-do-check-action) cycle. In other
words, the items listed in Table 3.3 are all interrelated, and we may
start with any one we choose. The shortcomings of the items listed in
Fig. 2.2 will be corrected regardless of where one starts, as long as
implementation follows and the PDCA cycle is repeated, with the
utmost effort, toward company-wide improvement. Of the items
listed in Table 3.3, we should first introduce quality control as a
policy issuing from the highest level and then aim for overall improvement in the company's position and product quality.[2]

TABLE 3.3
Rank ordering of major items in the introduction and promotion of quality control

Ranking	Major items	Order or selection 1	2	3	4	5	6–10	Sum of frequencies	Sum of points
1	Set and clarify policies, objectives, and plans	卌 ////	卌 //	/	/		//	20	98
2	Thoroughly develop awareness for control, management, and quality	卌 ///	//	///		/		15	76
3	Conduct training programs and follow up	///	/	卌 /	////	//	///	19	66
4	Conduct quality and QC inspection			///	卌 /	卌 /	卌 //	22	49
5	Clarify control plans and control items		/	////	///		//	11	36
6	Clarify priority policies	///	//				/	6	29
7	Systematize and improve QC system	/		//	//			5	20
8	Standardization		/		/	//	////	8	16
9	Clarify measures of evaluation		/		/	/	///	6	13
10	Clarify duties and rights		//				///	5	13
11	Information control and management		/			/	////	6	11
12	Company-wide participation		/		/	/		3	10
13	Development of QC techniques				/	/	////	6	9

The authors have been fortunate in having participated in numerous discussions regarding the promotion of total quality control in different companies and examining in detail the problems of policy management. This section is based on experience gained from these discussions through the cooperation of various companies and is intended to serve as a guide for policy management. Out of this participation, the seven new QC tools emerge as highly effective QC techniques for policy setting and implementation.

This section provides a brief description of the use of each technique at each step of policy management and notes where to use caution. Policy management concerns effective implementation of decisions made by top management; this procedure is not directly applicable to the decision-making process involved in entering a new field of industry and embarking on a new overseas market, which are more properly the domain of top management. However, the procedure described in this section will be useful for gathering information to be used for such decision making.

Promoting policy management

Figure 3.2 outlines the procedure for policy management. Listed at the top of the figure are points of caution and results that may be anticipated for each step.

It is clear that among the steps involved in the control cycle, policy management requires a most careful and serious planning effort. In various fields, the psychological and organizational climate of Japanese companies harbor elements that hinder planned policy management.[3] For this reason, successful promotion of TQC through effective policy management depends on dispositional reform of companies.

Step 1:   Determine policy and direction

Be certain of the needs for policy and direction. Identify problems of quality, quantity, and cost. Keep in mind that the ultimate goal is to upgrade achievement levels and to train staff resources.

a. Clarify the policy, implementation items, implementation process, levels of achievement and criticisms for the previous year or preceding period. In doing this, we should not be concerned exclusively with the levels achieved, but rather should focus on evaluation of processes involved.

b. For the current year or period, list fully business conditions, problems that may arise in connection with planned projects, and problems that may be encountered in one's own department.

c. Whether a problem is one of quality, cost, or timely production quantity, it ultimately becomes a quality problem. For example, improving the rate of operation may appear to involve problems related to improving the timing or quantity of production, but the underlying problem really may be that of quality, such as insufficient materials and inadequate facilities.

d. As mentioned in the preceding item, various functions, including quality, cost, and production volume, i.e., delivery (QCD), are interrelated in a complex way. Therefore, it is important at this stage to construct a relational diagram for the implementation items of each function. Figure 3.3 is a hypothetical simplified relations diagram of policy and implementation items at the division level.[4] From this figure we learn that an examination of suppliers' products is necessary to maintain acceptable levels. To improve the quality of outside products, we may provide guidance to the supplier or shift production from outside to inside the company if the supplier is not amenable to quality improvement. In this situation, we would need to improve efficiency further and embark early on the training of personnel and the adjustment of specification instructions and facilities. Although Fig. 3.3 is incomplete, it helps to clarify the relationships between departmental policies and implementation items.

 e. The format of a relations diagram is not restricted to that shown in Fig. 3.3. We may place problems, business environment, and projects at the center, write around these entries the policies and implementation items of top management, and note the lower-level management's implementation items outside those of top management. In this way mutual relations are easier to discern.

 f. For each position, the implementation items can be divided into three categories: items to be implemented personally, those to be delegated to subordinates, and those to be implemented by other departments. We underscore items to be implemented personally because regardless of one's position, whether one is a division chief or a departmental chief, one must execute certain items if top management's policies are to be fulfilled successfully. Delegation of tasks to lower-level personnel is never sufficient. Managers must think about what they themselves ought to do. A systematic diagram is often used for developing the implementation items for each position.

 g. List the needs $(g_1, g_2, \ldots, g_L)$ determined by business condition, project, and problems of each department, and through the KJ method or brainstorming, generate as many small implementation items $(d_1, d_2, \ldots, d_m)$ as possible that respond to these needs. Group them to obtain large implementation projects $(D_1, D_2, \ldots, D_n)$ and remedies $(P_1, P_2, \ldots, P_r)$. Be careful, in this process, that no implementation items are omitted for any position.

 h. Since experience has accumulated on quality, cost, and delivery over many years, it is customary to revise improvement plans for the current year on the basis of cumulative experience. By analyzing

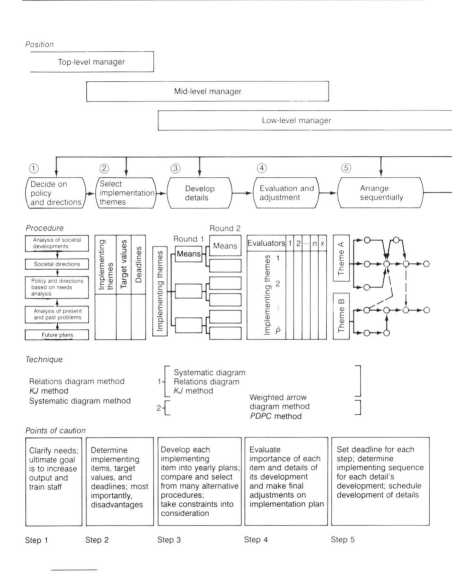

FIGURE 3.2
Outline of the policy control procedure

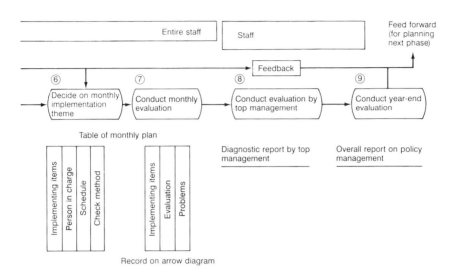

Table of monthly plan

Diagnostic report by top management

Overall report on policy management

Record on arrow diagram

| Put down as much detail as possible; establish monthly objectives | Make certain that evaluation is forward-looking not backward-looking | Adjust policy and implementation themes; grasp importance of making adjustments among divisions | List accomplishments and problems; select items worthy of consideration in next year's planning |

Step 6   Step 7   Step 8   Step 9

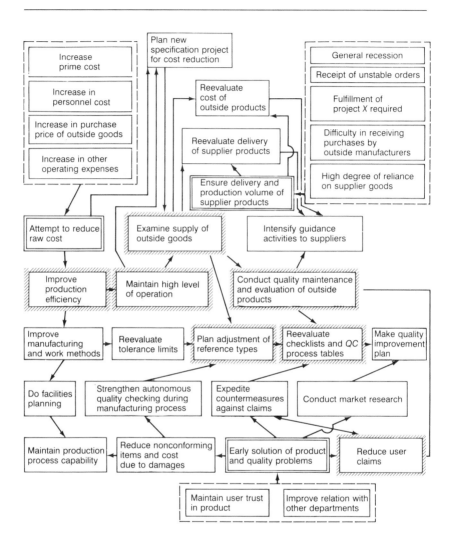

FIGURE 3.3
Simplified relations diagram for selection of implementing items

past experience with the PDPC method, we find that it is frequently possible to generate new ideas for implementing this year's objectives.

i. The implementation items mentioned here are those that require sustained implementation for the current year or period for a given position; developing detailed steps is described in step 3 and thereafter.

j. The policies determined by the steps described up to this point can be consolidated. It is helpful to capture in a few sentences the background or need for such policies and their relation to implementation items.

Step 2: Select implementation activity items

Select activity items and determine their projected value and delivery dates. Weighing the costs and benefits of an activity is most important here.

a. Build on the results of the first step by selecting activity items for each grouping. In doing this, determine not only the target and delivery date, but also the required resources (human, technical, and monetary).

b. Establish whether the targets assigned to lower-ranking positions are related to accomplishment of the overall objective assigned to the department. Through this process activities at different levels can be brought into harmony.

c. Consider any constraints. In discussing quality (Q) improvement as an implementation activity item, we should ask whether it raises problems of cost (C), production volume (D), safety (S), the environment (E), or morale (M). If there are grounds for concern, we should naturally come up with activities that counteract this constraint. Similarly, it is necessary to give full attention to the potential of negative effect of cost reduction (C) on quality, production volume, safety, the environment, and morale. It is a common situation for cost reductions to result in claims of inadequate quality, which nullify the profit gained. Since product longevity is not readily controllable by inspection, this requires much more attention and consideration.

d. Another aspect of the cost-benefit analysis deserves comment. One should ask whether an improvement in one's department or segment of the production process may cause problems in the preceding or subsequent portions of the process. An improvement from one's standpoint may hinder or adversely affect the next phase of the production process.

e. An activity may be consistent with today's purpose, but we should ask whether the situation may not change if production volume or equipment facilities change in the future. Our thinking should be oriented toward the future.

f. The target level should be a value that can be achieved only with considerable effort, and it should be expressed in specific numerical terms. It is meaningless to set a goal that is beyond reach. There is a general tendency, however, not to set high targets. Since the spirit of policy management is to evaluate not only the results, but also the process, it is important that personnel realize that projected values should be set high. A reasonably high target poses a challenge and inspires people toward achieving it.

Step 3: Detailed development of activity items

Consider all options for proceeding, then select a suitable goal and make certain that constraints are taken into consideration.

a. When activity items for each position are established using the steps described above, it is necessary to develop those items further for the current year or period. For example, assume that receiving outside supplier parts shown in Fig. 3.3 has been selected as an activity item. A delivery date and quantifiable objectives are fixed. We note that there are many items to investigate. For example, we may need to ask what type of products should be obtained, from where, when, and what coordination should be made with other departments. In addition, we need to determine how and when to coordinate with other departments. Handled in this manner, each activity item develops into several implementation items for the current year or period. As shown in step 3 of Fig. 3.2, we mainly use the systematic diagram method to develop detailed plans. Figure 3.4 illustrates the development of a portion of a problem into a systematic diagram.

b. Although a delivery date and objectives may have been decided on for an activity item, there is more than one way to achieve our goal. Presented with one yearly plan, we should always ask if it has been selected after considering all the alternatives. Often there are obvious ways of proceeding that even outsiders are able to list. Simple plans, evaluations, and status surveys do not have much

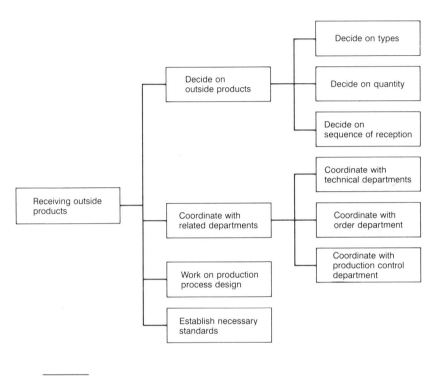

FIGURE 3.4
Detailed development of an activity item

meaning unless they are accompanied by the thoughtful evaluation of alternatives. Even for a matter as simple as training, we need to think about such things as who is best qualified to be trained, how a trainee should be selected, how to follow after training, how to train, and what training materials should be used.

   c. In the preceding item, we underscored the selection of one method from a set of alternatives. What should guide the selection is the economic effect on resources. *Resources* here refer to budgetary resources, human resources, and technical resources. All these resources may boil down to the question of expense. If the solution to a problem requires the renovation of existing facilities and the building of new facilities, the resulting expense may turn out to be prohibitive and the solution impractical. However, constraints can sometimes be resolved by means of positions. The cooperation required for a solution may not be feasible at lower levels in the organization, although the same cooperation may be easy to obtain at a higher level. For this reason, upper management should be involved in assessing whether the constraints identified genuinely pose significant obstacles.

   d. If a disadvantage is anticipated for an implementation activity item (part c in step 2), this fact also should be kept in mind in developing details for this step. If the creation of an activity item depends on the cooperation of another department, detail development must occur between the related departments. The detailed tasks developed for each implementation item are the keys to successful achievement of company objectives. For this reason, there must be clearly defined ideal criteria to guide our selection of objectives.

Step 4: Evaluate the importance of individual activity items and then finalize plan for implementation

Prioritize activity items through evaluation. Consensus should be a guiding principle in modifying the plan.

   a. The completion of steps 2 and 3 result in an increased number of activity items and their details. Since it is often not possible to implement all these items, it almost inevitably becomes necessary to evaluate the importance of activity items and select a manageable number for implementation. Rarely will all items need to be implemented in a given year or period. It is appropriate to defer some items of lesser priority. Indeed, certain items may increase in importance at a later stage.

   b. Evaluation can take place immediately after either step 2 or step 3. Use the number of items to be evaluated as a guide in determining the timing.

   c. Several methods of evaluation are available.[5] If P items are to be evaluated by N persons, a simple method is to use a 5-point scale for each item, where a score of 5 indicates the greatest importance and a score of 1 stands for the least importance. The evaluation score of an individual item is reached by the mean X of evaluation scores; the dispersion of evaluations among evaluators is expressed by the range R of evaluation scores. If $R = 4$ for an item, we know that one judge has given a score of 5, while another judge has assigned a score of 1. One judge thought it was the most important, while another judge thought it was the least important, reflecting diametrically opposed views. In such cases, we might discuss the evaluation criteria to reduce the R value. (Evaluation can also be done on a 10-point scale.)

d. Activity items and their detailed development are to be brought up for policy management in the order of evaluation ranks found in item c above.

e. In assessing the importance of items, as many people familiar with the evaluation items as possible (drawn from many fields and positions) should serve as judges. This objective can be accomplished by making a file of pertinent information available to the potential judges.

f. Prioritization is not the only goal of evaluation. It is better to develop a common perspective and consensus among those participating in the evaluation, even if misleading or incorrect values are sometimes obtained.

g. It is meaningless, even dangerous, for a majority of lower-level personnel to evaluate an item that is properly a decision for top management. Although the results of such evaluations may be considered by top management, the decision ultimately should be made by top management. It is, in fact, the duty of top management to make heart-wrenching, difficult decisions.

Step 5: Schedule implementation activity items

Determine how much time is needed to carry out the details of each step and develop a schedule. Identify the critical step upon which completion of an objective depends. Arrange the necessary steps in a chronological time sequence using an arrow diagram.

a. Through step 4, we have clarified the selection of items and their detailed development. Our next task is to determine the time to be allocated for implementing each step.

b. For each step in an implementation plan, there is a natural sequence to be followed. Implementation of one step might depend upon completion of several preceding steps. If the completion of a step depends on cooperation or input from other departments, fulfillment of their obligations by other departments is a prerequisite, and enough time should be allowed for coordination.

c. By going through this process, we determine the implementation sequence and deadlines for detailed development of each step. An arrow diagram is a suitable way to express this. We need not consider it a difficult task; rather, we should simply try to specify the connections among the detailed steps of each activity item and their delivery dates. For items that rely on another department's participation, mark the necessary delivery date clearly and make certain that the participating department agrees on the date. Furthermore, for activity items that depend on another department's input, make sure that the item is clearly incorporated into the work plan of the participating department and that the department's completion date matches the required date.

d. Clarify which steps are critical to final completion and fulfillment of the objective. Does an item that must be executed pose a deadline problem? Is there an item on which a technical or resource problem can be expected? When these problems are analyzed in greater detail, what emerges as the critical link? If a problem is expected, would additional personnel help? Would allocating more funds be of help? Would assistance from another department be of any help? It is necessary to think through possible solutions like these to enhance the probability of successful implementation.

e. In general, evaluation of situations described in item *d* should precede actual implementation. Frequently, only easy items are executed, deferring difficult ones to a later time. This makes it difficult to accomplish all activity items, however, and inevitably disrupts the following year's plan.

f. Typically, we proceed from planning to execution; we then discover problems, adjust our plan, return to execution and discover more problems. Despite the fact that the PDCA cycle appears to progress forward, achieving objectives sometimes turns out to be very time consuming. In such a situation, it is necessary to ask whether the person in charge could have anticipated the problem at an earlier stage. It is not uncommon to find in various companies that certain problems could have been anticipated at the planning stage and thus prevented. For purposes of early identification and prevention, it is necessary to have a contingency plan for each step in the detailed development of an activity item — a plan of countermeasures and alternatives in case the primary plan fails to proceed as expected. Although a plan is usually based on the presumption that everything will proceed normally, it is helpful to have a contingency plan for areas where difficulty is conceivable.

A way to promote steps 3 through 5: the PDPC method

Steps 3 through 5 are sufficient if the execution sequence and the details of each activity item can be specified fairly clearly, such as with construction or assembly. With a development project or a complex quality-improvement task, however, the detailed execution plan laid out at the early planning stage can hardly be complete. During execution, we need to revise and develop the detailed plan on the basis of the results of implementation or research up to that point. In recent times, the PDPC method has been used to determine the process that can best bring about the desired outcome despite conceivable complications.

Consider the situation where parallel efforts on each activity item by all participating departments are needed to bring about the desired state B_p from the initial state A_0 (Fig. 3.5). A_1, A_2, and A_3 refer to the series of activity items assigned to each department. Discussion among the participating departments midway through the execution period increases the tightness and cohesiveness of the subsequent portion of the plan. Sometimes we need to revise the policy or activity items during an execution period, but use of the PDPC method will automatically do this.

In interim discussions each participating department comes to recognize the role it plays in the expanded detail development and to better appreciate what is required of it. Consensus is reached and the departments become better motivated to fulfill their obligations regarding the delivery target.

Series A_1, A_2, and A_3 of activity items shown in Fig. 3.5 represent independent paths from A_0 to B_p. When there are discrepancies in execution among the series, the PDPC method can be used to remedy the situation. At one company, in response to a request to reduce NO_x, five possible measures were listed in decreasing order of cost

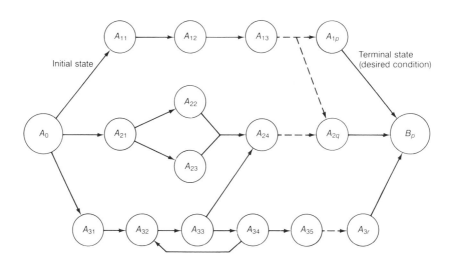

FIGURE 3.5
PDPC diagram to arrive at desired state

while always keeping the target date in mind. By this means, the company was able to achieve its goal with the least investment.[6]

Use of the PDPC method for policy-management is still under development. Depending on the situation, we can develop activity items using the systematic diagram in step 3 and further develop them into a chronologic sequence through the PDPC method. This point will be discussed further in the PDPC method section in Chap. 9.

Step 6: Decide on monthly activity items

Work out the plan in as much detail as possible. Set monthly goals for activity items.

   a. Each month, set activity-item implementation goals for the month. At the early stage of policy management it may be difficult to set up a detailed plan for the year. Even in such a situation, however, it is possible to work out activity items for the current month to at least aim toward the desired year-end result.

b. It is advantageous to specify as much as possible who is in charge, the length of the execution period, and the promotional measures for each activity item. In general, daily routines and fixed schedules keep people very busy, which often results in cramming most of the monthly improvement activities in toward the end or completing schedules in less than a fully satisfactory manner. It thus becomes necessary to determine what activities are scheduled for each week.

c. Establish clear objectives for each month. This is an important step in terms of the following month's evaluation. Within the context of detail implementation for a given month, it may not be possible to link monthly activity goals with the ultimate objectives of quality, cost, and delivery. In this case it is necessary to decide in advance how evaluation is to be conducted.

Step 7: Conduct monthly evaluations

Evaluation should focus on what lies ahead; an evaluation process should not reflect the past.

a. Evaluation is undertaken to ascertain if the proposed activity has taken place and to determine the level of achievement. Concerning the problem of standardization, for instance, we can ascertain the level by asking how the discussion progressed, what was discussed, and what was the result of trial testing.

b. An evaluation should not center on shortcomings in results and blame. What is important is to gain information and knowledge regarding how one may guide subordinates, what should be implemented in the following month, and how it should be implemented. Such an evaluation is what we call a forward-looking, action-oriented evaluation.

c. Steps 6 and 7 should take place simultaneously each month during the execution period. The main point of discussion, however, is to determine what must be achieved in the following month.

Step 8: Conduct a diagnosis by top management

Carry out adjustments regarding policy and activity items. Grasp the importance of interdepartmental coordination.

a. During the current year or period, it is necessary for the president or other top managers to conduct a diagnosis of the success of implementation activity related to the basic policy of each department or division.

b. Departmental policies and activity items must remain flexible so that they can be revised and supplemented in response to changing market conditions, problems of new standards, and progress status within each implementation year or period. One of the purposes of the diagnosis by top managers is to verify that such revisions and additions are instituted voluntarily by rank-and-file workers.

c. At the early stage of policy implementation, it is common for interdepartmental cooperation to be not so smooth, even though such cooperation may have been clearly specified. Another purpose of the top-management diagnosis is to evaluate the level of existing cooperation and to generate ways to bring about the needed cooperation if it is deficient.

d. Top management diagnosis is important from the standpoint of assessing progress and learning about the underlying process. It also contributes to an understanding and furthering of quality control at the top-management level itself.

Step 9: Conduct an overall year-end evaluation

List accomplishments, and assemble a list of problems. Identify items necessary for incorporation in next year's policy.

a. At the end of the year, list accomplishments for each activity item derived from the underlying policy. Rather than worrying about the results, pay attention to the process. The PDPC method may be useful for this purpose.

b. Problems listed and analyzed from the current year can be used as basic data for next year's policy management.

c. Acting out our commitment to policy management, we learn how to improve the quality of the policy-management system itself, including policy setting and daily schedule planning.

d. An analysis of problems that arise in the functional management of quality assurance, production volume and delivery, and cost may serve as a useful reference point for setting policies for the following year.

Conclusion

Regarding the seven new QC tools and policy management, further research and development are needed in the following areas:

Establishment and promotion of company-wide policies

It is hoped that efforts will be made to apply the technique of policy management discussed in this section to the establishment and promotion of company-wide policies. We look forward to the use of the seven new QC tools within the policy management system in order to harmonize top-management decisions with staff support activities and to advance company-wide TQC activity in an appropriate direction.

Coordination with a profit-control system

The preceding section focused primarily on the establishment and promotion of policies. In the policy management of individual companies, however, securing profit is important. This relationship between policy management and the profit-control system needs further study.

Standardization of the policy-control system

For the policy-management system discussed in this section to be introduced, established, and developed in individual companies, it will be necessary for such companies to announce the standardization of the system and to issue various processing forms as a systematic company policy.

Accumulation of experience on the use of each technique for policy management

Typically, in working toward a solution to a plant problem, a plant manager may meet with group leaders and collectively construct a relations diagram. Each group leader carries the group's tasks back to the group, which, in turn, constructs its own relations diagram and works toward the common goal of solving the problem. Also in some cases the promotion of company-wide policy management is expressed in an arrow diagram format and the solution of individual problems relies on the PDPC method. The former aims at a wider dissemination of knowledge, whereas the latter promotes the goal in terms of specific details.

Figure 3.2 is an example of such an application. In applying our techniques at each step, we hope our readers' cumulative experience will lead to many suggestions for the solution of existing problems as well as to the articulation of new problems.

We have discussed several points of general caution as well as the application of the seven new QC tools to promote policy management. In our experience the system described in this section helped to increase the likelihood of success at the stage of policy establishment. The greatest advantage reported by managers is the ability to obtain a comprehensive overview of the progress of improvement. We hope to see continued improvement in applications based on feedback from various fields.[7]

Notes

1. Mizuno, Asaka, and Ishikawa (eds.), *Dai Ikkai Hinshitju Kanri* (*The first quality control symposium*) (Tokyo: JUSE Press, Ltd., 1965).

2. A number of Japanese authors have considered the important issue of promoting policy control, for example, Ishihara Katsuyoshi, "Procedures for Establishing Quality Control Policy," *Hinshitsu Kanri* (*Quality Control*), vol. 27 (October 1976), pp. 8–12; Ikazawa Tachuo, "Managing Quality Control Policy," *ibid.*, pp. 13–15; Tamura Shoji, "Promoting Management Policy," *ibid.*, pp. 16–19.
   Mizuno Shigeru has also addressed the related problems involved in planning and programming in "Planning and Programming in Business," *Quality Control*, vol. 20 (November 1969), supplement pp. 1–4.

Koura Kozo has studied the relationship between objectives control and the QC team in "Examples of QC Teams," *Quality Control*, vol. 19 (October 1968), pp. 32–37.

Finally, a number of studies have been done on policy setting, implementation and promotion at different companies, for example, Ishihara Katsukishi, et al., "Staff's Role in Developing QC Policy and Plans (Nos. 1–4)," *Quality Control*, vol. 21 (November 1970), supplement, pp. 68–86; Yamamoto Mitsuo, "Examples of Policy Management in 1976," *Quality Control*, vol. 28 (June 1977), supplement, pp. 9–13.

3. Matsuda Takehiko, *Keikaku to Joho* (*Planning and Information*) (Tokyo: Nippon Hoso Kyokai Publishing Co., 1969).

4. In the field of quality control, the relations diagram was first introduced in Senmochi and Mizuno, *Hinshitsu Kanri no tameno Keizaikeisan* (Economic calculations for quality control) (Tokyo: JUSE Press, Ltd., 1971).

5. For more on evaluation *see* Shigeru Mizuno and Yoji Akao (eds.), *Hinshitsu Kino Tenkai* (Development of quality and function) (Tokyo: JUSE Press, Ltd., 1978).

6. Eguchi, Kagoyama, and Kishimoto, "On Reducing Nitrogen Oxide in LPG Boiler," in *Hin QC Nanatsu Togu Katsuyo irei Happyokai Jireihsyu* (Applications of the seven new QC tools) (Tokyo: JUSE Press, Ltd., 1978).

7. This chapter is based on research reported in Nayatani Yoshinobu, "Applying QC Techniques in Policy Management: *Hinshitsu* (*Quality*), vol. 8, no. 4 (1978), pp. 25–31.

PART
TWO

Details of the Seven
New QC Tools

4

The Relations Diagram

The relations diagram clarifies intertwined causal relationships in complex problems or situations in order to find appropriate solutions.

The method

Many problems confront modern businesses, problems that pervade such areas as

- Quality assurance
- Cost control
- Delivery schedules
- Resource economy
- Product liability prevention
- Environmental protective measures

- Reliability
- Automation
- Personnel economy
- Energy economy

Moreover, these problems involve complexly interrelated causal factors. Even if a problem were limited simply to quality control, there would still be many intertwined causal factors. Such problems cannot possibly be solved through conventional problem-solving methods, which rely on the efforts of a single staff member eliminating the causal factors one by one. Today, teamwork must be widely and effectively used. The relations diagram method is suitable for such complicated modern problems.

The relations diagram shown in Fig. 4.1 employs arrows to show the cause-and-effect relationships among a number of problems and factors that influence them. The relations diagram method utilizes this type of diagram as a technique for problem resolution. The relations diagram method could further be defined as a technique used to solve problems that have complex cause-and-effect and objectives-means relationships through

1. Isolating all factors related to the issue
2. Expressing these factors freely and concisely
3. Identifying logically the cause-and-effect relationships and depicting them using arrows in a relations diagram
4. Producing a complete picture
5. Extracting the key factors

When this technique is used, diagrams should be drawn up and revised a number of times by several people. During this process, issues can be identified clearly, a consensus can be obtained, and ideas can be developed. In other words, the relations diagram method is an effective technique for reaching the root of a problem and devising solutions.

The relations diagram method was developed into a problem-solving method from diagrams used in management indicator relational analysis.[1] During an attempt to apply relational analysis, after

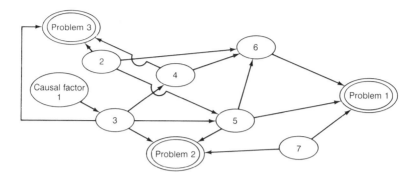

FIGURE 4.1
Sample relations diagram

the cause-and-effect relationships had been reorganized a number of times using relations diagrams, it suddenly became clear that the greater part of the problem had been solved. With this starting point, the use of relations diagrams has been expanded to other areas. Having been confirmed as a useful tool, the relations diagram has come to be viewed as one of the seven new QC tools.

Application fields

The relations diagram is used not only for problem resolution in business activities, but also for the analysis of social phenomena in other fields. In QC operations, this technique has been effective in

- TQC advancement operations
- Quality assurance (QA) and QC policy development

- Measures developed to counter manufacturing-process deficiencies
- The promotion and development of small group activities
- Market claim-prevention policies
- Operations improvement

There are many other fields in which the relations diagram can be used.

Special characteristics

The relations diagram can be used to organize information to highlight cause-and-effect relationships. The key characteristics of this technique are as follows:

1. It is a useful means for organizing problems that have complex factor relationships.
2. From the planning stages on, it provides a means for examining problems from a broad perspective.
3. It allows major factors to be accurately identified.
4. Its use facilitates consensus-building among participants.
5. Because it allows opinions to be expressed freely and does not restrict them with forms or models, problems and causes can be readily identified.
6. Because the diagram itself is not restricted to any specific framework, the conception and development of ideas are facilitated.
7. It helps in eliminating preconceptions.

Those who have successfully used the relations diagram have agreed that it has merits not found in characteristic cause-and-effect diagrams. This is so because, as stated earlier, a complete relationship can be mapped out without restricting expression or dictating the use of a specific framework; this, in turn, facilitates the conception and development of improvement ideas.

When the relations diagram method is introduced to study groups, many ask about the differences between this method and the KJ method. Both processes involve teamwork, the use of brainstorming sessions to develop ideas, and the use of a diagram to organize factors. Ideas are developed, and a consensus is reached. However, in contrast to the KJ method, which uses subjectivity in creating diagrams, the relations diagram method is a logical technique which connects the cause-and-effect relationships among factors by arrows. Moreover, it is a method that incorporates important factors and items from broad perspective, and in this respect, it varies greatly from the KJ Method.

Based on a number of case studies, the advantages and disadvantages of the relations diagram method are presented below.

Advantages

- Problems can be simplified into several major points, and this assists the development of improvement measures.
- The relationships among several departments can be clarified, and problem solving becomes easier when diverse groups are able to work in concert.
- Comments can be entered as they are stated, without restrictions.
- After a number of revisions, the key issues and substantiating points in problem resolution become apparent.
- When further information is added, it is easy to organize connections between factors, making forecasts possible.
- The relations diagram simplifies explanation of a complex problem to others (especially upper management).

Disadvantages and comments

- Since the format is unrestricted, the resulting diagrams differ from team to team, even if the same problem is being tackled (however, the conclusions ordinarily are similar).

- If factors are expressed too simply, arrows may point in misleading directions.
- If the diagram is too complicated, it becomes difficult to understand. When this occurs, important factors may be overlooked in drawing conclusions.
- Despite appearances, constructing an adequate diagram is a surprisingly difficult process.
- It is necessary to redraw the diagram in response to changing situations, a process that can be time-consuming.

Major uses of the relations diagram method

There are two major uses of the relations diagram method: single- and multiple-objective problem solving.

Multiple-objective problem solving (multiple-objective model)

Here the relations diagram is used in cases where there are two or more issues to be considered, such as TQC advancement, policy management, or operations improvement. The relations diagram is effective when applied to multiple-objective problem solving and demonstrates special characteristics not found in other techniques.

In order for a number of departments to cooperate in the development of a plan of action, the items essential in implementing these actions must be enumerated. After grouping all items to express their functional relations in a relations diagram, the major items are extracted. Generally, in such cases, it is also necessary to consider such objectives as quality, volume and delivery, cost, and safety, since the issue of quality control involves all these factors. For example, in order to raise productivity, it may be necessary to increase the speed of the machines used. However, such a step may adversely affect quality. For this reason, the process also may involve modifying material distribution so that when the machine speed is increased, quality products will still be produced.

Single-objective problem solving (single-objective model)

Here the relations diagram is used to solve problems having a single objective, such as decreasing product nonconformities, devising claims-prevention policies, or reducing schedules. Independent measures taken by individuals on the basis of their own view of a problem may result in a loss or no change in conditions. In most cases, it will be difficult to achieve beneficial results. It is therefore necessary to bring together the responsible personnel as a team to allow them to present their opinions. By constructing a relations diagram, a consensus can be obtained and an effective means to solve the problem can be devised.

Basic structure of a relations diagram

In a relations diagram, short sentences or phrases expressing factors or problem points are enclosed in rectangles or ovals, and cause-and-effect relationships are indicated with arrows. The goal to be achieved or the problem point to be solved is enclosed in a rectangle or oval, and important items or factors are shaded in so that they can be more readily identified. As a rule, the arrow in a cause-and-effect format points from the cause to the effect. Likewise, in an objectives-means format, the arrow points from the means or measure taken to the objective. However, where measure B is required in order to achieve objective A, it is sometimes better understood if the arrow points from A to B. Depending on the issue, however, an arrow pointing in the opposite direction may be more effective. It is necessary for the group in charge to determine beforehand the direction the arrow will point and its significance when creating a relations diagram.

Whether phrases or sentences are used is decided by the members of the group creating the diagram; however, it is best if these are kept short and easy to understand. In most cases it is best if at least a noun and a verb are used. (Expressions involving only the use of nouns often are not clear enough, and the quality of the diagram suffers as a result.)

Format of the relations diagram

A special characteristic of the relations diagram is its unrestricted format. However, general format considerations are shown for a centrally converging diagram in Fig. 4.2, a directionally intensive diagram in Fig. 4.3, and a relationship indicating diagram in Fig. 4.4.

Centrally converging relations diagram

The major item or problem to be solved is located in the center, and the related factors are arranged around the item or problem in such a way as to indicate close relationships (Fig. 4.2).

Directionally intensive relations diagram

The major item or problem to be solved is located on one side of the diagram, and the various factors arranged in accordance with the flow of their major cause-and-effect relationships on the other side (Fig. 4.3).

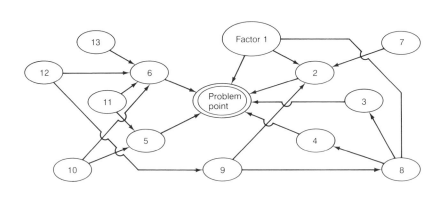

FIGURE 4.2
Centrally converging relationships

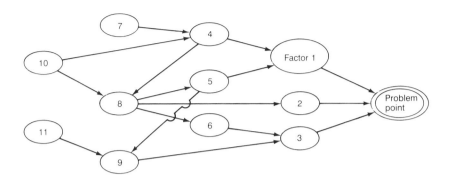

FIGURE 4.3
Directionally intensive relationships

Relationship indication relations diagram

There are no restrictions on this format because the main point is to arrange the cause-and-effect relationships of the application items or factors so that they are expressed in a straightforward manner in a diagram (Fig.4.4).

Application-format relations diagrams

Application-format relations diagrams are based on the three basic types of diagrams discussed above. This format includes diagrams in which the structure of the diagram is based on organizational structure, processes, the 5M's (man, machine, material, method, measurement), and other such items (Fig. 4.5). Other applied formats include diagrams in which a number of factors are collected, as in the KJ method (Fig. 4.6), and diagrams in which the interrelationships are entered after systematic development (Fig. 4.7).

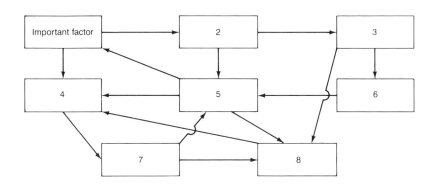

FIGURE 4.4
Relationship indication diagram

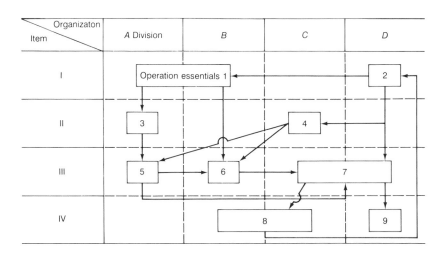

FIGURE 4.5
Applied relations diagram

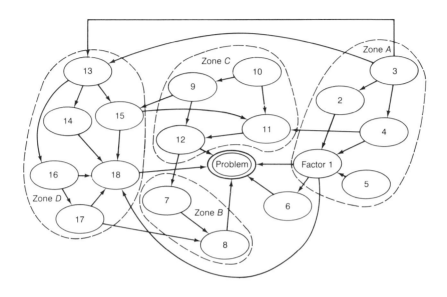

FIGURE 4.6
Applied relations diagram with collected factors

Of these diagrams, centrally converging, directionally intensive, and applied relations diagrams with systematic development
are more often used in single-objective formats, whereas relationship indication and applied relations diagrams, both with organizational structure and with collected factors, are directed toward
multiple-objective formats.

Relations diagram application process

As stated in the first section of this chapter, the relations diagram is a
problem-solving technique. A problem is not solved simply by constructing a relations diagram, but the skillful use of such diagrams is
an integral aspect of problem solving.

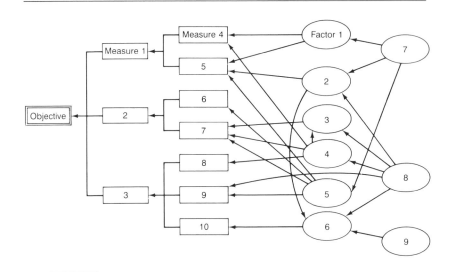

FIGURE 4.7
Applied relations diagram with systematic development

Multiple-objective format

Although methods of application vary significantly depending on the issue involved, multiple-objective models are generally applied in the following step-by-step manner:

1. *Formation of teams in response to problems.* In the case of policy development, for example, a team may be composed of department managers and their staffs.

2. *Close examination of factors and major items through team meetings.* Brainstorming or similar processes are used to allow team members to express their opinions on the measures and policies required to achieve an objective.These, in turn, are concisely entered as presented on a blackboard or on paper (cards also may be used).

3. *Creating the relations diagram.* After the ideas have been exhausted, arrows are drawn in the diagram to indicate the cause-and-effect relationships among the various items. (It is best to combine similar items and organize the diagram for clarity.)

4. *Diagram revision.* The diagram is comprehensively reviewed, and additions and revisions are made where necessary.

5. *Extracting the key items.* Key items in the process are clearly marked by shading or by marking the borders with thick or double lines.

6. *Planning concrete actions concerning key items.* If authorization for action on the key items (step 5) is given, the respective department managers begin preparing their plans for implementation of these actions. (Further stages are best developed using a systematic diagram.)

7. *Review of the relations diagram.* It is very important for the relations diagram to be reviewed in response to any changes. Additions, revisions, and rewritings must be completed in order for this technique to be used to its optimal potential.

Single-objective format

Single-objective relations diagrams are applied in such cases as problems involving decreasing product nonconformities, devising claims-prevention policies, and reducing schedules, among others. This type of relations diagram is usually drawn up either by a team or by a single staff member. As a rule, teamwork is preferable. Even in the case of individual development, the single staff member will not arbitrarily create a diagram, but rather will gather opinions from concerned personnel and organize these in the relations diagram, keeping the expressions as close to the original as possible. Then the staff member determines the actions to be taken. Since the process involved is basically the same as that for a team, the step-by-step application procedure discussed here will be that of a team approach:

1. *Team formation.* The best team is composed of four to five persons concerned with the problem (for example, the line manager, section chief, supervisor, and staff members).

2. *Preparatory meetings.* In a preparatory meeting, members decide what the problem is, how the relations diagram is to be applied, and how to conduct the approach. This step can be omitted if it is not necessary.

3. *First meeting.* Meetings should be held once or twice a week for approximately two hours. At the first meeting

   1. Define and clarify the problem.
   2. Let everyone talk freely about possible causes of the problem. Even excuses and factors based on guesswork should be welcomed.
   3. On the blackboard or a large sheet of paper write down every factor mentioned by the members and circle them. Use a bold circle for the problem definition.
   4. Study the relations between the problem and the factors, asking why over and over to reach root causes. Use arrows to connect factors with the problem. Add other factors as they come up along the way.
   5. When the chart is completed, decide what everyone has to do before the next meeting before closing.

      a. The group leader checks the chart, makes copies and distributes them to the members.
      b. Every member should review the chart.
      c. Follow up on guessed factors to see if they are realistic.
      d. Use data to confirm.
      e. Investigate the points members noticed during the meeting, and if you come across possible solutions, test them and bring the results to the next meeting.

4. *Second meeting.* Everyone brings their assignment from the first meeting. At this meeting make necessary corrections or additions to the chart and rewrite it. When it is completed, from this chart, identify: (a) those items for which data are available and those for which data are not available; (b) those items for which data are required; (c) those items on which action should be taken and those items on which action is not required; (d) those items on which action *must* be taken; and (e) those factors which do not require further consideration. Such factors should be so marked (e.g., by using: o = most important; Δ = less important; x = unimportant). At this stage, a consensus should be reached among the members. Each member should be encouraged to disregard any preconceptions in order to discern the key patterns from either ideas presented or the total picture.

Each should attempt to grasp the specifics necessary for problem solution. Then preparations for the third meeting are the same as for the first meeting.

5. *Third and subsequent meetings.* In the third and subsequent meetings, the following points should be covered: (a) the results of actions based on the relations diagram drawn up during the second meeting should be examined; (b) the relations diagram should be revised to reflect changes in the situation or environment; (c) the key factors brought out during the second meeting should be analyzed further using the relations diagram. Further meetings should be held as necessary, and the results of all actions should be reviewed.

Points on creating and using relations diagrams

The following principles have been compiled from the numerous case studies: First, collect information from a wide range of sources. In this process it is important to talk directly with operators at the site and to speak freely during brainstorming sessions. Second, in constructing the diagram keep written comments as close to the original as possible. Concise phrases or sentences are preferable to isolated words. Third, draw up diagrams only after a consensus has been reached among group members. Someone outside the group may not fully understand the process, and problems may arise should differences of opinion be apparent in the resulting diagram. Fourth, make an effort to rewrite diagrams two or three times. It is essential that this revision process be carried out so that key items can be isolated. And finally, don't be distracted by intermediate factors, use them only as a means to track down fundamental factors.

When working with a single-objective model, the following principles are useful: First, using the question "Why?" as the key to establishing cause-and-effect relationships, makes construction easier. Second, using the question "Why?" is also effective should the process slow down. Third, follow up on any actions to be taken and examine key factors that come to light during the creation or revision process promptly. Lastly, determine whether or not factual relationships that appear to return to the same point can be cut at some point in the cycle.

Relations diagram method case studies

Multiple-objective format

Thorough policy management

A relations diagram was used at the S Company to develop the main items to be implemented by each division in accordance with the plant manager's plan. In the past at the S Company, each division established its main objectives on the basis of its interpretation of the plant manager's plans. However, it was difficult to confirm whether these objectives were appropriate or sufficiently developed. This time, however, through the use of a relations diagram, as shown in Fig. 4.8, related items were organized, key points were extracted, and a much more accurate plan was implemented.

Figure 4.9 shows part of the relations diagram used during this process. The main points extracted were the creation of a quality chart and the integration of products. A structure that was able to respond to new user demands was created.

TQC advancement

In promoting total quality control, personnel at all levels within the company must work together and this policy must be given top priority. Although obvious, quality, cost, personnel, and other factors are all related in an extremely complex manner. Because they are not restrained in terms of format, relations diagram use by various businesses, such as the one presented in Fig. 4.10, will probably be beneficial to TQC advancement.

Administrative operations improvement

Administrative operations involve more complicated social factors and human relationships than do technical operations. Accordingly,

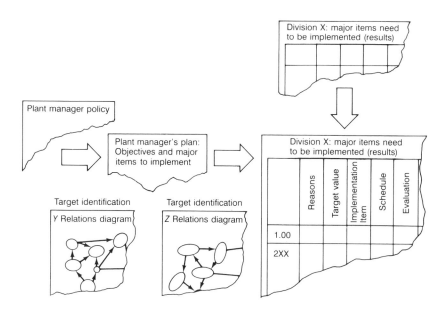

FIGURE 4.8
Policy management development and a relations diagram (partial)
Source: From *Shin QC Nanatsu Dogu Katsuyo Jirei Happyokai Tekisuto (Case Studies on the Application of the Seven New QC Tools)* (Tokyo: JUSE Press, Ltd., 1978).

it is important that the relations diagram be used to identify problems and extract key factors. In the relations diagram in Figure 4.11 the systematic connections can be readily identified.

Introduction of new production methods

In introducing new production techniques, staff and related departments, working with the support of the upper management, should prepare a careful implementation plan and seek uniform cooperation. Figure 4.12 provides a relations diagram used in the analysis subsequent to introduction of the just-in-time method, which is part of the Toyota production system. A superficial introduction of the

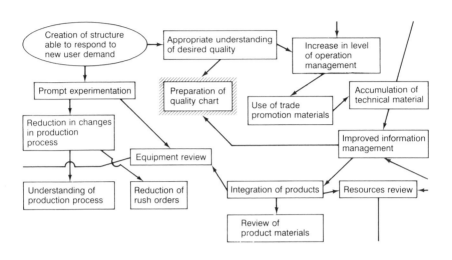

FIGURE 4.9
Policy management relations diagram (partial)

Source: From *Shin QC Nanatsu Dogu Katsuyo Jirei Happyokai Tekisuto (Case Studies on the Application of the Seven New QC Tools)* (Tokyo: JUSE Press, Ltd., 1978).

"just-in-time" method will not be effective. The analysis shows that in order to implement this plan, such fundamental aspects as thorough understanding of the concept throughout the company, standardization of production, and the creation of a supplier-management system must be addressed.

Single-objective format

Claim-prevention measures

Unexpected errors are often the cause of liability claims. Errors in labeling represent one form of such claims. Care must be taken, especially in terms of the human factor, to avoid errors in operating

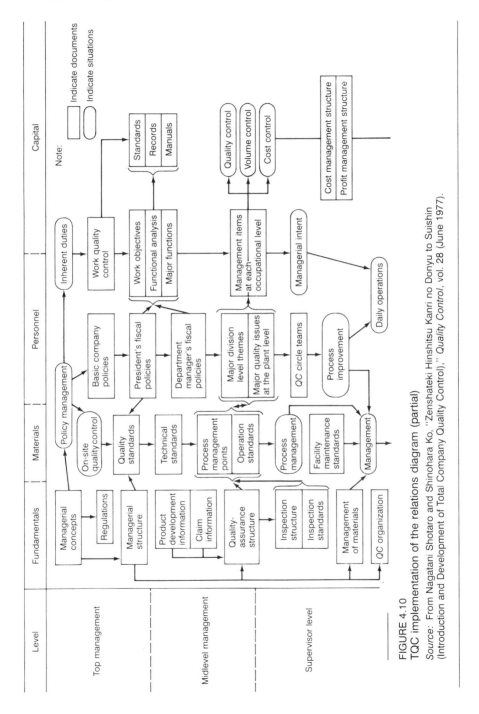

FIGURE 4.10
TQC implementation of the relations diagram (partial)

Source: From Nagatani Shotaro and Shinohara Ko, "Zenshateki Hinshitsu Kanri no Donyu to Suishin (Introduction and Development of Total Company Quality Control)," *Quality Control*, vol. 28 (June 1977).

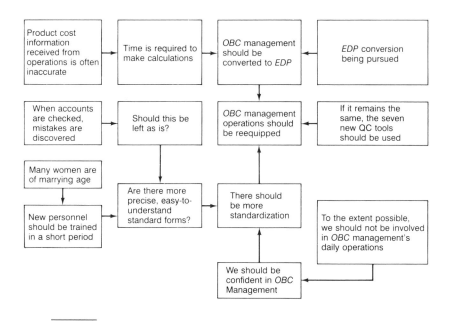

FIGURE 4.11
A relations diagram used in improving operations within the
administrative department

Source: From *Shin QC Nanatsu Dogu Katsuyo Jirei Happyokai Tekisuto (Case Studies on the Applications of The Seven New QC Tools)* (Tokyo: JUSE Press, Ltd., 1978).

instructions as well as errors in judgment on the part of operators. In such cases, relations diagrams can be extremely useful in establishing clear policy, as shown in Fig. 4.13. Such diagrams also have the advantage of listing the key items in a short note in the bottom right-hand corner.

Decreasing production-line nonconformities

At Company U, the seven tools for quality control had been used in an attempt to solve the problem of chronic nonconformities in the

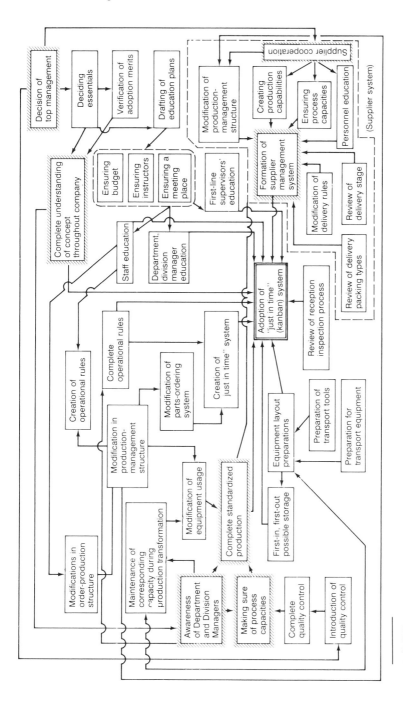

FIGURE 4.12
A relations diagram used in the introduction of new production methods

Source: From Shin QC Nanatsu Dogu Katsuyo Jirei Happyokai Mondaishu (A Workbook on Case Studies on the Application of The Seven New QC Tools) (Tokyo: JUSE Press, Ltd., 1978).

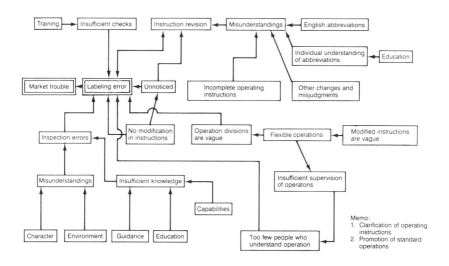

FIGURE 4.13
Use of a relations diagram in claim-prevention measures
Source: From *Shin QC Nanatsu Dogu Katsuyo Jirei Happyokai Mondaishu (A Workbook on Case Studies on the Application of the Seven New QC Tools)* (Tokyo: JUSE Press., 1978).

assembly line; however, the results were less than satisfactory. Behind this problem lay the interrelationships between such various factors as human issues, operations-management methods, and the methods of information sharing. The problem was reexamined using the relations diagram method.

Line-section managers and staff interviewed operators and collected their opinions about the reasons for the occurrence of nonconformities. During the process of creating a relations diagram, it was realized that nonconformities were caused by factors totally different from the earlier conclusion that the quality of the operators was low. Rather, the problem lay in such factors as incomplete

operations-management methods and the lack of an optimal equipment layout. With this understanding, a factor analysis was conducted.
Appropriate corrective measures were taken, and the number of nonconformities per month was greatly decreased. Furthermore, the operators' morale was greatly enhanced. The third and final diagram used
during this process is shown earlier in Fig. 2.3.

Reducing variations in product characteristics

An analysis process at the S Company was conducted to determine
measures for reducing variations in the hardness of the product *A*.
Various factors were arranged in a relations diagram similar to the
one in Fig. 4.14 in order to devise a method of dealing with this
problem. This type of relations diagram is best suited for situations
where there are complex interrelationships among various factors.

Reducing receipt inspection nonconformities

The responsibility for nonconformities evident at the time of receipt
is usually not placed on those receiving an order, but is more often
the responsibility of the sender or the partial responsibility of both
the sender and the receiver. However, the factors in this type of
problem frequently have complex interrelationships and often cannot be readily resolved. A relations diagram may be an effective
means of expressing the cause-and-effect relationships among the
factors and of isolating key factors. Although the single-objective
relations diagram could be used in this case, the multiple-objective
format is perhaps better suited to this type of situation.

Improving the pace in the assembly process

A slow assembly process can be caused by material, operators, equipment, and other factors, all of which are intertwined in a complex
relationship. This makes the production process extremely difficult
to control, especially in the case of individual items. Figure 4.15
presents a relations diagram (the third) created to analyze the reasons for slow assembly processes at the Company M's electric motor
assembly plant. During preparation of this diagram, many of the
points were changed, and it was found that in order to make improvements in the assembly process, it was necessary to conduct

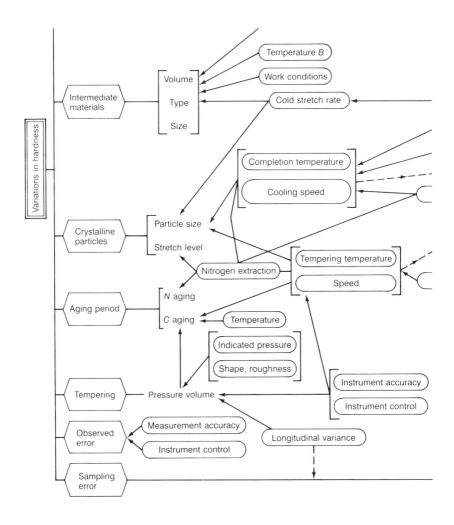

FIGURE 4.14
Relations diagram concerning variations in product characteristics

operations roughly according to a daily planning schedule. In this particular case, the relational analysis method also was used.[2]

Conclusion

This chapter presented the definition, application methods, and actual case studies of the relations diagram method. The relations diagram, in short, is the only effective QC technique for cases involving complex interrelationships. A problem cannot be solved simply by drawing up a relations diagram; nonetheless, through the revision process, which is usually carried out several times, the measures necessary to solve a problem are clarified, and in this sense, the relations diagram is truly effective.

Because the format of the relations diagram is unrestricted, it also can be used in QC circles. However, because it is a technique for use in problem solving involving large-scale issues having numerous factor interrelationships, it is best applied by managerial staff.

Here we would like to touch on relational analysis. This process is formally referred to as "management indicators relational analysis" and was developed by Professor Toshio Senju at Keio Gijuku University for application in industrial relations analysis.[3] In this analysis, problems having linked cause-and-effect relationships are numerically analyzed. Disadvantages of the method are that two sets of data are required for each factor; furthermore, the calculation process is time consuming. Nonetheless, this technique is sure to see future applications.

The relations diagram method is still a relatively new QC technique. Accordingly, it remains a technique with potential for expansion into new fields of application. Various problems that may have seemed too complex to tackle can now be challenged by teams of managers and staff using this method.

In conclusion, we would like to thank Professor Senju Toshio of Keio Gijuku University for his guidance and advice in the development of the relations diagram method. We also thank those who helped in the preparation of these diagrams.

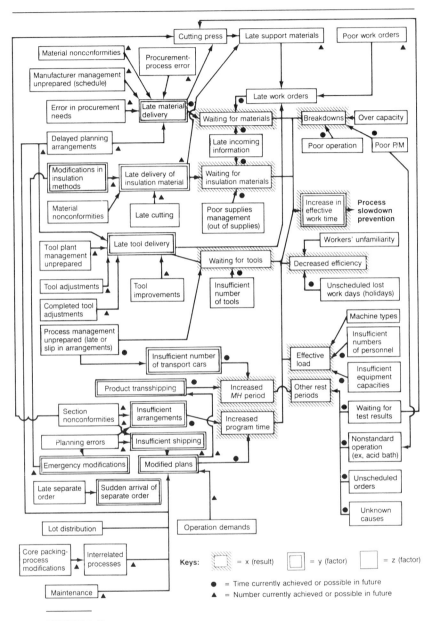

FIGURE 4.15
Relations diagram for a slow assembly process

Notes

1. Senju Toshio and Mizuno Yukiichi, *Hinshitsu Kanri no tame no Keizai Keisan* (Economic planning for quality control) (Tokyo: JUSE Press, Ltd., 1971); Senju Toshio and Fushimi Michio, *Keizaisei Kogaku* (Economic engineering) (Tokyo: Japan Management Association, 1967).
2. Yagishi Seichi and Kurabayashi Mikihiko, "Kanri Shihyokan no Renkan Bunseki Shuho" (Management indicator relational analysis), *Quality Control*, vol. 26 (May 1975), special issue, pp. 213–217.
3. Senju and Mizuno, *Economic Planning*, 1971; Senju and Fushimi, *Economic Engineering*, 1967.

Other references

Nagao Seigo, *Sangyo Renkan Bunseki Nyumon* (Introduction to industrial relational analysis) (Tokyo: JUSE Press, Ltd., 1970).

Nagao Seigo et al., "Relational Analysis," *Operations Research*, vol. 17 (September–December 1972).

Nagatani Shotaro and Shinohara Ko, "Zensha teki Hinshitsu no Donyu to Suishin" (Companywide quality control: introduction and advancement), *Quality Control*, vol. 28 (June 1977), special issue, pp. 5–9.

Fujita Shinji, *Kanri Gijutsu Koza* (Lectures on management methods) (Tokyo: Japan Standards Association, 1975).

Kumatani Tomoe, "Toyota Seisan Hoshiki no Tokushitsu" (Special characteristics of the Toyota production system), *Kojo Kanri* (Factory Management), vol. 24, no. 13 (1978), p. 155.

5

The KJ Method: Affinity Diagram*

The KJ method clarifies important but unresolved problems by collecting verbal data from disorganized and confused situations and analyzing that data by mutual affinity.

The KJ method and the seven new QC tools

The KJ method was developed and popularized by Kawakita Jiro. The principal tool in the KJ method is an affinity diagram. The seven new QC tools help solve problems not only through the repeated application of the affinity diagram, but also through the combined use of other diagrams. Table 2.1 shows the differences between the KJ method and the statistical method; Fig. 2.4 shows the similarities between the two methods.

---

*Permission to use material on the KJ method in this chapter granted by Kawakita Jiro, Kawakita Research Institute.

Description of the affinity diagram of the KJ method

The affinity diagram of the KJ method is designed to collect facts, opinions, and ideas about unknown and unexplored areas which are furthermore in a completely disorganized state. Like the first two stars in the sky at sunset, the data arrange themselves according to mutual affinity. Then the data areas are reduced to narrative rather than quantitative form.

Uses of the affinity diagram

Recognizing facts

Information about unknown and unexplored fields is difficult to obtain. It is important to collect facts about a field, one by one, to learn how it is organized. When we collect data in such a situation, it is important to do so with a completely open mind. Otherwise, we can make mistakes by interpreting these data in terms of previously formed opinions and hypotheses. This often occurs when we try to obtain information about an unknown. It also occurs when we try to understand consumer reactions or the reactions of manufacturers and retailers to highly unique products or to measure the effectiveness of a new factory or an existing factory operated by a new manager.

Forming ideas

When we have almost no information about a new field, we start from scratch, hoping to form our own ideas and concepts. In such a case, it is necessary for us to collect information about the target field, examine the opinions of other people, and write down our own opinions and ideas as they come to us. By organizing these data in an affinity diagram, we can build our own system of thought. We can use the same method when we are assigned to a new position and want to determine how to carry out the new assignment.

Breaking away from old approaches

We may face some difficulty in performing our duties if we are victims of our past experience. In a situation such as this, we must overcome the difficulty and formulate new ideas. Here, as in the previous example, the ultimate goal is also the formulation of new ideas, but unlike the previous situation, we must start by destroying the status quo. Old ideas and their systems are broken down into unstructured bits out of which we build a new way of thinking using the affinity diagram.

Adaptation

Any subject matter has a system of thought and a theoretical base. It is often useful to comprehend and then build upon that base by adding improvements and refinements. This process is analogous to destroying the status quo. First, we read books and papers and transfer pieces of information from these sources to cards; then we build a new concept by arranging the cards in an affinity diagram. In this way, we adapt the opinions and ideas of others and use them to build our own theoretical foundation.

Organizing a planning team

A diverse group of people brought together for the purpose of planning has no particular organization at first. Such people must come to an understanding and organize themselves into a team designed to take part in planning. Group members share experiences and exchange opinions in a brainstorming session, record these exchanges on cards, and individually arrange their thoughts into an affinity diagram. Members explain their thoughts using the diagram and hear the thoughts of other members. This is a way of promoting mutual understanding and teamwork. This method can be used to help form project teams for the promotion of total quality control or QA project teams, as well as to revitalize existing teams. It also can be used to create and revitalize teams in the workplace and in QC circles.

Thorough communication of management policies

Management cannot succeed in making employees understand its ideas and policies thoroughly through one-sided communication imposed from the top down. Management must be receptive to dialogue so that employees can understand management policy completely.

Management should participate in meetings with employees and hold brainstorming sessions with them on target subjects. Management personnel should allow employees to speak out freely about management policy, and the whole process should be recorded. Members of the managerial staff should not make direct rebuttals of opposing opinions expressed by employees; instead, management should also express its ideas and clarify its policies by accommodating opposing points of view as much as possible, in accordance with the rules of brainstorming.

As illustrated in Fig. 2.5 in chapter 2, an affinity diagram is constructed with the information gathered in these brainstorming sessions. The diagram can then be used to transmit management's ideas and policies to the employees. Thus management is able to study employees' opinions by hearing them, and management's ideas and policies are thoroughly understood by employees through brainstorming and the oral presentation.

In organizing teams to participate in planning, employees should be allowed to draw affinity diagrams. In other situations, however, only management should use affinity diagrams. This approach is effective in promoting a sense of participation in the planning process by employees.

Functions of the brain in relation to affinity diagrams

Impairment of all or part of the left half of the brain results in malfunctions in the right half of the body; impairment of all or part of the right half of the brain causes the left half of the body to suffer from motor disturbances. These phenomena are known from study of various mental and physical handicaps caused by cerebral hemorrhage due to high blood pressure, automobile accidents, or injuries to the brain during war.

The brain controls motor functions as well as cognitive and other functions. The left half of the brain controls the speech function, rational thinking, logical thinking, causal thinking, and analytical and discriminating thinking. The right half controls the ability to think instantaneously, intuitively, emotionally, and synthetically. The corpus callosum, located between the right and left halves, has the function of connecting the two halves.

Ordinarily, the thoughts and behavior of an adult are controlled by the left half of the brain. The left half is logical and critical, but not creative. Therefore, it is possible to develop the function of creative thinking by stopping the work of the left half of the brain and revitalizing the right half with more energy. In recent years, through research and training, techniques have been designed to increase creativity.[1] The KJ method is a creativity-mobilization technique that has been developed for practical purposes.

Of the seven new QC tools, six depend on the left half of the brain. The affinity diagram is the only one that depends on the right half of the brain (Fig. 5.1).

A relations diagram comes closest to an affinity diagram as a technique for arranging disorganized data. However, a relations diagram depends on the left half of the brain for logical thinking (the relationships of cause and effect), whereas an affinity diagram depends on the right half of the brain, which serves the function of feeling.

Drawing an affinity diagram

An affinity diagram is created through the following steps:

1. Selecting a theme
2. Collecting narrative data
3. Transferring narrative data onto cards
4. Sorting the cards
5. Labeling the cards
6. Drawing the diagram
7. Oral or written presentation

Many people, including Kawakita Jiro, have written in detail about the steps involved in preparing an affinity diagram for the KJ method.[2] This section will briefly discuss the most crucial points.

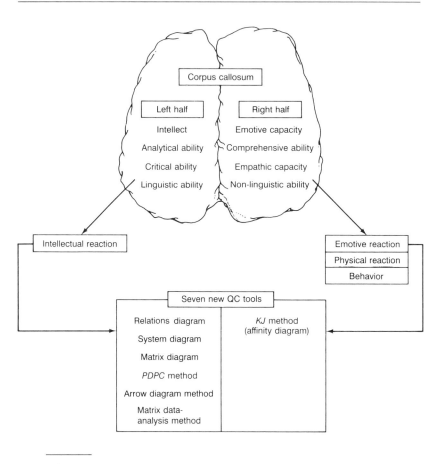

FIGURE 5.1
Function of the brain in terms of the seven new tools

Selection of methods

The seven new QC tools include six other techniques in addition to
the KJ method. Accordingly, in selecting the appropriate method,

the main focus is on (1) who, (2) what, (3) when, (4) where, and (5) with what technique. From the point of view of the PDPC technique (see Chap. 9), the appropriate selection of an affinity diagram for problem solution is most important. The process of selecting the best technique for various stages of problem solving was discussed in the second section of Chap. 2 (see Fig. 2.14).

The affinity diagram, along with the relations diagram, is used at the plan 1 stage, where data are arranged and the problem is defined. It can be used in six different ways, as discussed in the third section of this chapter. Therefore, one must select the most appropriate technique for achieving the specific goal. The seven new QC tools constitute a system of diagraming and thinking. With the proper use of a diagram, a thinking pattern can be changed completely.

Management personnel and staff members, as individuals, have specific ways of thinking with both strong and weak points. Accordingly, the full use of the best technique for the job at hand is recommended. However, conscious attempts should be made to learn to use unfamiliar diagrams so that our abilities are increased.

The seven new QC tools also sum up patterns of thinking. As such, they are convenient for the development of *new* ways of thinking. When we give assignments to employees, we should be careful to bring together the right person with the appropriate technique.

Selecting a theme

Affinity diagrams are appropriate for use within the following limits:

- Facts are uncertain and hard to understand; they need to be grasped systematically.
- Thoughts are uncertain and disorganized; they need to be arranged.
- Pre-existing notions make it difficult to achieve a goal; current ideas must be eliminated and a new way of thinking must be adopted.
- The existing thought system and ideology need to be dismantled; a new system needs to be established.
- No unity exists in a group of heterogeneous people; teamwork must be promoted for mutual understanding.

● Management needs to listen to employees and clarify its ideas and policies.

As described in the preceding section, you are able to think with feeling with the help of affinity diagrams by reducing the dominance of the left half of the brain and revitalizing the function of the right half. Accordingly, use of an affinity diagram is appropriate (1) when there is a strong need for a solution of any form, (2) when an easy solution is not available, and (3) when much time is needed for solution of the fundamental problem. The affinity diagram should not be used for solving problems that require instant solutions (Fig. 5.2).

Collecting verbal data

Several methods exist for the collection of verbal data (Fig. 5.3). The following subsections discuss these methods.

Direct observation

We may do field work, making direct observations by seeing, hearing, and experiencing. Whereas quality control as "fact control" (management based on fact) emphasizes fact finding, the KJ method uses the term *external exploration* to emphasize the importance of fact finding in the field. Exploratory fact finding is important in quality control.

Interview and reference-search method

There are many methods of obtaining information, such as reviews of literature, interviews of people, and group sessions designed to elicit the opinions of many people. There are limits to the use of direct, on-the-spot, and personal fact-finding methods. Therefore, the indirect method is useful for the collection of data from various sources. Furthermore, these are the only methods of obtaining opinions and ideas of other people.

Individual thought

There are two types of thought: *recall*, in which past experiences are recalled and used as data, and *reflection*, in which one's inner

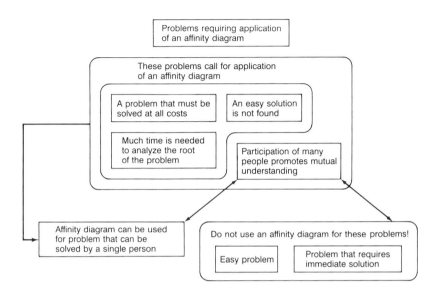

FIGURE 5.2
Problems that can use affinity diagrams

This diagram is drawn on the basis of material available in Japan Management
Association (Eds.), *Introduction to the KJ Technique for Management: Creative Technique
Born Out of Practical Experience.* (Tokyo: Japan Management Association, 1974).
Appreciation is extended to the author.

thoughts about a theme are explored in depth. Brainstorming by a
single person may make the recall method and the reflection method
more effective. Kawakita calls this individual contemplation an
"inner exploration."

The collection of spoken or narrative data varies with the application and purpose of the diagram (see Tables 5.1 and 5.2). The following subsections describe the various purposes of data collection.

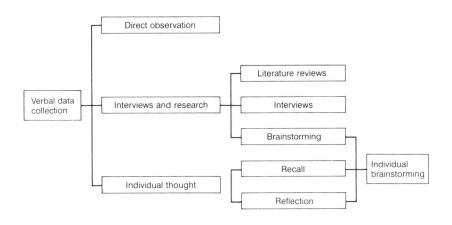

FIGURE 5.3
Methods of verbal data collection*

This chart is based on material appearing in Kawakita Jiro and Makajima Shiniichi,
Science of Problem-solving — The KJ Method (Tokyo: Kodansha, 1970).

Recognition of facts

In this case, fact gathering is important. We attempt to prevent opinions, ideas, and preconceived notions from confusing the facts. We make direct observations in the field by using our own eyes and ears and simply by being there in person.

The indirect data-collection methods, such as literature reviews, interviews, or brainstorming, allow for the potential influence of subjective opinions and judgments on the part of informants. This method should be avoided if possible. If indirect methods are necessary, we should make every effort to collect only objective facts.

When observed facts are reduced to spoken or narrative data, they should not be stated in the abstract. Retain the original flavor if

TABLE 5.1
Selection of methods for collecting verbal data (shown by matrix)

Purpose \ Type of Data	Direct Observation	Reference Search	Interview	Brain-storming	Recall	Reflection
Recognition of facts	●	△	△	△	○	X
Thought formulation	○	○	●	○	○	●
Breakthrough	●	○	○	●	●	●
Adaptation	△	●	●	X	○	○
Organization of planning and participation	X	X	X	●	○	○
Policy implementation	X	X	X	●	○	○

● = often used   ○ = used   △ = seldom used   X = not used

TABLE 5.2
Selection of collected data (shown by matrix)

Purpose \ Type of Data	Factual Data	Opinion Data	Thought Data
Recognition of facts	●	X	X
Thought formulation	○	●	●
Breakthrough	●	○	●
Adaptation	△	●	○
Organization of planning and participation	△	●	△
Policy implementation	△	●	○

possible. When data are collected in abstract form, they cease to be objective because of unavoidable observer bias.

Formulation of thought

If you must organize your thoughts from scratch, it is important to comprehend the facts while at the same time giving a great deal of thought to them. Useful data may be based on opinions and ideas as well as on quantifiable factual data. On some occasions, these two forms of data may be mixed. We should distinguish factual data from opinion data at the time of data collection.

Breakthrough thinking

If it is necessary to eliminate existing concepts, it is important to remember these points: (a) reexamine facts without prejudice; (b) make every effort to collect a variety of opinions; (c) the existing ideas need not be discarded, but they must be approached as data after they are analyzed; and (d) use the individual brainstorming method with all the preceding data in order to formulate new ideas (see the section on individual brainstorming below).

Organizing participative planning

In this case we collect data through brainstorming.

Transferring verbal data onto cards

Collected verbal data are broken down into individual thoughts units in the form of independent sentences with one clear, single meaning, and one sentence is recorded on one card. Abstract terms and complicated expressions should be avoided in these sentences; use ordinary everyday expressions. The use of abstract expressions makes the data almost useless at later stages.

Card grouping

The cards should be shuffled well to eliminate pre-existing order and then spread around so that every card can be easily seen. Each card should be read slowly two or more times. Cards containing similar items are grouped together and on the basis of their affinity. This sorting is done not on the basis of reason, but on the basis of feeling. The cards should not be grouped on the basis of the sorter's ideas and preconceptions or according to existing categories. The term "feeling" refers to a state that precedes logical consciousness. The cards should be grouped with the help of the *right* half of the brain.

What is desired is the "impression" that the cards group them-selves. The cards are not to be gathered according to a certain clas-sification scheme or on the basis of certain key words, because they are not supposed to be classified but simply to be grouped. (Use a matrix diagram if they are to be classified; to connect them logically, use a systematic diagram and a relations diagram.)

After two or three cards are grouped, they are labeled. Sometimes five or six cards are collected, but this kind of collection often indicates that they did not group themselves but were classified into certain established categories. This is similar to the grouping of letters and postcards into prearranged boxes. When two cards are grouped, a procedure similar to making nameplates should begin.

Labeling the cards

The grouped cards should be read one more time and checked to see if they are properly grouped. Cards that are suspected of being "strange" or inappropriately filed are taken out of the group and returned to the presorting pile. The cards that appear to be properly grouped are given a label that represents succinctly the characteristic of the group; the label is written on a blank card. The essence of labeling lies in retaining the nuances of the cards with lively, ordinary expressions. The label is supposed to convey the meaning of the cards fully, but not to say more than they do. It is inappropriate to express the meaning in abstract terms. Once the label card is completed, it is placed on top of the cards it covers and a rubber band is put around them. The labeled groups of cards are treated as single cards, and the procedure of card sorting continues.

Drawing the diagram

Some cards are left out in the process of sorting and do not fall into a specific group. These are called "lone wolf" cards or "isolates." They should be left alone, and no attempt should be made to force them into a sorting scheme. The process of sorting continues with "lone wolf" cards counting as individual groups until the number of groups is about 10.

After the groups are arranged, a diagram of the groups is drawn. For this purpose, the groups of cards that are the last to be collected are positioned so as to show their mutual relationships. These cards are pasted on a sample sheet, and symbols are used to indicate their mutual relationships.

Oral presentation

The content of the diagram is then explained orally. The meaning of each card is explained along with ideas that come to mind at the time of the presentation.

Written presentation

A written report is composed along with the affinity diagram. In explaining the data, include new ideas that come to mind. Such expressions as "It is," "I think," and "It appears" are encouraged.

Brainstorming techniques

Twenty-five years have passed since the brainstorming technique was introduced in Japan in 1952. It is widely used and well known, but it is often not used properly. In order to make effective use of the brainstorming technique, one must follow some basic rules:

1. *Criticism forbidden:*   No expression of criticism or opposition to statements by others is allowed.
2. *Complete freedom:*   Everyone must have complete freedom to express thoughts.
3. *Accommodation of many ideas:*   It is better to have many ideas.
4. *Combination and improvement:*   Opinions of other people are adopted and improved; statements of other people are to be pursued for possible adoption.

First of all, these basic rules must be followed faithfully. Second, self-examination is needed when things do not go well. Among the problems that may be encountered are the following: There may be no sense of urgency or immediacy in solving the problem. Leaders must motivate members to participate. Participants may make little effort to formulate ideas about the collected data. It is frequently necessary to give members homework so that they are well prepared for active participation. Participants may be reluctant to express their opinions, hampering the free flow of ideas. To avoid this, each member could be asked to make a presentation. There may be a sense of too little freedom; members may be too serious and depend too much on common sense. Statements should be kept as concrete as possible, using ordinary language. General and abstract statements do not comprise good data. Statements made without adequate awareness of the problem and with insufficient knowledge of facts and thought tend to become abstract.

Individual brainstorming method

The individual brainstorming method applies the principle of brainstorming to promote individual thinking. This may be assisted by taking notes.

It was pointed out in the section on method selection that a diagram is a method of thinking, and there are many types of thinking. One type of thinking is through language. Japanese-speaking people think in Japanese, and English-speaking people think in English. Language thinking is expressed in spoken language as well as in writing. "Note-taking thinking" is thinking with letters and writing. Albert Einstein, famous for his theory of relativity, said, "New ideas are born in my mind one after another while I am speaking."

Thinking is also done in images. According to Dr. Edward De Bono, famous for his concept of lateral thinking, one way of avoiding the rigidity of language is to think not with speech, but with images.

Note-taking thinking is taking notes about what goes on in one's mind while thinking. Reading these notes helps to develop ideas further, with hints from the notes. It helps to continue the thinking process while one "talks" with notes. This is why this method is called individual brainstorming.

Unless notes are taken, thinking may ramble, wander, and derail. Ultimately, the process becomes unproductive if this occurs. Note-taking helps the thinking process by preventing rambling and derailment. It may result in generation of a new thought.

The following is an example of an individual brainstorming session:

Book (thesis) is written with the KJ method.

It is called a KJ diagram.

It is called seven new QC tools along with other diagrams.

Is it different from the KJ method, even if it is called the KJ diagram?

No, it is not different; the essence of the KJ method lies in its diagram.

How is it done?

Take notes.

Take as many notes as possible.

Notes taken on any idea can be sorted out using the KJ method.

Don't pay attention to structure; simply take notes.

Arrangements of notes is the same as data collection.

Conduct external exploration completely; conduct internal exploration.

Try to change the surroundings from time to time.

Unless you change the surroundings, you may go around and around.

Many books have been written about the KJ method.

Is there any sense in writing a book about the subject?

It is the KJ method as seen by QC advocates.

Could the feature of the method be brought out by that method?

Think about it.

KJ method as seen by QC advocates.

KJ method for quality control.

The KJ method for quality control is a method that is supplementary to statistical techniques.

Statistical techniques and the KJ method are comparative theories.

Include new viewpoints and a way of thinking as opposed to the KJ method.

Let the KJ method serve useful purposes as a guide for those who want to use the method.

Introduction to the Study of Problem Solution — KJ Method Workbook is excellent as a guidebook.

Introduction to the KJ Method for Management is also a good book.

I wish to make this as valuable as the above-mentioned books.

This is a book about the KJ method; write a book by using the KJ method.

It is common practice in writing a book to begin with a table of contents (structure) and then write the text (content); actually a book will begin where the author feels like starting, and the entire book will be completed as a whole later. This is the way the KJ method is used.

Following the preceding guidelines, notes should be taken about anything that comes to mind. When a mental block occurs, relax and turn your attention to other things or work on something else. Frequently, going outdoors for a walk is helpful in producing a lead to follow.

KJ method case studies

How should research and development be carried out?

This case is based on a seminar conducted at the KJ Method Workshop (with Mr. Kawakita as a speaker) held at the Hakone Hotel in 1970 (Fig. 5.4 was drawn at that time). The workshop was conducted with a team composed of 10 engineers and engineering managers from different manufacturers, including Kataoka Hirō of the Japan Paint Company. Various affinity diagrams were drawn in the first and second rounds by faithfully following the rules of the KJ method. Figure 5.5 is an affinity diagram drawn in the first round that shows the presentation of a problem. Figure 5.6 was drawn in the second round and shows an understanding of reality.

These figures were drawn with the participation of various manufacturers, but it was a homogeneous group because it was

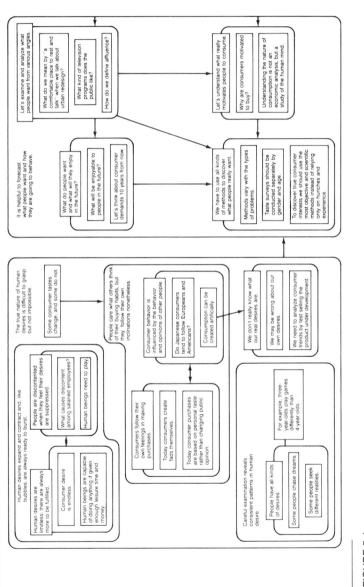

FIGURE 5.4
Example of an affinity diagram (one segment)

made up entirely of engineers. A group can be formed of people from the same industry as well as from different industries, such as banking, business, advertising, publishing, and film. The more people from different industries, the more lively will be the brainstorming and the more new findings will emerge in the affinity diagram.

How can QC circles be managed properly?

This case centers around the theme, "What is the best way to lead a QC group?" The case involves affinity diagrams drawn on the basis of data collected from brainstorming by a group of QC engineers representing different manufacturers.

Two diagrams (Figs. 5.7 and 5.8) were drawn on this theme because members were divided into two groups of 10 each and these two groups conducted separate brainstorming sessions. Two different teams were organized because the number of members in each group should be limited to a manageable brainstorming number and because the two teams were pitted against each other to increase productivity.

The same theme can produce entirely different data (verbal information on pieces of paper) if different members are involved. Furthermore, with different data, the same person could draw entirely different affinity diagrams. The drawing of similar diagrams would mean that the drawer probably predetermined the appearance of the diagram, and this kind of diagram cannot be expected to be truly creative.

What is the future of quality control?

With the same data (information on pieces of paper), two different drawers could produce entirely different affinity diagrams. First, brainstorming is done in groups, and each member shares data (e.g., fact cognition, opinions, ideas). Each member, using the same data, draws an affinity diagram independently, expressing his or her ideas. Then each member takes turns making oral presentations on

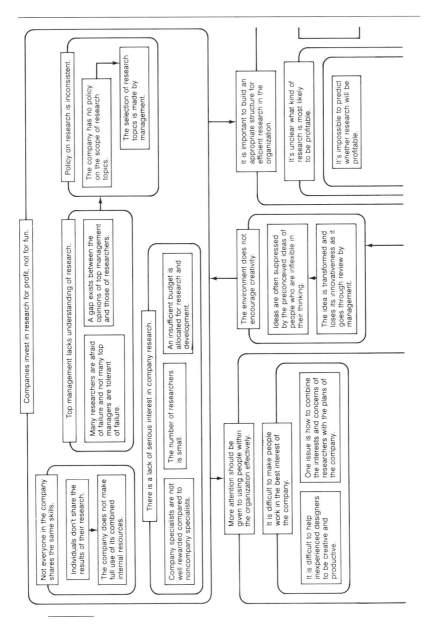

FIGURE 5.5
The process of developing research (the first round: asking questions)

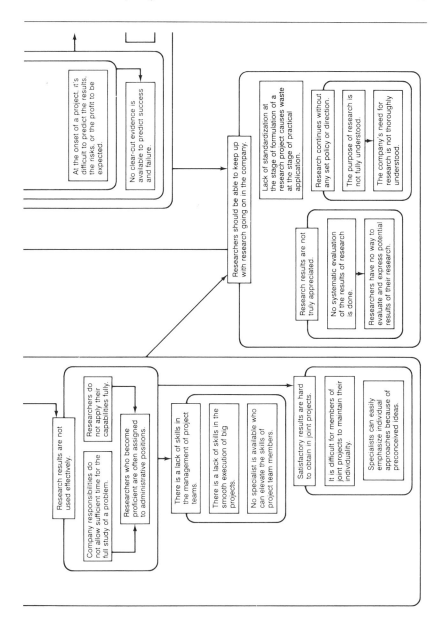

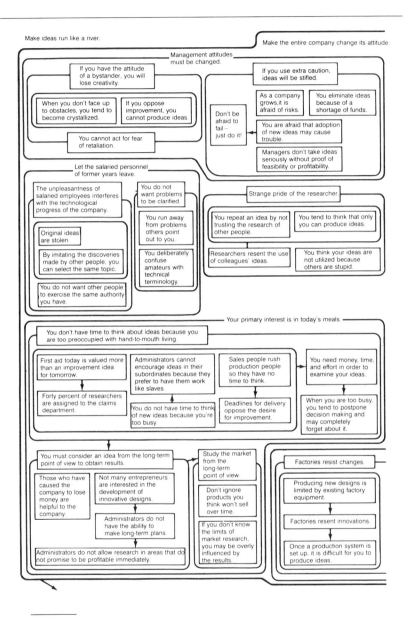

FIGURE 5.6
The process of developing research (the second round: understanding reality)

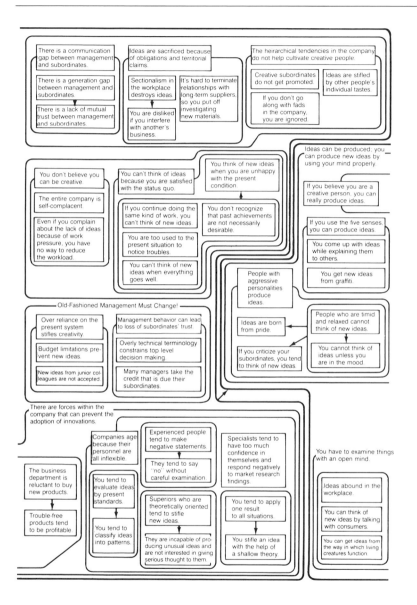

There is a communication gap between management and subordinates.

There is a generation gap between management and subordinates.

There is a lack of mutual trust between management and subordinates.

Ideas are sacrificed because of obligations and territorial claims.

Sectionalism in the workplace destroys ideas.

It's hard to terminate relationships with long-term suppliers, so you put off investigating new materials.

You are disliked if you interfere with another's business.

The heirarchical tendencies in the company do not help cultivate creative people.

Creative subordinates do not get promoted.

Ideas are stifled by other people's individual tastes.

If you don't go along with fads in the company, you are ignored.

Ideas can be produced; you can produce new ideas by using your mind properly.

If you believe you are a creative person, you can really produce ideas.

If you use the five senses, you can produce ideas.

You come up with ideas while explaining them to others.

You get new ideas from graffiti.

You don't believe you can be creative.

The entire company is self-complacent.

Even if you complain about the lack of ideas because of work pressure, you have no way to reduce the workload.

You can't think of ideas because you are satisfied with the status quo.

You think of new ideas when you are unhappy with the present condition.

If you continue doing the same kind of work, you can't think of new ideas.

You don't recognize that past achievements are not necessarily desirable.

You are too used to the present situation to notice troubles.

You can't think of new ideas when everything goes well.

People with aggressive personalities produce ideas.

Ideas are born from pride.

People who are timid and relaxed cannot think of new ideas.

If you criticize your subordinates, you tend to think of new ideas.

You cannot think of ideas unless you are in the mood.

Old-Fashioned Management Must Change!

Over reliance on the present system stifles creativity.

Budget limitations prevent new ideas.

New ideas from junior colleagues are not accepted.

Management behavior can lead to loss of subordinates' trust.

Overly technical terminology constrains top level decision making.

Many managers take the credit that is due their subordinates.

There are forces within the company that can prevent the adoption of innovations.

Companies age because their personnel are all inflexible.

Experienced people tend to make negative statements.

They tend to say "no" without careful examination.

Specialists tend to have too much confidence in themselves and respond negatively to market research findings.

You have to examine things with an open mind.

The business department is reluctant to buy new products.

Trouble-free products tend to be profitable.

You tend to evaluate ideas by present standards.

You tend to classify ideas into patterns.

Superiors who are theoretically oriented tend to stifle new ideas.

They are incapable of producing unusual ideas and are not interested in giving serious thought to them.

You tend to apply one result to all situations.

You stifle an idea with the help of a shallow theory.

Ideas abound in the workplace.

You can think of new ideas by talking with consumers.

You can get ideas from the way in which living creatures function.

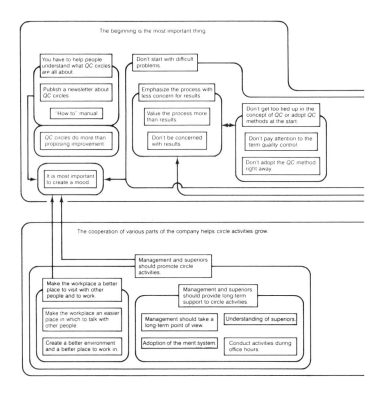

The beginning is the most important thing.

You have to help people understand what *QC* circles are all about.	Don't start with difficult problems.
Publish a newsletter about *QC* circles.	Emphasize the process with less concern for results.
"How to" manual	Value the process more than results.
QC circles do more than proposing improvement.	Don't be concerned with results.
It is most important to create a mood.	

Don't get too tied up in the concept of *QC* or adopt *QC* methods at the start.

Don't pay attention to the term *quality control*.

Don't adopt the *QC* method right away.

The cooperation of various parts of the company helps circle activities grow.

Management and superiors should promote circle activities.

Make the workplace a better place to visit with other people and to work.	
Make the workplace an easier place in which to talk with other people.	
Create a better environment and a better place to work in.	

Management and superiors should provide long-term support to circle activities.

Management should take a long-term point of view.	Understanding of superiors.
Adoption of the merit system.	Conduct activities during office hours.

FIGURE 5.7
What is the best way to promote the smooth operation of QC circles?

the basis of his or her affinity diagram, sharing ideas with everybody else. At this stage, participants learn about the ideas of other members and may think of new ideas. Through these stages, thought productivity is enhanced to the maximum and the search for a solution to the problems is pushed forward.

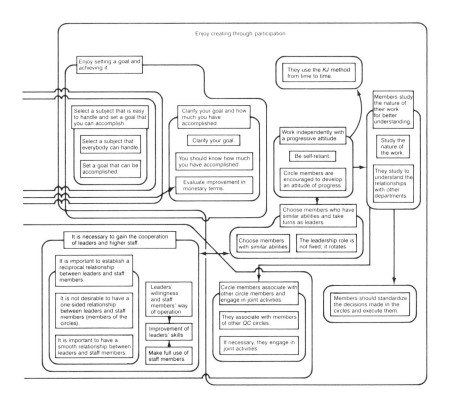

Notes

1. Ko Takahashi, "Lecture Notes of the Kansai Self-Study Group—Luthe Research Society of Creativity and Development" (recorded by Kago), 1977.

2. *See* Kawakita Jiro, *Thought Method II* (Tokyo: Chuo Koronsha, 1970); Kawakita and Makajima Shiniichi, *Science of Problem-Solving—KJ*

Method Workbook (Tokyo: Kodansha, 1970); Japan Management Association, eds., *Introduction to KJ Method for Management — A Practical Approach to a Creative Technique* (Tokyo: Japan Management Association, 1974).

3. Material in this section and the following sections on card sorting and labelling, drawing diagrams, and making written and oral presentations is drawn from Kawakita, *Thought Method II*, 1970; Kawakita and Makajima, *Science of Problem-Solving*, 1970; and JMA, eds., *KJ Method for Management*, 1974.

4. Mita and Ishizaki, "What Will Happen to QA?" in *Summary of Tasks 3, 4, and 6 — Seven New QC Tools Study Group* (Tokyo: JUSE Press, Ltd., 1978).

5. Mita and Ishizaki, *Summary of Tasks*, 1978.

Additional references

Japanese Union of Scientists and Engineers — QC Methods Development Division, *Proceedings of the QC Methods Development Division Conventions — Seven New QC Tools* (Tokyo: JUSE Press, Ltd., 1978).

————, *Introduction to Seven New QC Tools for Management and Staff* (Tokyo: JUSE Press, Ltd., 1978).

Futami Ryoji, *VE Manual* (Tokyo: Sogogiken Publishing Co., 1978).

Motoaki Hiroshi, "Science Illustrated #2: Psychology of Perception," in *Betsatsu Science* (Tokyo: Japan Economic Journal, 1976).

Tsukada Yuzo, "Science Illustrated #4: Brain," in *Betsatsu Science* (Tokyo: Japan Economic Journal, 1977).

Takahashi Hiroshi, *Training of Creativity* (Tokyo: Japan Industrial Training Association, 1970).

Kawakita Jiro, *Study of Party* (Tokyo: Shakai Shiso Sha, 1964).

————, *Teamwork* (Tokyo: Kobunsha, 1966).

————, *Exploration of Knowledge* (Tokyo: Kodansha, 1977).

Umezao Tadao, *Technology of Intellectual Production* (Tokyo: Iwanami Shoten, 1969).

Nakayama Masakazu, *All About NM Method* (Tokyo: Sanno Publishing Co., 1977).

Tokinori Norihiko, *Story of the Brain* (Tokyo: Iwanami Shoten, 1962).

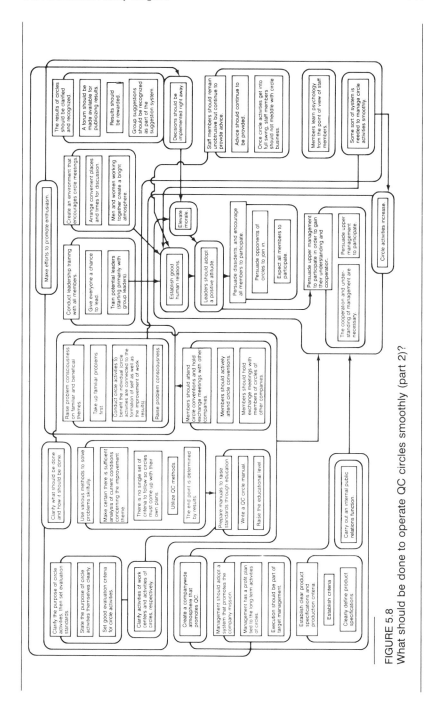

FIGURE 5.8
What should be done to operate QC circles smoothly (part 2)?

6

The Systematic Diagram

The systematic diagram is a technique developed to search for the most appropriate and effective means of accomplishing given objectives.

The method

The systematic diagram represents events in the form of a tree and its branches. This type of systematic diagram, sometimes called a dendrogram, has been used in family tree charts and organizational charts for a long time.

When means to achieve a goal are selected, secondary means are necessary to secure the primary means; thus the principal means become the goal of the secondary means. Figure 6.1 illustrates this relationship.

The systematic diagram displays the means necessary to achieve specific goals and objectives, clarifies the essence of the

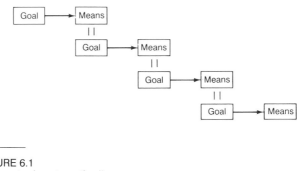

FIGURE 6.1
Conceptual systematic diagram

problem by making the subject matter visible, and searches for the most suitable means of realizing the objectives. This method is efficient not only in clarifying key control points in QC activities and developing effective improvement methods, but also in training business people to think in terms of means and objectives. Caught up in daily business activities, it is often difficult for business personnel to have clear notions of means and objectives. The systematic diagram alleviates this difficulty.

Uses of the systematic diagram

The systematic diagram can be applied in many phases of quality control:

- developing design quality for new products
- coordinating the development of quality assurance to the QC process diagram to ensure QA activities
- utilization of the cause-and-effect diagram

- developing solutions to various internal problems such as quality, cost, and production volume and delivery
- developing objectives, policies, and activity items
- clarifying departmental and control functions and promoting increased productivity

Constructing a systematic diagram

The diagrams used in the systematic diagram method can be classified into two major categories: the *component-development type*, which displays the component elements in terms of their purposes and means, and the *means-development type*, which systematically develops the ways and means for solving problems or achieving objectives.

Procedure for constructing a systematic diagram

To begin, obtain about 10 large (3′x4′) sheets of paper, 50 to 100 cards (3x5 in size), and several markers in two or three different colors.

Step 1: Establish objectives and goals

Clearly indicate on the cards the ultimate objectives or goals to be achieved. As a matter of principle, express goals and objectives in simple language, such as "Do X to obtain Y." If necessary, a short sentence or a phrase may be used. Most important here is that the expression be simple, direct and understandable to everyone. If there are conditions to be satisfied in achieving the goal, they must be clearly recorded. In establishing the goal, ask for what purpose the goal is to be attained. The answer to this question will help clarify a principal goal, which in turn will ensure that the proposed goal is an appropriate one.

Step 2: Deduce the means

The means thought to be necessary to achieve the established goal are deduced and recorded on paper, one by one. In deciding on the means, use the following guidelines: (a) start with the principal means and go to the secondary ones through association; (b) start with ideas of means considered to be least important and arrange these in groups, building up to more important ideas; and (c) simply pick up ideas of means without questioning their importance. Selection procedures will depend on the nature of the subject matter or the view about it. When collecting ideas for means, make sure they come from as many different points of view as possible. Make use of the divergent experience and knowledge of participating members through techniques like brainstorming. It is useful to express ideas for means in the form of a transitive verb and its object: "To (verb) to _____ (object)." The procedure here is basically the same as in step 1.

Step 3: Evaluate the means

The means deduced are evaluated for their adequacy before moving on to the next step. Constraints, if there are any, should be taken into consideration in sifting the means according to their adequacy. In evaluating means, the marks $\bigcirc$, $\triangle$, and X are used. The mark $\bigcirc$ means "practicable"; the mark $\triangle$ means "uncertain practicability without further investigation"; and the mark X means "impractical." Those marked $\triangle$ need to be investigated promptly and should receive either an $\bigcirc$ or X marking.

In evaluating the means, it is important to take into consideration the following: (a) avoid superficial evaluations and hasty rejections of means; (b) an idea that at first seems impractical may be improved through incorporation with other ideas and further refinement; efforts should not be spared to help generate ideas and nurture them; (c) unusual ideas tend to be considered impractical, but when they are made practical, they sometimes bring great results; and (d) new ideas often occur during evaluations of other ideas; remain open to new ideas, because they may lead to good, practical ones.

Step 4: Prepare means cards

The means selected in step 3 are recorded on cards in large letters.

Step 5: Systematize the means

Place the goal cards made in step 1 in the left half of a sheet of paper. If there are constraints, record them below the goal cards.

Pose the following question with regard to each goal card: "To achieve this goal, what is the most necessary means?"

From the means cards made in step 4, sort out those containing an appropriate answer to this question and place them to the right of the appropriate goal cards. If more than one means card can be used to answer the question, place them side by side.

Now the relationship between the goal and the means necessary to achieve it has been made clear. This state of affairs, however, cannot by itself lead to concrete actions. Further secondary means must be found until the least and most practicable means are identified.

Next, pose the following question regarding each means card placed to the right of each goal card: "If this means is considered a 'goal,' what further means will be necessary to achieve this goal?" From among the means cards made during step 4, locate those which respond to this question and place them to the right of the means card in question.

Proceed by repeating the second question, locating the corresponding means cards among those prepared in step 4, and arrange them in order of their relevance to the goal and its means. When all the cards are arranged, connect them so as to display the goals and means. The result is a systematic diagram displaying the goal established in step 1 and all the means necessary to attain it.

In the process of constructing a diagram, new ideas other than those listed in step 4 sometimes occur. Needless to say, these new ideas must be added, and unnecessary ones should be weeded out.

This process of diagram construction is the most important part of the systematic diagram method. Hasty diagram construction, which merely arranges means in some systematic fashion, should be avoided. What is most important here is continual and careful scrutiny of the viewpoints from which a system of means is developed so that any omission or oversight is precluded.

Step 6: Confirm the objectives

Although the systematic diagram was constructed in step 5, we confirm whether the high-level means are adequate as the objectives of

their corresponding secondary means. Starting with the least important means, the following question is asked: "Can the principal
means ('goals') really be achieved by these means or by part of
them?"

If the answer is "yes," raise the same question about the next
levels, one after another. Confirm the attainability of the goal established in step 1 exclusively through the means developed in step 5. If
the answer to the preceding question is "no," this reflects the insuf-
ficiency of the means developed in step 5 and the need for adding
other means in order to realize the established goal.

The above-mentioned confirmation completes the development of the means to achieve the purpose and goal. This, in turn,
completes the systematic diagram. Figure 6.2 illustrates these steps.

Application to quality designing

In the field of quality control, the literature defines the concept of
quality designing as follows:[1]

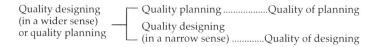

Quality planning means deciding, as the primary policy, on the
quality that will satisfy the users, i.e., the true quality characteristics.
Quality designing (in a narrow sense) refers to replacing the quality
desired by the users (the true quality characteristics) with a group of
controllable substitute characteristics through inference, translation, and conversion.

Speaking in general terms, the concrete application of quality
designing may be divided into two major categories: The first is
transformation and development of the planned quality (the top
policy), determined by quality planning, into the designed quality
(controllable substitute characteristics) and buildup of an image of
the product that satisfies the planned quality, i.e., *quality designing for*

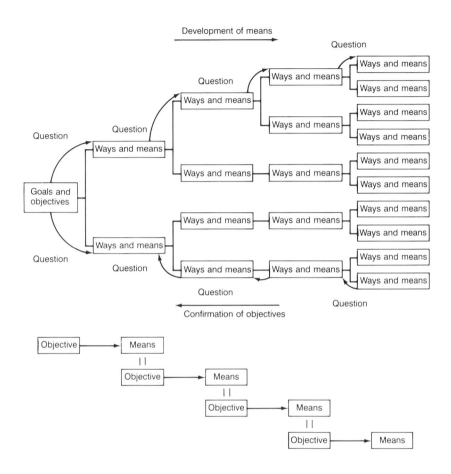

FIGURE 6.2
Constructing a systematic diagram

Note: In branching, *and/or* can be used when ideas are in the developmental stage. If a distinction between *and* and *or* is necessary, use the logical symbols employed in fault tree analysis (FTA).

the purpose of developing a new product. The second is transformation of the quality to be guaranteed to users into controllable substitute characteristics and determination of items and levels to be controlled together with the intracompany method of control, i.e., *quality designing for the purpose of quality assurance.*

Development of new products

The process of developing a new product can be thought of in the following manner. After the quality desired by users is defined based on research and speculation, the planned quality is designated as the primary goal. Then, through quality designing, planned quality is replaced (substitute characteristics). Next, from the viewpoint of function and production design, design and production methods are chosen so as to realize the designed quality most economically. Figure 6.3 illustrates this process as a system of corresponding objectives and means. The systematic diagram method can be utilized effectively in the quality designing of a new product, which we can call a systematic diagram for quality design. An example follows.

Example 1. Developing design quality for a new product, a television UHF tuner. When UHF broadcasting was promoted actively in Japan in March of 1969, Corporation M foresaw the demand for higher production and quality improvement for the all-channel television tuner. In response to this forecast, the company organized a project team to develop a new all-channel tuner. The goal assigned to the team was to develop, by October of the same year, a competitive, high-quality, high-productivity, low-cost product that would make its own contribution to the anticipated full-scale spread of all-channel TV receivers. The team members examined and evaluated existing products and those of competitor companies in terms of quality, capacity, productivity, and cost. Their discussions were guided by the criteria of practicability within the fixed period of time and by the certainty of securing full priority at the time of project completion. They constructed a systematic diagram for quality design (as shown in Fig. 2.7) and presented it to the development council. Having obtained the approval of top management, they started the actual development operations.

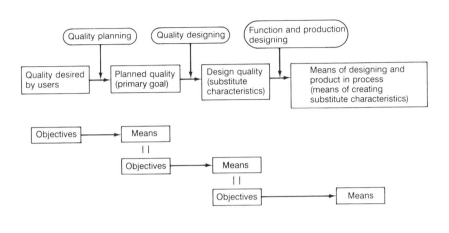

FIGURE 6.3
A systematic diagram for quality designing in new product
development

In this manner it was possible to harmonize the plans of top
management and the thinking of those charged with development
by making a systematic diagram for quality design. Moreover, when
changes were considered necessary in the development process, it
was possible to incorporate them quickly along the established line
of objectives-and-means relationships.

Figure 2.7 has a column designated "Undecided Items." When
planning a new product, it is not always possible to develop all the
means in detail to satisfy quality design. (As a matter of fact, it is
generally impossible to do so.) In such cases, the items which cannot
be detailed or which require further investigation or experimentation should be singled out and put in proper places in the development plan. Making a place for undecided items often brings about
good results.

As soon as a development plan for a new product is decided on,
a systematic diagram for quality design of the new product should

be constructed; then the development process should be carried out on the basis of that plan. This procedure will clarify the direction of development efforts, help accommodate needed changes in the process rapidly, and preclude counterproductive opinions, thereby effectively promoting the development of the new product.

Application to QA activities

Quality-assurance (QA) activities are control activities that clarify the quality desired by users and secure the level of quality that is satisfactory to them. Since the quality demanded by users, however, is generally understood only qualitatively, it is hard to control. Therefore, it is necessary for QA activities to transform the quality desired by users into controllable quality characteristics.

In other words, the quality demanded by users is first transformed through quality design into substitute characteristics (designed quality). Then this quality is correlated with control quality characteristics and their level (in many cases, the standard specifications and characteristics of the product). Next, control specifications and methods are established to realize these control quality characteristics and levels. In this manner, it is possible to clarify the object and method of control to realize quality assurance.

This process also can be reduced to an objective-and-means system, as shown in Fig. 6.4 This systematic diagram used for quality assurance activities is called a quality assurance systematic diagram. An example follows.

Example 2. Developing assured quality for a television VHF tuner. Figure 6.5 is a systematic diagram for assured quality that shows how the quality of a VHF tuner can be developed as part of the QA activities for color television receivers. The diagram shows how the required quality of a VHF tuner was derived from the design quality developed by the maker. It also shows how the required quality of a tuner was correlated to its design quality, and then how this design quality was developed to the standard specifications and level of the product. Furthermore, it shows the design check items and control points in the process. Because such a systematic diagram for assured quality was constructed, it was possible, when such problems as market claims occurred, to proceed systematically to determine

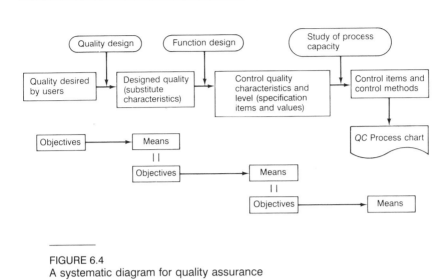

FIGURE 6.4
A systematic diagram for quality assurance

whether there had been slippage in control quality characteristics or whether the control quality level was too low. This determination could be conducted by examining the diagramed means to the product quality. Use of this method made it possible to develop appropriate countermeasures.

Example 3. Developing assured quality for automobile brakes. Corporation N, which specializes in automobile brakes, is extremely strict in securing the stipulated quality of its products. Moreover, ithas to ensure that its products can be assembled into the final product, i.e., automobiles, in such a way that the brakes function exactly as they are intended to.

Management established "a brake that works without failure" as the required quality. Based on this requirement, management derived secondary required qualities such as braking power, strength, durability, safety, operability, and feasibility of inspection

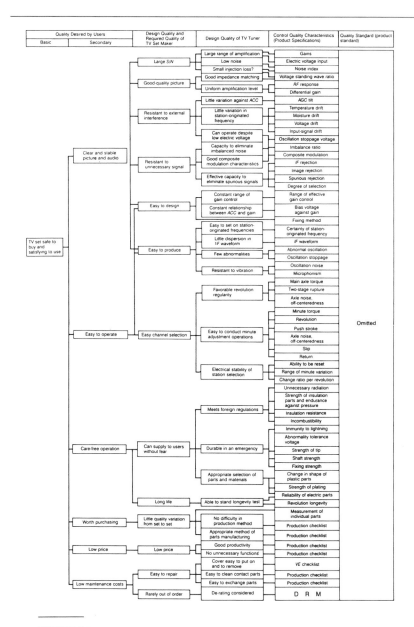

FIGURE 6.5
Systematic diagram for quality assurance of a television VHF tuner (a
systematic diagram of the component-development type)[2]

and maintenance. Each of these items was then considered as a basic required quality, from which secondary and tertiary design-quality levels were derived and control specifications were established.

Because the corporation's production process was insufficient to guarantee control specifications, QA activities were carried out at every step in the production process, from the manufacturing of brake parts to their assembly in automobiles. Accordingly, the control specifications were examined in relation to the suppliers of parts, the production process, and inspection of the brake manufacturer and the automobile makers.

This process of examination made it possible to diagnose problems, provide guidance to the part suppliers for their quality control, incorporate appropriate details into the company's own QC process chart, and make requests to the automobile makers. Figure 6.6 shows a portion of the systematic diagram for automobile brake quality assurance, which was useful in establishing the QC system.[3]

Application to quality improvement

Used as a cause-and-effect diagram

Needless to say, a cause-and-effect diagram is simple and effective. However, we encounter minor inconveniences in the following cases:

1. When causes at the sample level need to be compared, examined, and evaluated.
2. When the influence of each cause is quantified and expressed in a diagram similar to that in number 1 above.
3. When the number of causes is very large.
4. When the lowest-level causes need to be examined in relation to necessary measures, procedural details, or a list of standards.

In such cases, one solution is to arrange causes and effects in the form of a systematic diagram. A systematic diagram that expresses

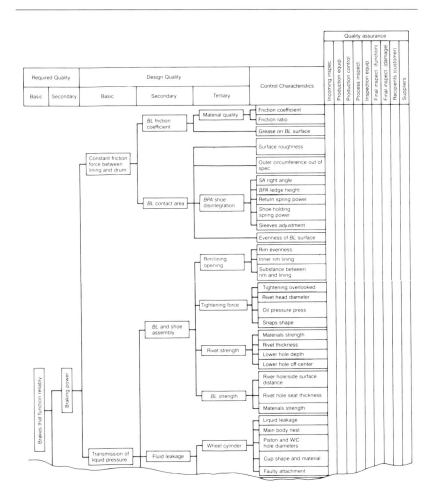

FIGURE 6.6
A systematic diagram for quality assurance for automotive brakes
(component-development type)

causes and their effects is called a cause-and-effect systematic diagram.

As can be seen in Fig. 6.7, a cause-and-effect diagram and a cause-and-effect systematic diagram express an identical event or process in two different forms.

Application to the reduction of nonconforming items

Such problems as the presence of abnormalities and the inability to reduce them can be dealt with in one of two ways.

Case 1

Consider the situation where the necessary means of production have been determined and are in use, such as parts, materials, facilities, repair tools, operational procedures, and finishing requirements. The appearance of nonconforming items indicates that these means either have deteriorated or have deviated from the standards occasionally. Dispersion of the so-called four M's (material, machine, method and man) includes use of substandard parts and materials, loss of precision of machinery, facilities, and repair tools, and nonobservance of operational standards. In such a situation, all the production means presently in use should be displayed in a systematic diagram and examined one by one. A priority list should be established for this process on the basis of the extent of each item's influence. In addition, those means with large dispersion must be located and corrected, since they are the source of abnormalities.

Case 2

Sometimes the production means currently in use are found to be inadequate for producing the quality characteristics in question. Such a situation may be due either to insufficient process planning or to the fact that while the required quality has become more and more exacting, the process has remained the same. When this is the case, it helps to reexamine and redefine the goals and collect ideas about effective means using a technique such as brainstorming with persons of diverse viewpoints. Such ideas may then be refined and developed into concrete measures for improvement.

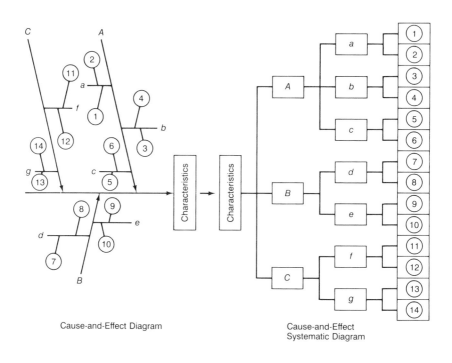

Cause-and-Effect Diagram

Cause-and-Effect
Systematic Diagram

FIGURE 6.7
A cause-and-effect diagram and a cause-and-effect systematic diagram

In either case, the first thing to do is to clarify the quality characteristics (objectives) to be attained. Next, the means for reaching objectives must be developed and examined, and measures for reducing nonconformities must be specified. In this process of developing objectives and means, a systematic diagram will help you to gather and organize information, pursue the cause(s) of abnormalities, and devise countermeasures.

The existence of so-called chronic abnormalities means that despite various measures taken in the past, the situation has not improved. The systematic diagram method has often been effective in eliminating such chronic abnormalities.

Example 4. Reducing dispersion in the thickness of wall-covering materials. Corporation D, which produces wall-covering material, experienced persistently conspicuous fluctuations in the thickness of its product. Although various measures were tried, the capacity of the production process, C_p, dropped to 0.647. The company decided to go back to the starting point. The firm had all personnel concerned enumerate the factors that could have caused the problem and summarize the results in a systematic diagram. Figure 6.8 shows that diagram.

Discussions about the diagram were held by all personnel concerned, while examination of the degree of influence of each factor was divided and assigned to several people. As a result, it was found that factors that had been thought to be of little importance, such as a change of speed, had a surprisingly large effect. (A change of speed occurred when the operation was started or the product type was switched.) A countermeasure to this problem was devised and implemented. In addition, the method of adjusting the steam pressure was standardized and the roll balance was improved. As a result, the process capacity was improved to 1.20.

The cause-and-effect systematic diagram used in this example is similar to a cause-and-effect diagram of the dispersion-analysis type. Since the causes of the thickness irregularities were investigated with a systematic diagram, it was easy to compare the causes of dispersion with one another and to correlate them with the operation standards and control sources. Furthermore, it also became easier to determine the priority of the measures to be implemented and to follow up the results of that implementation. In this case, the merits of the systematic diagram are fully apparent.

Example 5. Reduction of loss caused by cross-sectional rupture of book-cover cloth. Corporation D, a producer of book-cover cloth, faced the problem of cross-sectional rupture, which occurred as often as 59 times a month on average during the production process. When such a rupture took place, the machinery had to be stopped to reconnect the ruptured parts, and each stoppage caused the loss of 80 to 90 meters of the product, resulting in an enormous overall loss.

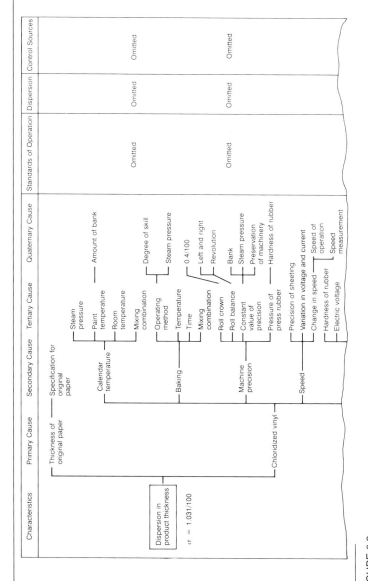

FIGURE 6.8
A cause-and-effect systematic diagram for the dispersion in the thickness of wall coverings[4]
(component-development type)

Consequently, an objective of minimizing the loss was established. This objective was divided into two parts: one was prevention of ruptures, and the other was minimizing the loss caused by ruptures. Regarding each of these new objectives, suggestions were collected through brainstorming, and after sifting through the ideas, a systematic diagram was constructed, as shown in Fig. 6.9. The ideas at the bottom of the diagram were thoroughly evaluated, were given practicable forms with implementation directions, and were carried out one by one. After a period of 6 months there was a decrease in the number of ruptures to an average of 13.2 per month and the loss of the product was reduced to an average of 35 to 45 meters per rupture.

Other applications

The systematic diagram method helps us find the starting point in problem solving by arranging the branching phases of the problem into understandable relations between an objective and the means to achieve it. It is applicable not only to quality design and quality improvement, as was explained earlier, but also to other aspects of the manufacturing process. Several applications will be briefly mentioned below.

Developing policies and goals

If top-management policies or departmental objectives are to penetrate to lower-level personnel and be implemented by them, it is necessary to analyze problems in appropriate ways and develop concrete solutions. The development of goals and policies results in a system of goals and means, and it is here that the systematic diagram method becomes applicable.

Developing administrative functions

The systematic diagram method is effective in promoting efficient management because it clarifies both departmental and control functions within a company. In planning to increase departmental

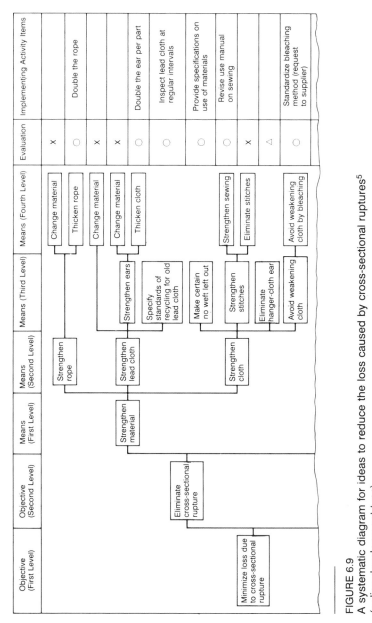

FIGURE 6.9
A systematic diagram for ideas to reduce the loss caused by cross-sectional ruptures[5]
(policy-development type)

efficiency and reduce personnel, it is not desirable to analyze current assignments too deeply. One may encounter the unwelcome situation where close examination of inefficient or unattended tasks leads to a staff increase. A better strategy is to develop a systematic diagram of "target conditions" for work in each department and to clarify the purpose of that work. This will promote the discovery of new approaches to achieving departmental objectives as well as improvement in the administrative structure itself.

Other areas

In addition to the preceding examples, the systematic diagram method can be applied to various other problem areas, such as

- Developing means for promoting productivity
- Generating ideas for improving bookkeeping
- Developing implementation specifications for design standardization
- Developing ways to activate the QC circle
- Developing ways to reduce claims
- Developing practicable means for the effective promotion of research and development
- Developing means for effective project team management
- Developing ways to promote TQC activities
- Comparing production costs with rival makers through function comparison
- Functional analysis to improve the production process

Techniques employed with the systematic diagram method

Function analysis

Function analysis is used in value engineering (VE) to evaluate how well a product design fulfills user requirements in relation to cost. A brief explanation is given at the end of this chapter.

Correlation-tree method

This technique is used in planning assistance through technical evaluation of relevant numbers (PATTERN). It establishes an objective, arranges the means necessary to achieve the objective in several levels of the system, and helps visualize the relations between the goal and each means. This technique effectively promotes decision making in technological developments.[6]

Reverse PERT (program evaluation and review technique)

PERT is an effective technique used in developing a new product. It relates project plans and pertinent research to the development goal, clarifying where to start.

PERT networks are used in making day-to-day plans. When we plan a route to a final goal in this manner, however, we often become exhausted along the way. The reverse PERT proceeds backwards from the final goal, reversing the order of steps used to create a PERT network.[7]

A reverse PERT begins with the final goal of development and enumerates all the resources needed to attain that goal, such as technology, parts and materials, production methods, measuring methods, and so on, including resources that have not yet beendeveloped. It then arranges them in reverse order until the practical means that can be implemented are reached. In this manner, the route to the goal can be charted.

Decision tree

A decision tree is a technique used to facilitate decision making. It represents the subject matter in the form of a tree with numerous branches and twigs. A decision tree contains points that can be decided on by the decision makers (determined points of selection are indicated by ☐) as well as points that are decided on by outside elements (probable points of selection are indicated by ○). These points are connected one by one to form twigs and branches that represent various phases of the process, leading to a final result. Ifthe probability of phases or events and the gain derived from the anticipated results can be quantified, the most suitable "decision" can be calculated.[8]

Fault-tree analysis (FTA)

Fault-tree analysis as well as failure mode and effect analysis (FMEA) are techniques used to analyze and evaluate the reliability of systems. They were originally developed as techniques to analyze the causes of fatal accidents. Fault-tree analysis determines things that are unfavorable to an object system and their causes and connects them in parallel (*and*) or series (*or*) by logical gates according to their cause-and-effect relationship. It presents them all in the form of a tree, which helps visualize how the unfavorable phenomena occurred. Because fault-tree analysis arranges and analyzes occurrences and their causes by logical circuits, it is called logic diagram analysis (LDA).[9]

The YS technique

This technique was introduced by Yabiki Seiichiro as a method for solving problems that range from expansion of sales to the lifelong plans of newly employed staff members of a firm.[10]

The PC technique

This is a variation of the correlation-tree method that consists of four steps: consideration of purpose, prospective concepts, clearing of problems, and planning and communication.[11]

A few words on functional analysis in value engineering (VE)

The functional systematic diagram (FAST* diagram), used for functional analysis in value engineering, is probably the best systematization and application of the systematic diagram among control techniques. The concept of and procedure for functional analysis will be explained, in terms of the functional systematic diagram.

------

*FAST = Functional Analysis Systems Technique developed by Charles Bytheway in 1965.

Functional analysis and a functional systematic diagram

Functional analysis clarifies and evaluates the essential functions of a product and its component parts in order to discover ways to improve the product and its cost.

Functional analysis consists of a series of analyses: First, functions are *defined* in a way that clearly expresses the functions to be performed by the product and its component parts (sub-assemblies, units, parts, materials, etc.); next the functions of each component part are *arranged* systematically in the functional systematic (or FAST diagram) in terms of their goals-means relations to one another (see Fig. 6.10); finally the functions are *evaluated* to determine which parts of the product design can be improved to obtain the most significant results.

Steps of functional analysis

Step 1:

Determine the objective of functional analysis. Here the reason for conducting the analysis is established and the product structure and its components are clarified.

Step 2:

Define functions. The functions of a product and its component units are succinctly described in short phrases such as those shown in the box below. Keep in mind that there are functions as objectives and functions as means.

Function = verb + noun
To (*verb*) (*object*), e.g., "transfer torque," "connect components," "rotate assembly"

Step 3:

Prepare function cards. Each defined function is recorded on a small card (about half the size of a business card).

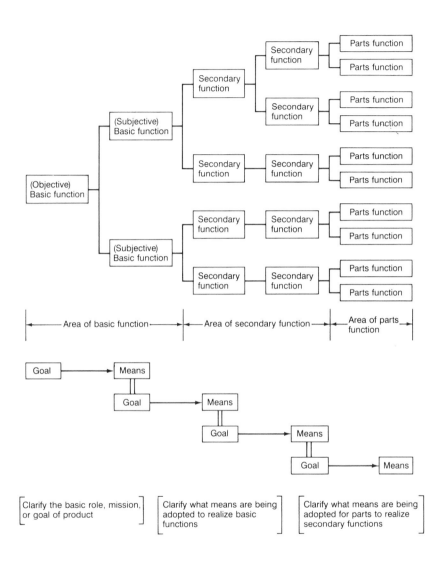

FIGURE 6.10
A functional systematic diagram

Step 4:

Determine primary- and secondary-level functions. Apply the following questions to each function card and determine its primary or secondary positions: (1) "What objective must the means on this card achieve?" (2) "What means is necessary to achieve the objective on this card?" The function answering question (1) becomes a primary-level function (objective) in relation to what the question is applied to on the card. In a similar manner, the function that answers question (2) becomes a secondary-level function (means) in relation to what the question is applied to on the card.

Step 5:

Construct the functional systematic diagram. This diagram is constructed by arranging the cards in terms of their primary or secondary levels and connecting them by lines.

Step 6:

Evaluate functions. Each function-series in the functional systematic diagram is evaluated: functions generating ideas for improvement are identified and investigated, and the potential effects of proposed improvements are evaluated. [12]

Finally, we are very grateful to the Matsushita Electric Parts Company, the Nissei Textile Company, and the Dainik Company for their permission to use the diagrams in this chapter.

Notes

1. Editorial Board for Quality Control (Ed.), *Understanding and Promoting Quality Design* (Tokyo: JUSE Press, Ltd., 1967).

2. Futami Yoshiharu, "Analysis of Quality Characteristics Using the Function Analysis Technique," *Hinshitsu Kanri* (Quality Control), vol. 26, Supplement (May, 1975), pp. 208–212; Tsutsuya Yutaka and Futami Yoshiharu, "Technique to Sustain Management During Low Growth Periods — The Technique and Implementation of Value Engineering," *Kojo Kanri* (Factory Management), vol. 21, no. 4 (1975), pp. 6–63.

3. For more on the development of quality and quality functions see Mizuno Shigeru and Akao Yoji (Eds.), *Hinshitsu kino Denkai* (Development of quality and function) (Tokyo: JUSE Press, Ltd., 1978).

4. Futami, *Quality Control*, pp. 208–212; Yutaka and Futami, *Factory Management*, pp. 6–63.

5. Futami, *Quality Control*, pp. 208–212.

6. *See* Mizuno Keizi, *Jishyu Gijutsu Kaihatsu* (Do-it-yourself technology development) (Tokyo: Sanno Publishing Co., 1971) and Makino Noboru, *Gijutsu Nyumon* (Technology forecasting for beginners) (Tokyo: Nikkan Kogyo Shimbunsha, 1969).

7. Makino, *Technology Forecasting*, 1969.

8. *See* Saito Yoshihiro, "An Approach Toward Decision (1): Rationale and Technique," *Operations Research*, vol. 12, (August 1967), pp. 16–21; Saito Yoshihiro, *Kettei no Hanashi* (Decisionmaking) (Tokyo: JUSE Press, Ltd., 1969); R. V. Brown, A. S. Carl, and C. Peterson, *Decision Analysis: From Introduction to Application* (translated by Fujita Tsuneo) (Tokyo: Sanno Publishing Co., 1974).

9. Shiomi Hiroshi, *Kosaiseki to Shindan* (Breakdown analysis and diagnosis) (Tokyo: JUSE Press, Ltd., 1977); Japanese Union of Scientists and Engineers, Division of Machine Reliability, eds., *FMEA and FTA Explained* (Tokyo: JUSE Press, Ltd., 1978).

10. Yabiki Seiichiro, *Handan to Kettei no Kagaku* (Science of judgment and decision) (Tokyo: Japan Management Association, 1975).

11. *See* Mizuno Keizi, *Genjo Daha no Shikoho* (Getting to breakthrough) (Tokyo: Dobunkan, 1973).

12. Tamai Masatoshi, *Kinobunseki* (Function analysis) (Sanno Publishing Co., 1967); Futami Yoshiharu, *VE Manual*, 1978; Tsutsuya and Futami, *Factory Management*, pp. 6–63.

7

The Matrix Diagram

The matrix diagram method clarifies problematic spots through multidimensional thinking.

About the matrix diagram method

The matrix diagram method is designed to seek out principal factors from a plethora of phenomena concerning a subject under study. As shown in Fig. 2.8, it indicates the relationship of L factors and R factors at the point of intersection. Factors $L_1, L_2, \ldots, L_i, \ldots, L_m$ are arranged horizontally, and factors $R_1, R_2, \ldots, R_j, \ldots, R_n$ are arranged vertically.

The matrix diagram helps to expedite the process of problem solving by indicating the presence and degree of strength of a relationship between two sets of factors. By using the intersecting points as starting points, the design allows us to (1) explore the problem under study from two points of view and (2) build a base for further two-dimensional problem-solving.

The systematic diagram method discussed in Chap. 6 is used to clarify a problem when its causes and the methods for solving it can be explained in one dimension. When there are two sets of factors and methods, however, the matrix diagram method, which can correlate these to each other, is more effective.

Uses of the matrix diagram method

Many kinds of quality control and management problems can be addressed through applications of the matrix diagram method. Some examples are as follows:

1. A new idea is needed for new product development or for product improvement, and this is accomplished correlating the hardware and software functions of the product system to each other.

2. The substitution of a feature affects many quality requirements and generates complexity, for this reason a systematic diagram cannot be used for quality development.

3. A system of quality assurance must be established by clarifying the relationship between required quality characteristics and the related control functions of the quality assurance department.

4. The system of quality evaluation must be strengthened by clarifying the relationships among quality characteristics, testing and measurement items, and testing and measurement equipment.

5. Many factors that contribute to the production of a nonconforming item should be eliminated by clarifying the relationships between the defect phenomena and their causes (when the defect phenomena have common causes).

6. Matrix diagram method is also the best method of organizing data in order to apply multivariate analysis.

Types of matrices

Successful matrix diagraming depends on proper expression of the subject matter in the matrix chart. Various patterns of matrix diagrams can be constructed; the choice of a particular pattern depends on its purpose.

L-type matrix

This is a basic matrix diagram with one set of data expressed in two dimensions employing rows and columns. Figure 7.1 shows that it is composed of A factors and B factors. The L-type matrix can be used for associating goals and the means to achieve them, as well as for drawing conclusions about the relationships between consequences and their causes.

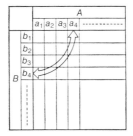

FIGURE 7.1
L-type matrix

T-type matrix

As Fig. 7.2 shows, the T-type matrix combines a matrix of A and B factors with a matrix of A and C factors. In other words, it is a matrix of A factors corresponding to B and C factors, respectively. The T-type matrix shown in Fig. 2.9, illustrating defect phenomena by cause and process, is a good analysis method for defect-reducing activities. Also, when exploring a new use of materials, this T-type matrix can be used to analyze ingredients and components of the material by characteristics and usage.

Y-type matrix

As Fig. 7.3 shows, the Y-type matrix is a combination of three L-type matrices (A factors and B factors, B factors and C factors, C factors and A factors). In other words, it shows how A and B, B and C, and C and A correspond to one another. For example, in its newspaper advertisements the Osaka Asbestos Slate Association used the Y-type

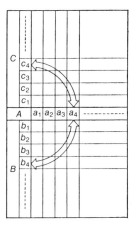

FIGURE 7.2
T-type matrix

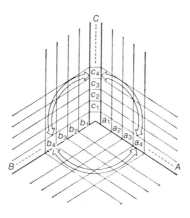

FIGURE 7.3
Y-type matrix

matrix to explain simply how material can be selected rationally by considering the place of its use, its features, and its shape.

X-type matrix

As Fig. 7.4 shows, this is a combination of four L-type matrices. This matrix shows the correspondence of four sets of factors, *A* and *B* and *AB* and *D*, *B* and *A* and *BA* and *C*, *C* and *B* and *CB* and *D*, and *D* and *A* and *DA* and *C*. Applications of this matrix are limited, however, as with the EDP (electronic data processing) system, it can be used to consider the correspondence of management functions, management items, output data, and input data.

C-type matrix

As Fig. 7.5 shows, the C-type matrix is expressed in a rectangular cube whose sides are represented by three elements, *A*, *B*, and *C*. The main feature of this cubic type of matrix is the "point of conception of the idea," which is determined by three elements of *A*, *B*, and *C* in three-dimensional space. This point of idea conception is difficult to

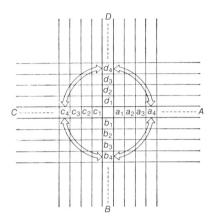

FIGURE 7.4
X-type matrix

show in Fig. 7.5, but it can be seen clearly in Fig. 7.6. This matrix may
be better understood if the L-type matrices, containing the corresponding sets of A and B, B and C, and C and A, are combined with
Fig. 7.5 or Fig. 7.6. Consider the relationship between Fig. 7.9 on the
one hand and Figs. 7.8, 7.10, and 7.11 on the other.

Other uses of the matrix method can be designed by combining
these five types of matrices. In short, the matrix to design is the one
that is most appropriate for one's purposes.

The systematic diagram and the matrix diagram

The most important point in designing a matrix is deciding how to
combine the sets of phenomena and the factors that correspond to
them. There is no single way to combine sets of phenomena because
the combinations depend on the nature of the problem under study.
The examples presented later will illustrate some of the possibilities.

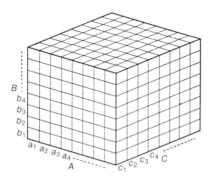

FIGURE 7.5
C-type matrix

Using a matrix diagram, the correspondence between phenomena is shown; then the relevant factors are developed to illustrate their level of significance. The systematic diagram is used to develop these factors. Another approach is to combine the systematic diagram with the matrix diagram, as shown in Fig. 7.7.

Applications of the matrix diagram

For a better understanding of matrix diagrams, a few examples of their application are introduced here.

Application of system products to functional design

Company Y planned to develop "a system of weight distribution of particles." The company decided to study the system to determine how to add new functions, how the company's own technology could be used to add new features, and how to increase added value.

The company analyzed the types of system requirements, drafted a new product plan, described the system in detail, and selected and defined one necessary function. The defined function

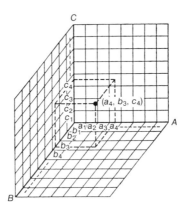

FIGURE 7.6
Developmental diagram of the C-type matrix

was divided into a hardware function and a software function; a functional system chart was drawn for each of the two functions. These functional system charts were combined to produce a matrix of the software-hardware functional system, as shown in Fig. 7.8. Furthermore, they decided to include function layout in the matrix, since the systems product layout function needed to be consistent with the current factory layout. They came up with the C-type matrix in Fig. 7.9. This type of matrix is called a function system matrix.

In the functional system matrix in Fig. 7.9, which is a C-type matrix, it is not easy to conceive of ideas, because the point of idea conception is a point in three-dimensional space. With the addition of Figs. 7.10 and 7.11, three L-type function system matrices were designed, including software-hardware, hardware-layout, and software-layout functions, and the point where they intersect was made the point of idea conception. The intersections marked ○ in the two charts are functions that specifically gave rise to many ideas. The intersections marked ● represent functions that correspond to the ● in the function system matrix of the entire system in Fig. 7.9.

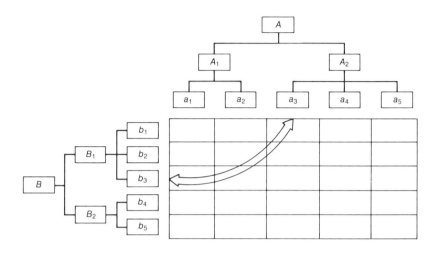

FIGURE 7.7
Combination of a systematic diagram and a matrix diagram

Although the content of the idea and its concrete manifestations cannot be discussed here, it is interesting to note that from this analysis, three new ideas led to patent applications.

When it is necessary to develop functions from various points of view, as in the case of a system product, designing a functional system matrix that uses the principle of matrix diagraming results in effective functional design and analysis.

Application to the quality development of component products

In the case of parts, a substitute feature may be used as a way of obtaining a required quality, and therefore, a systematic diagram can be used to explain its development. In this case, the process can be explained with a matrix, as in the following examples:

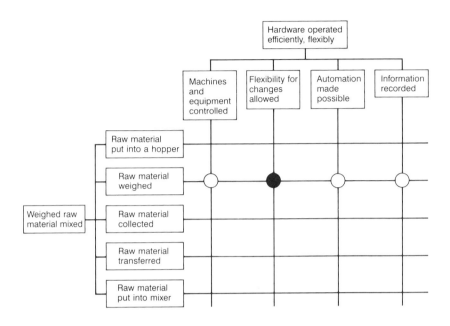

FIGURE 7.8
Soft-hard function system matrix[1] (L-type matrix)

In order to ensure a warranty for water-pipe fittings that had been put on the market recently, YK Company clarified the relationships among quality required by users, substitute product features, and manufacturing management items.

Connecting the required quality to substitute product features

First, two separate systematic diagrams were drawn for the quality of water-pipe fittings required by users and for the features of their substitute product, respectively, and these diagrams were arranged to correspond to each other in a matrix of required quality and

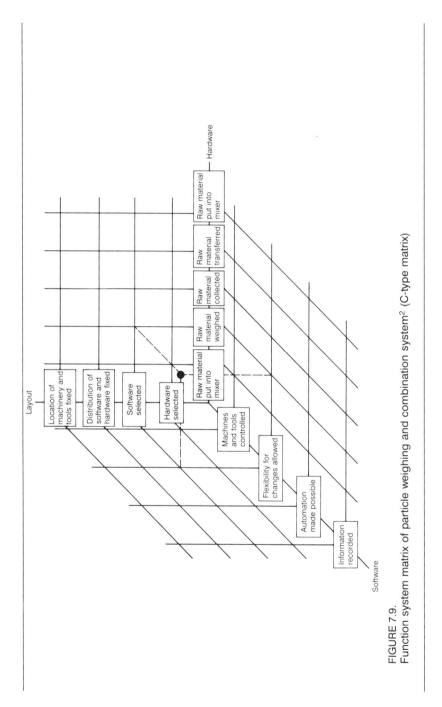

FIGURE 7.9.
Function system matrix of particle weighing and combination system[2] (C-type matrix)

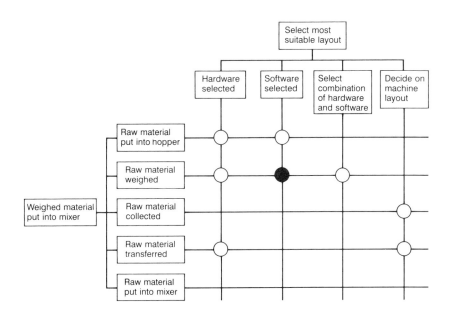

FIGURE 7.10
Matrix of hardware-layout function system[3] (L-type matrix)

substitute product features, as shown in Fig. 7.12. This matrix was used to evaluate the degree of correspondence between the quality required by users and the substitute product features. In addition, the degree of importance of the substitute product feature was sought. The acquired degree of importance was compared with the level of control, and measures were taken to eliminate the gap, if any existed between the two. Much improvement was made in terms of the large gap between the degree of importance and the current quality and management levels. The systematic diagram was used to develop a plan for this improvement.

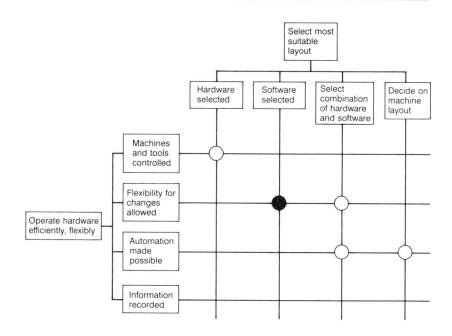

FIGURE 7.11
Matrix of software-layout function system[4] (L-type matrix)

Connecting substitute product features and manufacturing control items

Quality must be ensured during production. No matter how strict testing and inspection of a substitute product feature may be, they do not ensure quality. For this reason, a "matrix of substitute features and process control items" was constructed as shown in Fig. 7.13, which correlates substitute features with the process-control items of the QC process chart. In this matrix, the same degree of correspondence was evaluated, and the degree of importance of the manufacturing control item was obtained. As a result of reorganizing the

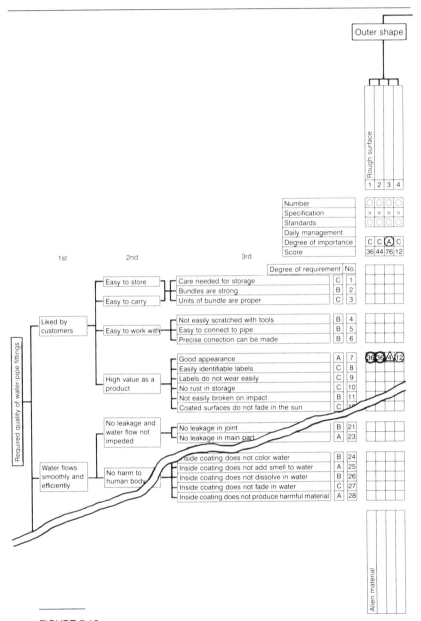

FIGURE 7.12
Matrix of required quality of water-pipe fittings and substitute features
(systematic diagram and L-type matrix)

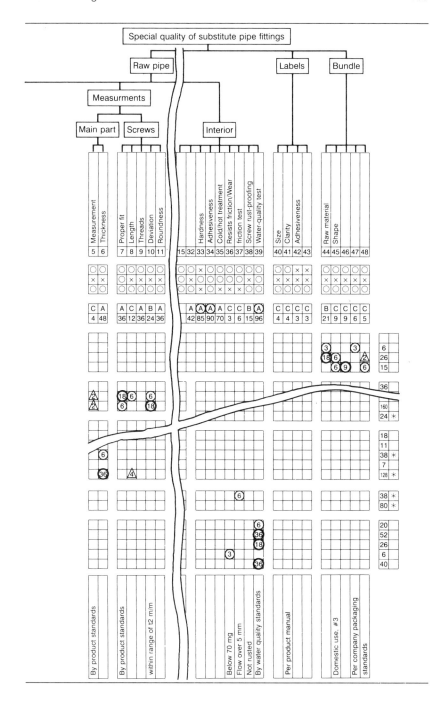

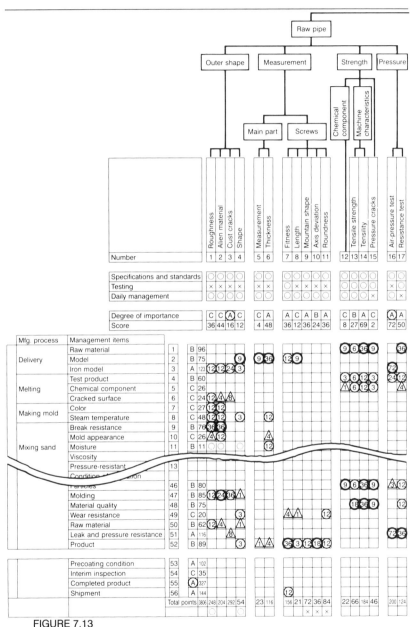

FIGURE 7.13
Matrix of substitute pipe fittings and manufacturing control items[7]
(systematic diagram and L-type matrix)

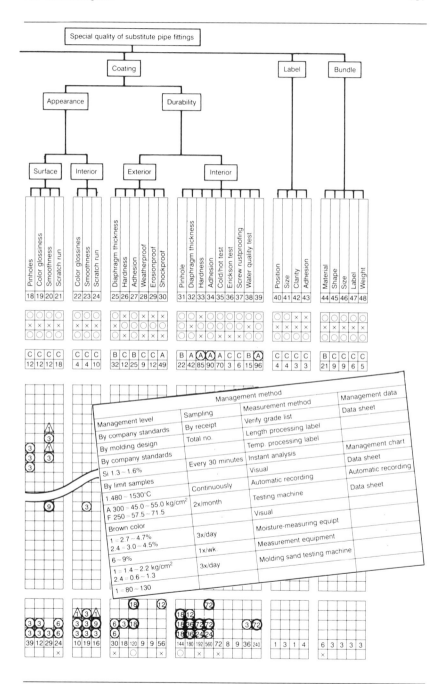

control system of production efficiency to reflect this degree of importance, control increased and the number of nonconforming items dropped.[5]

Application to improvement of the quality-evaluation structure

The testing department of Company N tests and inspects the quality features on many parts of an automobile brake system. The company undertook the current quality-evaluation program to strengthen the system and to make it more efficient because users' requirements for quality had become more strict. The development department had requested a greater number of tests on an increasing number of new products, and superior testing and measurement equipment was now available. In order to adequately plan for improvement of the system of quality evaluation, it was important to clarify the relationships among warranty features, test and measurement items, and testing and gauging equipment.

A warranty systematic diagram was used, and a T-type matrix was incorporated with the quality feature (control feature) corresponding to test and measurement items and test and measurement items corresponding to testing and gauging equipment, as shown in Fig. 7.14. Circumference rates were calculated by adding all the solid circles (●) in the rows and columns of the matrix; they were then arrayed in such a way as to provide a number of meanings and improvements, as shown in Fig. 7.15. From this, plans to make the quality system stronger and more efficient were implemented.

Application to a search for causes of poor quality

Company D manufactures book cloth and had a great deal of trouble with soiling. Recently, the company produced a large amount of light-colored cloth, which is easily soiled, and more than 10 percent of the product failed the final inspection. The company decided to find a way to reduce the soiling nonconformities by half.

Since there are many types of "soil," the company gathered inspection data and classified them into categories on the basis of the types of soil. These data were compiled into a pareto chart, as shown in Fig. 7.16. This pareto chart shows that one type of nonconformity

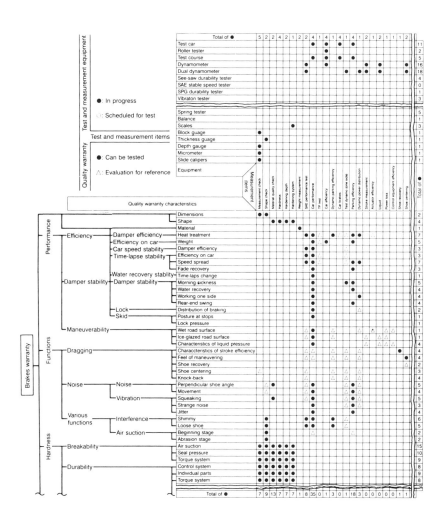

FIGURE 7.14
Matrix of car brake warrenty, test items, and test equipment
(T-type matrix)[8]

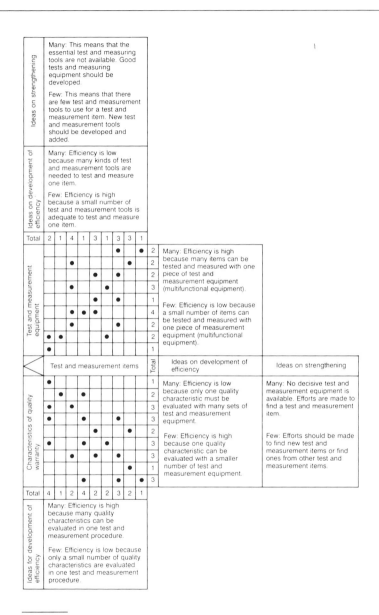

FIGURE 7.15
Ideas on improvement of quality-evaluation system

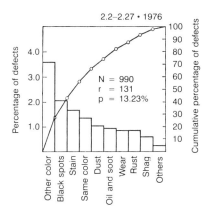

FIGURE 7.16
Pareto diagram of abnormalities due to soiling

represents the soiling event (e.g., unusual color, soiled spots, black spots), and the other type represents the causes of the soil (e.g., soiled with oil and soot or rust soil). The phenomena and causes of soil defects were separated, and an attempt was made to show the relationship between the two by correlating them on a matrix.

Furthermore, the relationship between the cause of soiling and the manufacturing process, which is the source of soiling, was shown in a matrix by drawing a correlation; a T-type matrix was designed to show the phenomenon, the cause, and the manufacturing process of the "soil defects," as shown in Fig. 2.9. After discussions about the problem possible solutions were considered and evaluated, and a list of countermeasures against soil defects was prepared, as is shown by Table 7.1. Notice the first countermeasure requires some time to examine and the third measure requires a great deal of discussion and does not include any concrete plans, but is simply a point of view.

TABLE 7.1
List of steps taken to prevent book cloth from soiling

Manufacturing process	Place	Causes	First countermeasure	Person responsible	Second countermeasure	Person responsible	Third Countermeasure	Person responsible
Paint mixing	Mixer	Oil	Clean blades					
		Rust	Replace cloth filter (2×/mo.)		Replace drums with stainless steel			
		Soot	Cleaning (esp. blades)					
	Drum cans	Attendance (others)	Clean drum dents					
		Attendance (self)	Replace lids					
	Raw material	Dust						
Paints *Machines* *Roll-out/roll-in*		Oil	No oil lubrication with light-color paint		Elevate roller position			
		Rust						
		Dirt from hands						
		Cardboard	Recycle cardboard					
		Paper						
		Black paint						
		Static electricity	Place cloth on roll-out machine		Install device to vacuum cardboard debris			
	Pump hose	Rust						
		Soot						
		Dust						
	Roller coating	Rust	Moisten cloth		Scrape rust from gluing dryer		Quick return device developed	
		Crease			Expand diameter of guide roller			
		Dew						
		Paint dregs						
		Black paint	Clean rubber roller with ammonia					
	Guide roller	Oil			Replace metal with bearings			
		Dew						
		Paint dregs						
	Cylinder	Soot	Clean air curtain (4×/yr.)		Improve drain system			
		Dust	Clean cylinder					
		Paint dregs					Cavity between joined parts narrowed	
	Clip	Oil	Clean cover		Prevent particles from dropping on heater			
		Rust						
		Dew						

The company implemented the countermeasures identified on this list, and consequently, the abnormalities dropped to less than 5 percent and have continued to drop since then.

When the relationships between abnormalities and their causes are analyzed, many people think that the information must be expressed in terms of numerical data. With numerical data, quantitative and objective analyses are carried out with the statistical quality control (SQC) method. At least one to two months are needed to obtain numerical data, however, and a considerable amount of time and labor is required.

The matrix design shows the degree of relationship between nonconforming phenomena and their causes with such symbols as ○ (relationship) and △ (possible relationship) (see Fig. 2.9). Here the subjective opinions of the evaluators are likely to be involved, and the objective analysis possible with numerical data cannot be expected. On the other hand, if people with much experience are involved, they should be able to evaluate the data in a very short period of time because of their long experience. It is difficult to determine which method is better, but the kind of data obtained on the basis of years of experience and expressed in ○ and △ can be more effective than numerical data. The matrix design has the advantage of drawing highly reliable data from observations made over a long period of time, analyzing these data skillfully, and finding a solution for the problem under study relatively quickly.

Different techniques used with matrix diagraming

The benefits of matrix diagraming have been well integrated with many widely used techniques, some of which are introduced here.

Morphologic analysis

This is a technique for forming ideas. First, the existence of a problem is established, then variables in the problem are listed and analyzed at all possible levels, and these are combined to form an idea. In other words, an L-type matrix is designed with two variables and a C-type matrix is designed with three variables; the point where all these variables intersect is a focal point for idea formation.

Matrix for determining objectives

This technique is one of many used for technological development. This technique sets an objective when technical forecasting is used as input and evaluation of a substitute plan is taken as output.[9]

The PESIC system

PESIC is an acronym for projects, elements, services, and information construction. It attempts to establish a system of management by arranging projects, products, elements, engineering, and services vertically, horizontally, and diagonally. This was developed by Tachiishi Electric Company, Inc., as a management system adaptable to all types of management.[10]

Finally, we would like to extend our deep appreciation to Yasukawa Electric Manufacturing Company, Inc., the Yoshitoshikaren Cast Iron Foundry, Inc., the Nisshin Textile Mill, Inc., and Dainik, Inc. for permitting us to use the charts reprinted in this chapter.

Notes

1. Futami Ryoji, "Uses of Matrix," *Kojo Kanri* (Factory Management), vol. 24, No. 9 (1978), pp. 6–15.

2. *Ibid.*

3. *Ibid.*

4. *Ibid.*

5. Yada Hiroshi, "A Quality Development System Applied at Sumikoto Joint," in *Proceedings of Regular Meeting of the Society for Study and Use of the Seven New QC Tools* (Tokyo: Japanese Union of Scientists and Engineers, 1978), pp. 3–22.

6. *Ibid.*, Futami, "Uses of Matrix," pp. 6–15.

7. Futami, "Uses of Matrix," pp. 6–19; *Proceedings*, 3–22.

8. Futami, "Uses of Matrix," pp. 6–19.

9. Makino Noboru, *Introduction to Technology Forecasting* (Tokyo: Nikkan Kogyo Shimbunsha, 1970).

10. Editorial Board for Handbook Study and Development, *Handbook on Research Development* (Tokyo: JUSE Press, Ltd., 1973).

Additional references

Mizuno Shigeru and Akao Yoji, *Development of Quality and Function* (Tokyo: JUSE Press, Ltd., 1978).

Futami Ryoji, "Using the Matrix to Come Up with Defect Causes and Countermeasures," *Kojo Kanri* (Factory Management), vol. 24, no. 3, (1978), pp. 15–19.

8

Matrix Data-Analysis

The matrix data-analysis method arranges the data presented in a matrix diagram so that the large array of numbers can be easily seen and comprehended.

The method

The matrix diagram arranges items in a column-row format, with the degree of correlation entered in the relevant column using symbols or numerical values. In Fig. 2.9, for example, the relationships among blemishes on printed cloth, the cause factors, and the place of occurrence or process are presented. Symbols are used in the relevant columns to indicate those factors believed to be important. In this case, concrete solutions can be developed through further examination of the causes of the blemishes, which, in this case, had been an area targeted for improvement.

Table 8.1 evaluates preferences among men and women, by age group, for 100 types of food items on a scale of 1 to 9, with 1 indicating the highest preference and 9 indicating the lowest. The numbers indicate the average preference values for each observed age group and food product. For example, the data show that while the preference for food product 1 varies by age group, the preference for food product 2 varies by sex. However, the data presented in Table 8.1 actually extend across a 10-row, 100-column matrix having 1000 items of data. Even if one were to examine these data thoroughly, the general extent of sex and age differences would still be unclear. Is there some way in which this can be organized in a clearer form?

One type of matrix data analysis is principal-component analysis. This technique is used in multivariate analysis and is detailed in the literature.[1] Unfortunately, because this technique is generally not well known, it is not used very often. Recently, however, an increasing number of Japanese companies have been introducing multivariate analysis methods, including principal-component

TABLE 8.1
Average Food Product Preference by Group

Group	Food Product 1	Food Product 2	⋯	Food Product 100
Men:				
15 years and younger	7.8	4.6	⋯	3.1
16–20 years old	5.4	3.8	⋯	2.8
21–30 years old	3.9	4.4	⋯	3.3
31–40 years old	3.5	4.0	⋯	3.0
41 years and older	3.0	3.5	⋯	2.5
Women:				
15 years and younger	8.1	6.2	⋯	3.9
16–20 years old	6.0	7.2	⋯	3.5
21–30 years old	5.4	7.5	⋯	3.0
31–40 years old	3.8	7.0	⋯	2.8
41 years and older	2.5	9.0	⋯	3.0

analysis, in both total company and organizational settings.[2] Furthermore, reports of the successful use of this method in the industrial sector continue to increase.

As stated in Chap. 1, even if it is impossible for all managers and staff to understand and use this method, it is still important because it is a method that is coming into greater use in the industrial sector.

Recently, along with the development of automatic calculation techniques, there has been an increase in the use of curves, rather than single values, to present data. Figure 8.1 shows a curve of the spectral distribution characteristics of a fluorescent lamp. Table 8.2 presents some of the spectral distribution characteristics of fluorescent lamps for each 10-nanometer interval. Similar readings taken for two other types of fluorescent lamps are also presented. Table 8.2 shows a 45-row, 3-column matrix data array similar to that in Table 8.1. When 94 types of spectral distribution characteristics of various fluorescent lamps, which vary in color quality, color, and luminescence, are entered, 45 rows and 94 columns of matrix data are obtained. For example, if one wishes to examine the spectral distribution shape characteristics for fluorescent lamps having good color characteristics using these data, the principal-component analysis method can be used.[3]

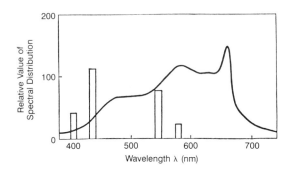

FIGURE 8.1
Example of spectral distribution of a fluorescent lamp (lamp F2 in table 8.2)

TABLE 8.2
Spectral distribution values for three types of fluorescent lamps

No.	λ (nm)	F1 S (λ)	F2 S (λ)	F3 S (λ)
1	380	5.4	10.7	23.0
2	90	5.6	12.0	27.5
3	400	5.8	13.9	33.4
4	10	6.1	16.8	43.6
5	20	7.4	20.8	55.0
⋮	⋮	⋮	⋮	⋮
18	550	82.3	88.4	99.8
19	60	100.0	100.0	100.0
20	70	113.2	110.4	101.1
21	80	125.7	116.0	102.7
22	90	112.9	115.3	102.7
⋮	⋮	⋮	⋮	⋮
38	750	1.0	6.6	11.0
39	60	0.2	5.2	9.0
40	70	0.0	4.0	7.3
41	80	0.0	3.1	6.0
42	404.7	27.2	42.3	77.7
43	435.8	84.0	112.1	182.4
44	546.1	77.7	77.7	100.8
45	577.8	23.7	23.0	29.1

Note: Values less than 404.7 nm correspond to the emission component.

Analysis of this type of matrix can be important in the fields of market research, new product planning and development, and process analysis. It is a technique that can be used to the greatest advantage in the PDCA plan and do stages when a large volume of data must be analyzed.

Calculation examples

In this section we will examine the results obtained through a calculation process, by computer, used in the principal-component analysis approach to a case study originally prepared by Toda.[4]

As shown in Table 8.1, an analysis was conducted based on average preference values presented in a matrix array for over 50 people categorized by sex and age. One-hundred food items, considered to be staple foods in the Japanese diet, were selected for this study. The breakdown of food categories selected is as follows: 19 types of staple foods, 4 types of soups, 10 types of meat dishes, 11 types of fish dishes, 3 types of side dishes, 14 types of drinks, 11 types of cakes and candies, and 4 types of fruit.

The purpose of this study was to determine how food preferences vary by sex and age. Should a difference in preference exist, ,group preferences for various types of foods should be made clear. In other words, the analysis did not determine whether each of the 10 age/sex groups preferred a particular food or not, but rather it illustrated the representative characteristics of these preferences instead.

Principal-component analysis was used to calculate representative characteristics. For example, using this method, the results of a science test, for subject i and student j, are expressed as x_{ij}. In this case, one representative characteristic of student j for the number of subjects taken, p, is expressed as:

$$w_j = \sum_{i=1}^{p} x_{ij} = x_{1j} + x_{2j} + \cdots + x_{pj} \tag{a}$$

Usually, a weighted value (l_i), which varies by 1 for each subject, is added and the representative characteristic is calculated using the following formula:

$$w_j = \sum_{i=1}^{p} l_i x_{ij} = l_1 x_{1j} + l_2 x_{2j} + \cdots + l_p x_{pj} \tag{b}$$

For example, just as a greater weight is placed on mathematics for a person who wishes to enter the technical section of a company, the representative characteristic allows for various selections to be made in response to a particular objective. Principal-component analysis is a selective measurement technique in which the representative characteristics can be mathematically calculated. These representative characteristics are independent. The weighted value l_i, which appears in the second equation, is referred to as a *characteristic vector*, and the representative characteristic corresponding to the base data for each representative characteristic is referred to as the *contributing ratio*.

An outline of the calculation process follows:

Step 1:

Each data item is assigned a term, x_{ij}, where $i = 1, 2, \ldots$, and $j = 1, 2, \ldots, 100$. The term i corresponds to the group evaluated, and j corresponds to the food item.

Step 2:

The correlation coefficient matrix is then calculated for each observed group. These results are presented in Table 8.3. That is,

$$r_{ii}' = \frac{1}{n-1} \sum_{j=1}^{n} z_{ij} z_i' j \qquad (c)$$

where

$$z_{ij} = \frac{x_{ij} - \overline{x}_{i\cdot}}{\sqrt{V_i}}, \overline{x}_{i\cdot} = \frac{1}{n} \sum_{j=1}^{n} x_{ij},$$

$$V_i = \frac{1}{n-1} \sum_{j=1}^{n} (x_{ij} - \overline{x}_{i\cdot})^2, n = 100.$$

TABLE 8.3
Correlation matrix for each group

	Men					Women				
	15 years and younger 1	16–20 2	21–30 3	31–40 4	41 and older 5	15 years and younger 6	16–20 7	21–30 8	31–40 9	41 and older 10
2	0.871									
3	0.516	0.759								
4	0.370	0.604	0.852							
5	0.172	0.402	0.726	0.874						
6	0.938	0.821	0.517	0.358	0.208					
7	0.811	0.838	0.658	0.488	0.354	0.889				
8	0.615	0.709	0.698	0.620	0.523	0.746	0.894			
9	0.500	0.647	0.701	0.721	0.710	0.621	0.768	0.852		
10	0.330	0.457	0.558	0.632	0.748	0.493	0.642	0.773	0.911	

Note: The diagonal is 1; the upper-right portion was omitted for symmetry

Step 3:

The characteristic values and vectors are calculated using the correlation matrix. This part of the sample calculation was carried out using a computer. The results are presented in Table 8.4.

The analysis process is itemized as follows: First, as can be seen in Table 8.1, the question addresses the degree of preference for each food item by evaluated group. These data should first be collected into a smaller number of representative characteristic groups. The size of the characteristic value indicates that perhaps a roughly similar representative characteristic can be extracted.

Second, each characteristic value in Table 8.4 (i.e., 6.83, 1.76, and 0.75) expresses the degree of preference for a certain food item; the larger the number, the larger is the representative characteristic. The first item (the first principal component) has a characteristic value of 6.83, and because the total fluctuation in the case of a 10×10 correlation matrix is 10, the influence exerted (contributing ratio) by the first principal component (individual food items not yet entered) is 0.683 (68.3 percent). Similarly, the contributing ratios for the second and third principal components are 0.176 (17.6 percent) and 0.075 (7.5 percent), respectively. By combining three preference patterns, the total fluctuation in the base data is 0.934 (93.4 percent). This is

TABLE 8.4
Characteristic value and vector values

Evaluated Group	First Principal Component	Second Principal Component	Third Principal Component
1	0.286	0.446	0.194
2	0.331	0.240	0.336
3	0.323	−0.166	0.442
4	0.299	−0.359	0.375
5	0.261	−0.507	0.128
6	0.309	0.408	−0.084
7	0.344	0.253	−0.171
8	0.348	0.032	−0.290
9	0.346	−0.164	−0.322
10	0.303	−0.267	−0.522
Characteristic value:	6.830	1.760	0.750
Contributing ratio:	0.683	0.176	0.075
Cumulative contributing ratio:	0.683	0.859	0.934

shown in the cumulative contributing ratio row. The characteristic value in the case of 10 × 10 correlation matrix is generally 10; however, this is gradually reduced to first, second, and third characteristic values, and a large part of the total fluctuation can be explained in ordinary numbers.

Next, the significance of the three principal components is applied by characteristic vectors. In Table 8.4, the numbers in the left-hand column represent the observed groups given in Table 8.1. There are 10 values in the first principal component column. These are characteristic vectors. Each of these values shows the relationship between each observed group and the preference pattern (principal component). Regarding the first principal component, all the coefficients have the same sign and are roughly equal. In other words, this shows a common pattern of preferences for all the groups. In the second principal component column, the characteristic vector value decreases as it moves down the column from groups 1 to 5 and shows a similar pattern for groups 6 to 10. Here observed groups 1 to 5 are men, while observed groups 6 to 10 are women. In other words, the value of the characteristic vector changes from positive to negative in accordance with age for both men and women; thus the preference pattern appearing in the second principal component column indicates a difference in preference in accordance with age. Similarly, the third principal component column shows positive preference values in relation to men and negative values in relation to women. From this it is seen that for this component there is a difference in preference based on sex. The preceding results thus reduce the food item preferences to a general preference (contributing ratio 68.3 percent), a preference affected by age (contributing ratio 17.6 percent), and a preference affected by sex (contributing ratio 7.5 percent). Furthermore, the total fluctuation for the three principal components is 93.4 percent.

Finally, we shall attempt to compile a matrix array based on the preference patterns for each food item. This is calculated using the following formula which is available in a computer program:

$$w_{mj} = \sum_{i=1}^{10} l_{mi} z_{ij} \qquad\qquad (d)$$

With $m = 1, 2, 3$ indicating the three principal components, the principal-component score is calculated for each food item, j, which is assigned a value $1, 2, \ldots, 100$. The value of the vector corresponding to i is in Table 8.4. When the first and second principal component scores are plotted on the horizontal and vertical axes, respectively, a diagram such as that shown in Fig. 8.2 is obtained.

In this diagram, the food items generally preferred appear as one moves to the right along the horizontal axis, while those food items not generally preferred appear as one moves to the left. Furthermore, those items preferred by younger age groups appear as one moves up the vertical axis, while those foods preferred by older age groups appear as one moves down the vertical axis. By plotting the first and third principal component scores in a similar fashion, information on general preferences by sex can be obtained.

Principal-component analysis is a method in which matrix data, as presented in Table 8.1, can be expressed more clearly through numerical analysis, as shown in Fig. 8.2. In this sense, it is a diagraming method that includes analysis.

Conclusion

This section presented a working example of principal-component analysis. As is clear from the results presented, this is a method of organizing and categorizing raw data that are difficult to grasp. A topic for future study in this same area will most likely be how this information can be used in the development of food products.

0–1 data: investigating new material applications: product A

To develop and market a new material effectively, we must know, prior to entering the market, how the new material can be used. The opinion of a specialist is considered, and then a process begins in

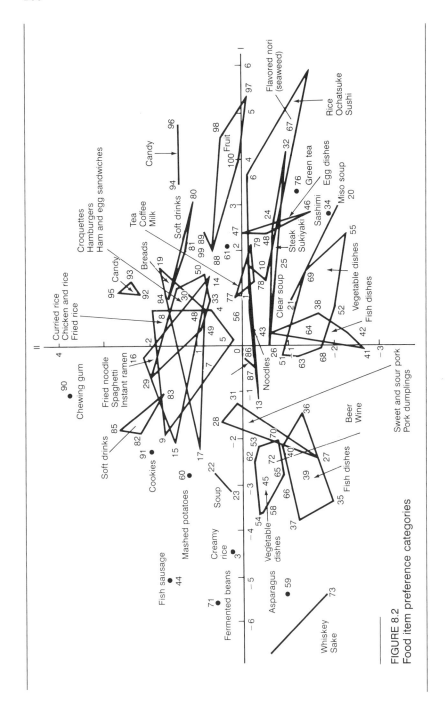

FIGURE 8.2
Food item preference categories

which trial products employing the new material are made and tested repeatedly. It is only after completion of this process that final decisions about applications of the new material are made.

Noguchi Hiroshi[5] has conducted various experiments involving a partially objective applications search process. Here we will provide an example of this method.

Prior to conducting an applications search for a new material, product *A*, a matrix array is compiled. This matrix shows the relationships among various applications, listed in the right-hand column, and desired characteristics of the material, across the top (see Table 8.5). In the table, a 1 is used to show whether the particular characteristic is desirable in relation to the application, while 0 indicates that the characteristic is not required. For example, in relation to men's summer wear, desirable characteristics include color-fastness in sunlight, stain resistance, ability to keep its shape, resistance to wrinkling, tears, and static, dryness, lightness, and breathability. The newly developed material *A*, which is listed in the last row of the table, satisfies these characteristics. Therefore, this could possibly be an area of application for the new material.

The principal-component method also can be applied to this type of 0–1 data matrix.[6] A diagram showing the locations of the first and second principal component scores has already been presented in Fig. 2.10. In this diagram, if the applications characteristics are similar, the scores will be closer, and conversely, if the difference in application characteristics is significant, the distance between the score locations will increase. Next, the principal component scores of the new material *A* are calculated. These are indicated in Fig. 2.10 with the symbol ○. As can be seen clearly in the diagram, applications for men's and women's summer wear, sports wear, pants, skirts, and raincoats are relatively close.

The desired characteristics shown in Table 8.5 also can be obtained using calculated data in addition to 0–1 data. Even if the matrix data appearing in Table 8.5 are complicated by having computed values and 0–1 values mixed together, principal-component analysis can be used.

TABLE 8.5
Various product applications and corresponding desirable characteristics

Desired Qualities, Item j:

1. Color-Fast in Sunlight
2. Color-Fast in Wash
3. Color-Fast Perspiration
4. Color-Fast Dry Clean
5. Stain Resistant
6. Ability to keep shape
7. Wrinkle Resistant
8. Wash and Wear
9. Nonchafing
10. Nonpilling
11. Tear Resistant
12. Breathability
13. Warmth
14. Absorbency
15. Water Repellent
16. Lightness
17. Wind Resistant
18. Drape
19. Stretch Recovery
20. Elasticity
21. Slip Friction
22. Electric Charge
23. Nonflammability
24. Chemical Resistant
25. Gentle to Skin

Group	Item i	Applications Item i	1	2	3	4	5	6	7	8	9	10	11	12	13	14	15	16	17	18	19	20	21	22	23	24	25
A	1	Men's, summer	1	0	1	1	1	1	1	0	0	0	1	1	0	1	0	1	1	0	0	0	0	0	0	0	0
	2	Men's winter	1	0	0	1	1	1	1	0	1	1	1	1	0	1	0	0	1	1	0	0	1	0	0	0	0
	3	Women's, summer	1	0	1	1	1	1	1	0	0	0	1	1	0	1	0	1	1	0	0	0	0	0	0	0	0
	4	Women's, winter	1	0	0	1	1	1	1	0	1	1	1	1	0	1	0	0	1	1	0	0	1	0	0	0	0
	5	Skirts	1	0	0	1	1	1	1	1	1	0	0	0	0	0	0	1	1	1	1	0	0	0	0	0	0
	6	Trousers	1	0	0	1	1	1	1	0	1	1	1	0	0	0	0	0	1	0	1	1	0	0	0	0	0
	7	Overcoats	1	0	0	1	1	1	1	0	1	1	1	0	1	0	0	1	1	1	0	1	0	0	0	0	0
	8	Raincoats	1	0	0	1	1	1	1	0	1	1	1	0	0	0	1	0	0	1	0	0	0	0	0	0	0
	9	Office	0	1	0	0	1	0	0	0	0	0	0	0	0	0	0	0	0	0	0	0	0	0	0	0	0
	10	Work	0	1	1	0	0	0	0	0	0	0	1	0	0	0	0	0	0	0	0	0	0	1	1	1	0
	11	Sports	0	1	1	0	0	1	0	0	1	0	1	0	0	1	0	0	0	0	1	0	0	0	0	0	0
	12	School	0	0	0	0	1	1	1	0	1	0	1	0	0	0	0	0	0	0	1	0	0	0	0	0	0
	13	Home	0	1	0	0	0	1	0	0	1	1	1	0	0	1	0	0	0	0	0	0	0	0	0	0	0
	14	Baby clothes	0	0	0	0	0	1	0	0	0	0	0	1	1	1	0	0	0	0	1	0	0	0	1	0	1
B	15	Dress shirts	1	1	1	0	0	1	1	1	0	0	1	1	0	1	0	0	1	0	0	0	1	0	0	0	1
	16	Blouses	1	1	1	0	0	1	1	1	0	0	1	1	0	1	0	0	1	0	0	0	1	0	0	0	1
	17	Sweaters	1	1	0	1	0	1	0	0	0	0	0	1	0	0	0	1	0	0	1	0	0	0	0	0	0
	18	Sports shirts	1	1	1	0	0	0	0	0	0	0	0	0	0	1	0	0	0	0	1	0	0	0	0	0	1
C	19	Night wear	0	0	1	0	0	0	0	0	0	0	0	1	1	1	0	0	0	0	0	0	0	0	0	0	1
	20	Summer underwear	0	0	0	0	0	1	0	0	0	0	1	1	1	0	1	0	0	1	0	1	0	0	0	0	1
	21	Winter underwear	0	0	0	0	0	1	0	0	0	0	1	0	1	1	0	0	1	0	1	0	0	0	0	0	1
	22	Foundations	0	0	0	0	0	1	0	0	0	0	0	0	0	1	0	0	1	0	1	0	0	0	0	0	1
	23	Baby wear	0	0	0	0	0	1	0	0	0	0	1	1	1	1	0	0	1	0	1	0	0	0	0	0	1
D	24	Towels	0	0	0	0	0	0	0	0	0	0	0	0	0	1	0	1	0	0	0	0	1	0	0	0	1
	25	Handkerchiefs	0	1	0	0	0	0	0	0	0	0	0	0	1	0	0	1	0	0	1	0	0	1	0	0	0
	26	Hats	1	0	1	0	0	0	0	0	0	0	0	1	1	1	0	0	0	0	0	0	0	0	0	0	0
	27	Mufflers	0	0	1	0	0	0	0	0	0	0	0	0	1	0	0	0	1	1	0	1	0	0	0	0	0
	28	Ties	0	0	1	0	0	0	0	0	0	0	0	0	0	0	0	0	1	0	1	1	0	0	0	0	0
	29	Scarfs	0	0	1	0	0	0	0	0	0	0	0	0	1	0	0	0	1	0	0	1	1	0	0	0	0
	30	Gloves	0	0	0	0	0	0	0	0	0	0	0	0	1	0	0	0	1	0	0	0	1	0	0	0	0
	31	Socks	1	0	0	0	0	0	0	0	1	0	0	0	0	0	1	0	0	0	0	0	0	0	0	0	0
	32	Umbrellas	1	0	0	0	0	0	0	0	0	0	0	0	0	0	1	0	0	0	0	0	0	0	0	0	0
E	33	Carpets	0	0	0	0	0	0	0	0	1	0	0	1	0	0	1	0	0	0	0	1	0	1	1	0	0
	34	Curtains	1	0	0	0	1	0	0	0	0	0	0	0	1	0	0	0	1	0	0	0	0	0	1	0	0
	35	Tablecloths	0	0	0	0	0	0	0	0	0	0	0	0	0	0	1	0	0	1	0	0	1	0	0	0	0
	36	Upholstery	1	0	0	0	0	0	0	0	1	0	0	0	1	0	0	0	0	0	0	1	0	0	0	0	0
	37	Mats	0	0	0	0	0	0	0	0	0	0	0	0	0	0	0	0	0	0	0	1	0	0	0	0	0
	38	Pillows	0	0	0	0	0	0	0	0	0	0	0	0	1	0	0	0	0	0	0	1	0	0	0	0	0
	39	Cushions	0	0	0	0	0	0	0	0	0	0	0	0	0	0	0	0	0	0	0	1	0	0	0	0	0
Material A			1	1	1	1	1	1	1	1	1	1	0	0	0	0	0	1	0	0	0	1	0	0	0	0	0

Applications in planning, development, and process analysis

An example of curve data analysis[7]

Fluorescent lamp spectral distribution characteristics are shown in Fig. 8.1 and Table 8.2. Data involving a total of 94 types of fluorescent lamps on the market that have various color and color-reproduction characteristics were collected. Then the data were arranged in a matrix comprised of 25 wavelengths and 94 lamps.

On the basis of these data, principal-component analysis results for the average and three characteristic vectors, $J(\lambda_i)$, $S_1(\lambda_i)$, $S_2(\lambda_i)$, and $S_3(\lambda_i)$, as shown in Fig. 8.3, were obtained.

Using these results, it is clear that all possible fluorescent lamp spectral distribution characteristics can be expressed using the following formula:

$$J(\lambda_i) = \overline{J}(\lambda_i) + k_1 S_1(\lambda_i) + k_2 S_2(\lambda_i) + k_3 S_3(\lambda_i) \tag{e}$$

In this formula, the coefficients k_1, k_2, and k_3 were determined, using characteristic techniques, from the values of the calculated fluorescent color (x, y) and color-reproduction characteristics (R_a).

On the basis of equation (e), a projection of the spectral distributions of fluorescent lamps was prepared reflecting those developed to date and those yet to be developed. The color-reproduction characteristics and luminescent efficiency were tested. The results for fluorescent lamps having the same color and various color-reproduction characteristics are shown in Fig. 8.4. Part (b) represents a fluorescent lamp that provides color characteristics close to those of daylight. Because part (d) shows characteristics that exceed the fluorescent light range of coefficients k_1, k_2, and k_3, this lamp was found to have the special characteristic of color reproduction that is better than that of daylight, which is both an advantage and a disadvantage.

Forecasting fashion cycles

Forecasting fashions is a major concern in many industries. Kawasaki Kentaro and others[8] have reported some interesting results in this regard.

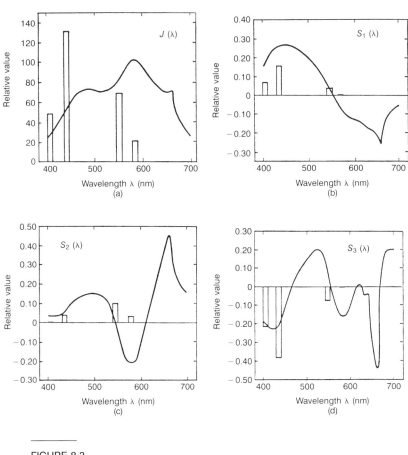

FIGURE 8.3
$J(\lambda_i)$, $S_1(\lambda_i)$, $S_2(\lambda_i)$, and $S_3(\lambda_i)$ distribution characteristics

Once, 53 representative fashions that appeared in *American Book* magazine were selected for each of the years from 1918 to 1974; these were then evaluated by 45 specialists employing 20 types of usage evaluation criteria. On the basis of these data, a matrix was constructed, the correlation array among the evaluation criteria was calculated, and principal-component analysis was conducted.

The result was that the following principal components were obtained: "contemporary elements," "feminine elements," and

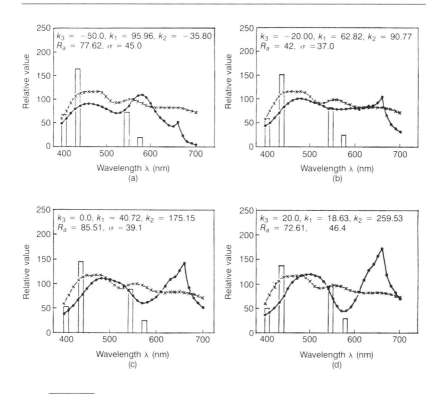

FIGURE 8.4
Spectral distribution for fluorescent lamps having daylight color and
color-reproduction fidelity levels, R_a.

"unique elements." Forecasts based on simple insertion or recurrence of evaluation criteria and an evaluation of the next fiscal year were prepared. Using these, the following year's principal-component estimate score values were obtained.

Analysis of desired car styles

Tamanaka Hiroki[9] and others analyzed the responses of 1041 subjects on 12 items concerning 10 types of passenger cars that were being marketed, including car A, which, at the time, was receiving a great deal of public attention. It was discovered that the one essential element explaining the good evaluation given to this car was that structurally this car was seen as having unusual interior space.

In order to discover the relationship between the actual dimensions of the car's interior and the "psychological feeling of space," 26 different measurements of 29 types of cars, including car A, were taken. These data were then compiled in a 26-location, 29-car matrix.

A principal-component analysis was then carried out on the basis of a correlation matrix between the measurements and three principal components. The contributing ratio for these three components was approximately 54 percent. Each principal component was examined individually for items that reflected overall width, sitting room conditions, and superior front-seat and back-seat room. Finally, following a detailed analysis of the locations of the component scores, the reason for the high evaluation given to car A was that although in a geometric sense the interior of the car was average for domestically produced cars, the roominess of the back seat was emphasized at the expense of the front seat but was offset by the sedan shape of the car.

Press manufacturing wrinkle analysis

Sumimoto and Kamimura[10] prepared an analysis of a method to prevent wrinkles in automobile front bumpers when using right-side press. Although both the left- and right-side presses produced good results, when a slight difference in essential standards or operation occurred in the right-side press, a wrinkle would appear.

A series of 20φ circles were drawn at 39 prescribed locations on steel plates, and the degree of circle deformation after pressing was measured. Then 18 sample pressings of the left-side front bumper and 27 samples of the right-side bumper were produced for a total of 45 samples. These data were compiled into a 45-sample, 29-location matrix for examination.

On the basis of the correlation matrix between the locations, principal-component analysis showed that the source of wrinkles was not located where the circles had been drawn, but rather was affected by the degree of deformation that resulted at pressings at other locations.

Finally, an additional analysis was conducted. The machinery, materials, shapes, and other factors having an influence on the degree of deformation at specific locations were examined, and a process-management method was established as the factors contributing to nonconformities were removed.

This is a good example of the use of a combination of characteristic technology and this type of analysis.

Other examples

It has been reported that despite a variation in the number of factors, a stable factor structure can be detected by applying principal-component analysis to the metallic surface nonconformity cause groupings obtained using major recurrence analysis. In other words, the defects occurring on the steel surface were analyzed using the major recurrence method, as a special value related to the nine variables believed to affect this. In order to extract a few factors from the nine variables, eight, six, and five types of variables were selected and three types of major recurrence methods were calculated. However, the deviation recurrence value differed greatly for each formula, and in some cases, positive and negative values were reversed.

Thus principal-component analysis was carried out using all nine variables, four principal components were extracted, and the representative characteristics of the factors were calculated. The surface nonconformity and these four representative factor characteristics were calculated and analyzed using the major recurrence method. Consequently, the cause factors influencing surface defects were made clearer.

At a photo-processing plant it was discovered that there were large variations in a process using a two-dye mixture and that the product light-absorption curve varied with each batch processed. Because of the kinds of variations, it was assumed that impurities were being introduced into the mixture or that variations in dye composition occurred. To determine the cause, the problem was analyzed using principal-component analysis.[11] Spectral absorption curves were calculated for a sample group obtained using an experimental production process. These curves were then compiled into a matrix comprised of wavelength and sample rows and columns.

On the basis of these data, the horizontal sum and product sum matrices for the wavelengths were calculated, an examination was conducted on the basis of the characteristic values and vectors, and contributing ratios were obtained. The results showed that the spectral absorption curve fluctuations among the samples were a result of variations in the composition of the two-dye mixture. It was thus determined that the introduction of impurities was not the cause. Furthermore, spectral absorption curves were obtained from experimental results calculated in conjunction with the characteristics technique. These results showed that the composition of the dyes varied in substance from the characteristics established by technical standards.

Conclusion

This chapter showed that by using matrices as one method of analysis to arrange data, more information can be obtained than could be obtained through a study of the basic data.

This type of method has already been converted into a computer program[12] and certainly provides advantages in the understanding of input and output data. For this reason, principal-component analysis should not be thought of as complex. It can be actively applied to those problems for which it is suitable and understood through experimentation. Using this process, the individual's technique can be strengthened when combined with a mathematical foundation. We trust that this method, including the different multivariate analysis techniques, will see more use in the industrial sector.

Finally, we would like to thank Mr. Toda and Mr. Noguchi for their permission to use their tables and figures.

Notes

1. *See* for example, Okuno, Kume, Haga, Yoshizawa, *Tahenryo Kaiseki-suho (Multivariate Analysis Method)* (Tokyo: JUSE Press, Ltd., 1971).

2. Takabatake Kunihiko, "Tokei Kaiseki no Suishin" (The advancement of statistical analysis), *Hinshitsu Kanri (Quality Control)*, vol. 29 (May 1978), special issue, pp. 194–196; Nakaso Nobutada, "Tahenryo Kaiseki no Taikenteki Donyu ni tsuite" (Concerning the experienced introduction to multivariate analysis), *Hinshitsu Kanri (Quality Control)*, vol. 29 (May 1978), special issue, pp. 197–202.

3. Noya, Kurioka, Shokugaki, "Enshokusei to Metamerizumu ni Kansuru Kenkyu, Sono 3" (Research on performance and *metamerizumu, Shomei Gakkai Zasshi* (Lighting Study Group), vol. 27 (1968), p. 190.

4. Toda Tanaka, "Shokuhin no Shiko Chosa" (Study of Food Preferences), *Dai 9 Kai Kanno Kensa Daikai Hobunshu* (Report on the 9th Sensory Inspection Conference), vol. 10 (1968), JUSE; Tanaka Toda and Jinbo, "Shiko kara mita Shokuhin Bunrui" (Categorization of food by preference), *Takeda Kenkyu Sho Nenpyo* (Yearly report of the Takeda Research Center), vol. 27 (1968), p. 190.

5. Noguchi Hiroshi, "Shinsozai Yoto Tansaku no Giho" (Method for investigating new material applications), in *Nippon Hinshitsu Kanri Gakkai Dai 10 Kai Kenkyu Happyo Kai, Kenkyu Happyo Yoshishu (Proceedings of the 10th Japan Quality Control Conference)* (Tokyo: JUSE Press, Ltd., 1977), p. 20; and Noguchi Hiroshi, *Kansai Tahenryo Kaiseki Semina—Tekisuto, Jishirei* (Kansai multivariate analysis seminar—text and case studies) (Tokyo: JUSE Press, Ltd., 1978), p. 37.

6. Mizuno, Nagae, Kamisugi, "Shitsugobyo no Sogoteki Hyoron Chi 0–1 score—Shuseibun Seki o Ooyoshite" (Aphasia evaluation 0–1 score—application of the principal-component method), *Gyodokeiryogaku* (Behavior measurement), vol. 3, No. 2 (1976), p. 1.

7. See note 3.

8. Kawasaki Kentaro et al., "Fashion Dynamics 3" *Seni Seihin Shohi Kagakkaishi*, (Textile product study group newsletter), vol. 17, no. 14 (1976).

9. Tamanaka Kiroki, *Kansai Tahenryo Kaiseki Semina—Tekisuto, Jishirei* (Kansai multivariate analysis seminar—text and case studies), (Tokyo: JUSE Press, Ltd., 1975).

10. Sumimoto and Kamimura, "Jidosha no Seizokotei ni okeru Tahenryo Kaisetsu Ooyorei" (Application of multivariate analysis in automobile manufacturing processes), *Hinshitsu* (Quality), vol. 6, No. 2 (1976), p. 59.

11. W. H. Lawton and E. A. Sylvester, Self-Modeling Curve Resolution, *Technometrics*, vol. 13 (1971) p. 617.

12. For example, Iguchi Haruhiro, *Tahenryo Kaisetsu to Komputa Purogramu* (Multivariate analysis and computer programming) (Tokyo: Nikkan Kogyo Shimbunsha, 1972), p. 61.

9

The Process Decision Program Chart (PDPC)

The process decision program chart (PDPC) method helps us select the best processes to use to obtain desired results by evaluating the progress of events and various conceivable outcomes.

The method

In the areas of policy control and total quality control, we make an effort to plan step by step in order to solve problems and reach our objectives. However, changing conditions often do not allow us to act as we anticipate, so we are forced to alter our plans. This occurs especially when we face the difficult problem of quality. Solution processes can be classified in two ways:

1. A solution can be anticipated based on prior knowledge.
2. A solution cannot be anticipated at this stage due to insufficient knowledge and unexpected changes in conditions or events.

Much of the research and development of new products belongs in the second category. In the investigative process, we often obtain new knowledge and encounter totally unexpected phenomena. For example, in the case of an extensive oil leak at an oil refinery or a train derailment, we may face totally new matters that are not anticipated under normal operating conditions. These cases also belong to the second category. To resolve problems involving new circumstances and unprecedented occurrences, we must be guided in the right direction (i.e., toward completion of research, prevention of accidents). Therefore, whenever new information is obtained, we review our plans and consider possible alternatives.

The process decision program chart is one of the methods used to solve problems in operations research and is introduced here to deal with problems that occur during the process of total quality control. The PDPC directs progress toward a desired goal in the planning stage, or during the design stage in research and development, by anticipating undesirable conditions and results. Moreover, the PDPC is an effective means of moving promptly toward one's goal at the very stage of the process where we encounter an unexpected problem. Therefore, the PDPC is used to define the solution process when we are dealing with problems that have more than one possible outcome. The PDPC is effective in preventing serious accidents; therefore, it is known as a chart for the prediction of serious accidents.

PDPC in operations research

The PDPC method is introduced here as a qualitative model in operations research. The definition of the qualitative model is a "change in a phenomenon and the reciprocal correlation between the substance and the nature of elements related to that phenomenon." Qualitative models are expressed in many cases with geometric figures and tree charts. If a certain condition occurs as a result of a certain action, and if the condition is not desirable, a proper solution should be sought. Suppose, however, that the solution causes various new conditions. In such a case, a chart is used to express a chronological and systematic picture of a phenomenon through the entire process.[1] Fig. 9.1 shows a PDPC for a Gemini space flight. The chart graphically illustrates the whole process from takeoff to recovery. For example, various alternatives are planned in the event of death of the astronauts right after ignition during the first stage. Of course, matters may not progress as anticipated. In that case, the PDPC should be redesigned. For example, if an emergency not included in the original plan in Fig. 9.1 occurs, the method of rescuing the astronauts without any serious harm, despite the disastrous situation, is promptly determined through communication between the astronauts and their base.[2]

The PDPC method and quality control

Now that the era of stability and prosperity has begun, competition among enterprises has intensified. To deal with this situation, our day-to-day operations have become more diversified and complex than ever before. The same can be said about problems of quality control. Conventional QC methods, where consequences are analyzed to determine actions, often provide the solution too late. Even if the process is initiated as soon as problems occur, small environmental changes might force the entire process to be redesigned. Without the ability to deal promptly with such situations, it is frequently too late to do anything, especially in dealing with problems of product liability.

In developing new products, it is important to introduce into the market in a timely manner products with high added value that respond to customer demand. For this reason, features desired by customers should be well integrated during the planning stage of new products. In the planning stage, it is also important to consider users and the environment in which they use the product in order to minimize adverse impacts. In addition, the process of planning production should be as effective as possible because of limited production periods and cost. In reality, however, unpredictable matters occur frequently and circumstances are likely to change over time. Conditions relevant to alternative solutions to any problem, both social and economic, change gradually. Under such circumstances, previous ways of dealing with problems, in which only

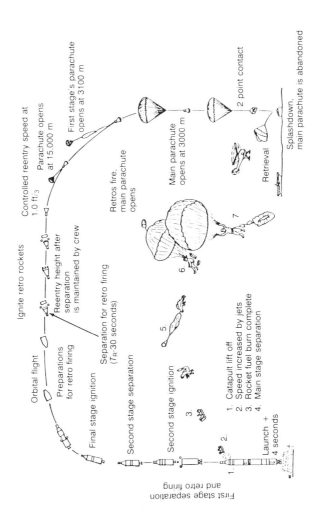

FIGURE 9.1
Graphic PDPC for a Gemini space flight

Source: From Jiro Kondo, *Operations Research* (Tokyo: JUSE Publishing Co., 1973), p. 131.

one solution is determined during planning, are not effective. We might not see a problem in the beginning, but later, in the face of changing conditions or the occurrence of unexpected results, we are forced to abandon our objectives because of slow response or lack of a proper solution.

As illustrated earlier, problems of development or product liability frequently put us in unanticipated or uncertain situations. To deal with these kinds of situations, a method that enables us not only to anticipate solutions, but also to respond to changing conditions is especially desirable. In light of this, the PDPC method is considered well suited. The PDPC method has no definite structural rules: Start with the present, suggest a possible solution under a conceivable future, anticipate undesirable outcomes, present a means of reaching a better result, and then decide on a course of action. If we are forced to face a new problem, information, or dimension that occurs during the process without previous warning or indication, we must review the process in a flexible manner, considering changes that accommodate the new conditions. Then, based on this review, we can proceed to redesign or correct the plan. Therefore, in the new era of quality, the PDPC method is quite useful for solving TQC problems.

Characteristics of the method

PDPC is a dynamic method

To solve a problem with defined parameters (e.g., building a house within a certain period of time), difficulties that occur during the process can be readily anticipated because of the building plan, which begins with planning and ends with the actual steps to reach the goal. However, problems often have to be solved under uncertain conditions. For example, if the elimination of defective products is set as a goal, it is impossible to determine exactly the process necessary to reach such a goal. Were it possible to do so, the problem would already have been solved earlier in the process. Therefore, the proper method for reaching a solution to the problem of product quality improvement remains to be discovered through new information and analysis at each step of the process. When the PDPC method is used for quality control, especially with problems related to important qualities, there are two steps:

Step 1

To apply the PDPC method during the planning stage, it is necessary to clearly describe the problem verbally, through previously established analysis, prior experience, and the proper techniques. It is important to describe all problems in the planning stage and to anticipate their solutions. For example, Fig. 9.2 indicates the process of moving from the present point A_0 (high percentage of defectives) to Z (tolerable percentage of defectives). In the first step of planning, a line from $A_1, A_2, A_3, \ldots, A_p$ is considered as a possible means to reach from A_0 to Z. However, when dealing with the problem of defectives, the matter is not so simple. As a result of discussion, A_3 is determined to be too technically difficult to implement. Thus, if not A_3, there is another line from A_2 to $B_1, B_2, \ldots, B_q$ to reach Z as a possible solution. If the two lines described above are not possible, there are others, such as $C_1, C_2, C_3, \ldots, C_r$ or $C_1, C_2, C_3, D_1, D_2, D_3, \ldots, D_s$, even though they are more costly than previous methods of reaching the goal.

So in the first step, to increase the probability of reaching the goal, not only one, but several lines of approach toward the desired condition Z should be considered. In actual practice, it is possible that each of the alternatives may be put into successive use, or if time is limited, several may be tried simultaneously.

Step 2

When dealing with the perpetual problem of quality, the first step described above is not always adequate because there is always the possibility that unforeseen technical problems will appear during the process of implementing a solution. On the other hand, there also exists the possibility that not only problems but also new perceptions will arise. For example, in Fig. 9.2, suppose that stages A_3, B_1, and C_3 were all reached, respectively, by processing through each line simultaneously and that a couple of months already have passed since this was started. If so, the possibility of success in progressing from A_p, B_q, C_r, and D_s to Z and associated problems becomes

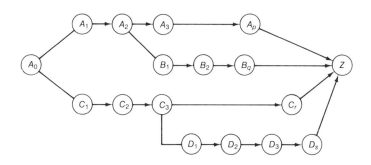

FIGURE 9.2
How to think in the PDPC method

clearer. Should it be proven that the lines described above are not adequate, it would be necessary to set new lines E, F, etc. based on the information learned. In this way, the second step is to be done every couple of months to increase the possibility of success in reaching goal Z through information learned. In quality control, it is said that the object of evaluation is not the result, but the process. Using a chart similar to Fig. 9.2 at each step, information about the adequacy of the original plan, the means of obtaining information, and the timeliness of response during the process is given as data. These data contribute largely to successive decision-making processes.

In the whole process of problem solving, the PDPC method promotes every possible means of solution. It also efficiently deals with conditions that work against a solution. For this reason, the PDPC method is characteristically quite dynamic in nature. Moreover, the PDPC graphically expresses the entire process for reaching a goal. Therefore, the PDPC method encourages ready summarization for executives and many new and inventive ideas from participants.

To understand the character of the PDPC method, let us compare it with other techniques that employ charts, their subjects, and their methods of use. The PDPC is similar in form to the tree chart. As lines progress from concept to actuality, the PDPC is certainly like a goal-method tree chart. But the tree chart is static because events progress within a fixed line of goal-method. On the other hand, in the PDPC, events in the process are linked by flow lines in chronological order; therefore, this method is dynamic. Arrow diagrams, as we shall discuss later, also arrange events in chronological order and are used for schedule control. With the PDPC method, schedule control is possible if dates are inscribed on the events in the process. However, the subjects of arrow diagrams are, in many cases, events under comparatively static conditions. Each step of an arrow diagram is precisely determined according to the planned date of completion. For example, in the case of building construction, based on past experience, each stage and its projected completion date can be determined quite precisely. When dealing with quality control, however, we often cannot visualize a solution from beginning to end. In these cases, the PDPC is more effective than an arrow diagram.

In the field of reliability engineering, two methods, failure mode and effect analysis (FMEA)[3] and fault tree analysis (FTA) are representative methods used to resolve system failures. FMEA starts from each function of subsystems or parts that make up a system or product and from the potential failure mode that might occur and evaluates its influence on the larger system and its significance. In other words, FMEA is oriented toward a bottom-up succession of analyses. FTA selects one "undesirable situation" and seeks the cause in a top-to-bottom fashion, in the manner of the branches of a tree, until it reaches the principle failure element to obtain a solution. In other words, FMEA deals with function and FTA deals with existing phenomena.[4]

As these examples illustrate, both FMEA and FTA are often used under static conditions. Unlike FMEA and FTA, the PDPC method can reveal not only logical phenomena, but also phenomena expressed in the light of new ideas. As a result of a detailed comparison of the PDPC method and FTA, PDPC can be characterized as follows:

1. Because the PDPC comprehends the actions of a system as a whole, we are able to make a comprehensive summarization (effective for identifying significant errors and problems, but not individual details).

2. We can view the progression of processes in the system in chronological order.

3. In the dynamics of the system, the relationship between initiating influence and terminating influence is shown. Therefore, causes of undesirable conditions can be followed through the course of their actions; undesirable conditions can be discovered by following the movement of actions starting from a certain initiating influence.

4. Because events are the basis of the PDPC, anyone who has a basic understanding of the system can use it easily. Thus, within the many possible directions of change and development of conditions, we are sometimes able to point out unanticipated fundamental problems. It is particularly effective in dealing with human factors engineering and with complex interactions between systems.

For instance, were the FTA chart in Figure 9.3 switched to PDPC, the following problems could be represented: 1) A fire prevention monitor inadvertently turns off the power to the alarm system; consequently, there is no alarm in the case of fire. To deal with this, switches such as those in the alarm system are to be set separately at night. 2) Poorly located lockers deflect the fire and delay the alarm system reaction until it is too late to do anything. To prevent this, notices are posted that nothing is to be placed around the sensor.

The PDPC enables us to readily discuss those problems influenced by human action or changes in the environment. In this way, it is possible to anticipate the consequences of major accidents and to prepare to deal with them in the planning stage. In this way, PDPC can increase the reliability and safety of system and products.

Decisions concerning reliability and safety are developed effectively through the combined methods of FMEA, FMECA, and FTA. Adding the PDPC enables the company to increase safety markedly.[5]

Patterns of PDPC

The PDPC method has no definite rules. One may distinguish the following two patterns.

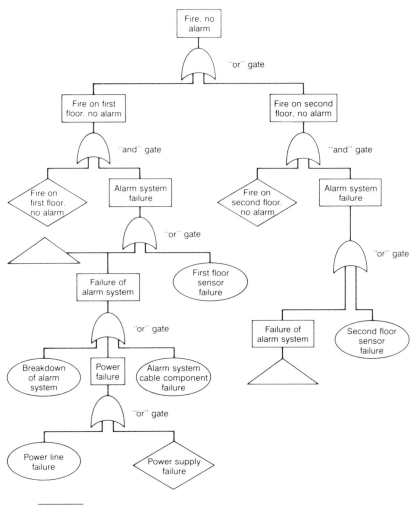

FIGURE 9.3
FTA fire warning system failure tree chart

Source: From Mizuno Shigeru (Ed.), Prevention Plan for Product Responsibility (JUSE Publishing Co., 1975).

Pattern I

In Fig. 9.2, the pattern I process starts with condition A_0 and proceeds to the desired condition Z in an organized manner. The process goes through $A_1, A_2, A_3, \ldots, A_p$, starting at A_0 and ending at Z. If as a result of the process A_3 is not possible, $B_1, B_2, \ldots$, etc. are considered as replacements. Although the preference of the planner is $A_1, A_2, A_3, \ldots, A_p$ or $A_1, A_2, B_1, B_2, \ldots, B_q$, lines C and D are set up as alternatives in case both these preferred lines fail. In this way, we plan to proceed from starting point A_1 and end with desired condition Z, because A_p, B_q, C_r, and D_s are closer to goal Z, they are more uncertain and can be described in less and less detail. We describe each event $A_0, A_1, A_2, \ldots, D_3$ in a brief sentence enclosed in a circle. Twenty to thirty of these circles are sufficient. Because of increased uncertainty associated with events far from event A_0, it is acceptable in the early stages of planning to provide less than complete details.

In Fig. 9.2, Z is set as a goal to be accomplished, such as establishment of a new technology, completion of research into a new product, prevention of claims, or reduction of the defective rate. But if Z becomes an undesirable condition, such as a major accident, it is necessary to cut the line between the present points A_0 and Z. This pattern is in the same category as pattern I.

For example, in Fig. 9.4, A_0 is set as the normal operating condition of the system. Suppose that through various influences on the system, normal condition A_0 changes to A_1, and then through other influences it finally reaches B_i ($i = 1, 2, \ldots, n$; where B_i is an undesirable condition). In this case, we develop policies to deal with each B_i, considering the risk of occurrence and its effect, if it occurs. For example, B_p represents cases of serious accidents and undesirable conditions. In this situation, we have to prevent the occurrence of A_0, $A_1, A_2, \ldots, A_p, B_p$. To accomplish this, it is necessary to stop that sequence of events and guide the process to A_3 or A_5. This is the way to use a PDPC for the prevention of major accidents. Figures 9.2 and 9.4 are described as pattern I.

Pattern II

In the second pattern, first the goal Z is set as a desirable or undesirable condition. Then the process from Z to the beginning point A_0 is developed with the inclusion of various alternatives from many points of view. In this process of development, it is necessary to note the nonlinear elements, especially the actions of human beings. If the goal Z (or undesirable condition Z) is linked to A_0, then we will

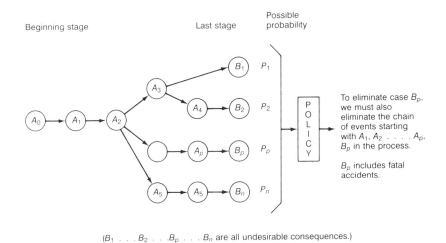

FIGURE 9.4
PDPC pattern I (anticipation of serious accidents)

determine a solution through detailed examination of the process, as with Pattern I. This is called pattern II and is shown in Fig. 9.5.

Where Z is desirable, we start with Z and attempt to link it to the beginning condition A_0. Should Z be an undesirable condition, we try to determine every possible chain of events that results in that condition and cut them off.

How to prepare a process decision program chart

Step 1

Participants in the project (preferably from various fields) meet to discuss the issues. To stimulate discussion, the leader can present one basic line as a possible solution.

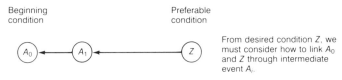

Beginning
condition

Preferable
condition

From desired condition Z, we
must consider how to link A_0
and Z through intermediate
event A_i.

When Z is an undesired condition, we must find a solution that cuts the chain
$Z \rightarrow A_i \rightarrow A_0$. Z is determined through other analyses, discussions, or examinations.

FIGURE 9.5
PDPC pattern II

Step 2

Discuss which issues must be examined.

Step 3

Once the issues are identified, consider and note down all the antic-ipated results. At this stage you have identified issues and some solutions; weigh the feasibility of each solution proposed and inves-tigate alternative solutions.

Step 4

Classify each issue according to its urgency, number of operations required, likelihood of occurrence, and difficulty. Consider the an-ticipated results and alternative solutions related to issues that must be addressed immediately, and link the items with arrows to the desired goal.

Step 5

Prioritize the different issues and consider them all together. Infor-mation related to one set of possibilities can influence another set; related items should be linked with a broken line.

Step 6

If the department that will handle a process involving several lines is determined, circle the process and write in the name of the department.

Step 7

Set a date for completing the examination period.

When the PDPC method is put into practice, it is possible that new information and problems will emerge at each stage. Therefore, it is a good idea for participants to have regular meetings to check progress in terms of the original PDPC. At such points, participants can correct or add to the plan in light of newly emerging problems or rewrite the chart starting at that point.

To understand how to prepare a process decision program chart here are two examples.

Example 1 (Pattern I). Suppose that a major defect has emerged in the mass-production test stage for a new product and that it remained totally undetected during the short-run test process. The PDPC to solve this problem is shown in Fig. 9.6. After various observations, the major defect is considered to be caused by a heat reaction of substance *MB*, so the product research center, the central research center, and the production department decide to cooperate to solve the problem. At the central research center, the defective part is analyzed and the substance causing the defect is sought. At the product research center, the ability of substance *K* to withstand heat must be confirmed. Therefore, if substance *K* can sustain heat in a satisfactory manner, the defect must be caused by the combination of substance *K* with other substances. In that case, the composition of the base material will be reviewed, and if that is the cause, eliminating it will solve the problem. However, if substance *K* itself is the cause, a substitute must be found. At this point, substances *L* or *M* can be considered even though they are more costly than substance *K*. In this case, if *L* or *M* are tested without defects, the problem is resolved.

On the other hand, the production department must confirm results at each job site, and analyzed data at the central research

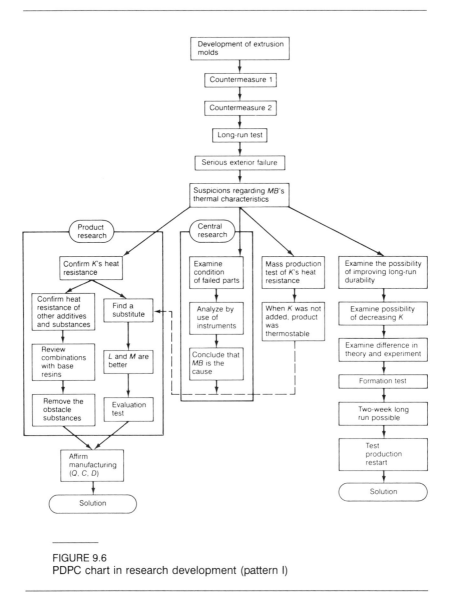

FIGURE 9.6
PDPC chart in research development (pattern I)

center must be passed to the production department. (This is indicated by a dotted line in the diagram.) After these three divisions have examined the problem simultaneously, it is determined that the problem lies in the additive amount of the material K, which had been determined at the development phase. Thus the amount of material K can be reduced in the production department, contributing to a successful two-week-long test run and solution of the problem.

Example 2 (Pattern II). Let us consider a PDPC analysis for a fragile crate that is being exported to a developing country. This crate should not be turned over. To make things simple and for the sake of clarity, we will limit examination to the process of delivery after the package has been unloaded (see Fig. 2.11). Let us assume unfavorable condition Z, in which the package is delivered upside down. First, condition Z is unavoidable if there is no warning label on the package. If an English language sign states "This Side Up" in red ink, provided that English is generally understood in the destination country, the delivery person should be able to determine correct handling methods by reading the warning label. Second, suppose a person who cannot read English is to handle the crate. A picture can be drawn for that possibility. Two different kinds of pictures may be required if the person does not understand one of the pictures. One of them should display a wine glass, indicating that wine would spill if the package were turned upside down; the other should display the hoisting of a chain so that down and bottom can be determined from the picture. Third, what would happen if the person did not notice the pictures? Condition Z can be assumed in this case also. If so, handles can be added. Fourth, although it is too heavy for a delivery person to carry, what might happen if that person were to decide to deliver it without assistance? He or she would probably roll the crate over. This would lead to condition Z. If so, what can be done to ensure that the crate is not rolled over? Consider using a pyramid-shaped package. When developing a PDPC chart for this idea, we can see the possibilities of connecting A_0 to Z and the countermeasures that must be taken in order to avoid unfavorable situations.

Different cases may be considered in order to connect A_0 and Z. Express these variable conditions in a brief sentence, which then is enclosed in a frame or is illustrated along with an explanation. Then link each condition with an arrow. When considering these countermeasures, surprisingly good results may be obtained if, developing related events, we also consider economic or psychological factors rather than being dependent only on specific technological knowledge.

In this example of crate transport, the four methods considered are shown below to illustrate "This Side Up": (1) instructions in English, (2) two kinds of illustrations, (3) adding handles, and (4) improvements in packaging design, such as making a pyramid shape or adding support to prevent the package from being rolled over. The chart for this example is illustrated in Fig. 2.11.

The method for drawing a chart for Pattern I (forecast of critical accidents) is basically the same as for Pattern II, but it may be enhanced by enclosing data within a double frame if the events in condition Z occur only under circumstances that could endanger human lives.

Applications of the PDPC method

Interdependent methods used to accomplish goals (an application for productivity improvement)

Suppose we want to improve current productivity from A_0 to Z by 20 percent (Fig. 9.7). At one point in process A, a 10 percent improvement is expected due to the increased use of automation. At this stage, new failures occur due to the increase in speed, and these require implementation of policy A_4 to cope with the problem. Then plan B_1 must be enforced, since continued machine failures can be expected. In addition, improvement in operating rates is planned in process C, from which the remaining 10 percent improvement is expected.

To improve operating rates, it is decided to work through lunch breaks. To adopt this, labor-management negotiations (C_3) are needed; the change (C_4) must be implemented and staff secured $(D_1$ and $D_2)$. If negotiations (C_3) fall through, then newly developed strategies (D_2) must be employed. Furthermore, as a more permanent plan, a plan for partial improvement of machinery must be added to process A.

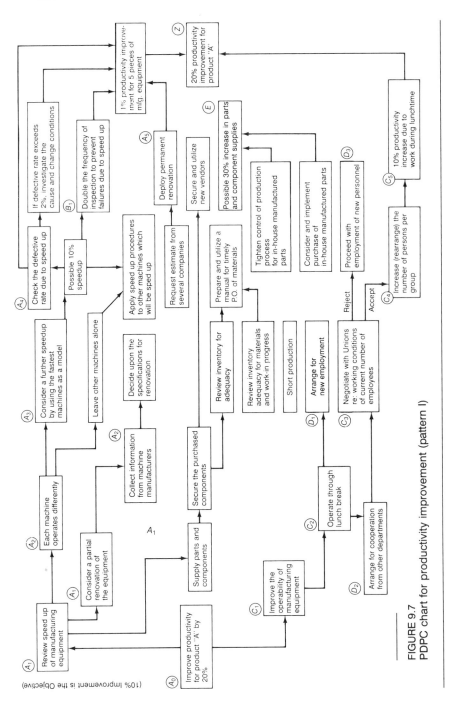

FIGURE 9.7
PDPC chart for productivity improvement (pattern I)

Therefore, corrective measures must be developed while maintaining organic links between processes *A, C,* and *E.* Along with increases in other areas of productivity, various problems related to the amount of raw material used and work-in-process inventory will result in implementation of more countermeasures.

When independent means exist and the order of implementation can be determined among them (an application for the prevention of environmental pollution)

Consideration was given, and policies studied, for reducing NO_x from the current 150 index of 100 or lower within a designated period. It was known from the beginning that the goal could be achieved if 20 million yen were invested in equipment. Avoidance of the investment was preferred. However, consideration was given to possible future investment in denitrating equipment. A total of five methods were identified and considered as capable of contributing to the reduction of NO_x; these included three boiler combustion methods and two equipment-improvement methods. After examining them from the aspect of cost-effectiveness and completion date, the goal was achieved, in cooperation with the boiler manufacturer, by implementing two methods for improving the boiler combustion system. In addition, the estimated investment cost was greatly reduced.[6]

When Fig. 9.8 is compared with Fig. 9.2, we can see that each process $A_3, A_4, \ldots, B_1, B_2, \ldots,$ and $C_1, C_2, \ldots$ is independent and that the priority of implementation is determined from a standard. We can understand that the reduction is accomplished if the first-priority processes $A_3, A_4, \ldots$ lead to achievement of the goal. If they do not achieve the goal, then processes $B_1, B_2, \ldots.$ will be implemented. Depending on the results, it may be necessary to adopt processes $C_1, C_2, \ldots.$

Implementing several almost independent methods for achieving a goal simultaneously (an application to technical development)

At a factory, goods developed by a research center were found to have a serious flaw that was not discovered at the research level. A

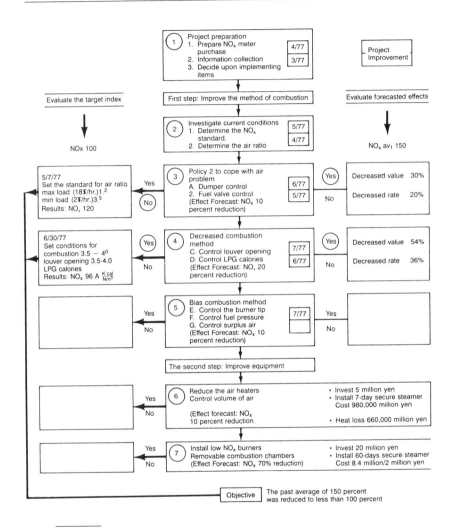

FIGURE 9.8
NO$_x$ Reduction Plan Using PDPC (Pattern I)

Source: Eguchi, Kagoyama, and Kishimoto, "Nitrate Oxide (NO$_x$) Reduction Activities in the LPG Combustion Chamber," quoted from *Examples from Application Study Meetings for the Seven New QC Tools*, (Tokyo: JUSE Press, Ltd., 1978).

source reports that competitors are going to introduce a similar product in the market. We would like to solve the problem within two months and commence line production. Therefore, four departments, two research centers, the engineering department, and the production department, meet and prepare a process decision program chart.

Consequently, it will likely be possible to correct the critical flaw with independent plans. On the basis of a PDPC each department is to examine and execute the process within its jurisdiction. Each department then corrects its PDPC after periodically discussing its progress with other departments. As a result of these interchanges, the plans developed by the production department are found to be superior to the others in cost-effectiveness and ability to meet the due date. So from that time on, all other departments join forces with the production department and solve the problem (see Fig. 9.9).

In this case, the two research centers and the engineering department were in charge of processes *4 and *5, design for a metal mold, which is illustrated in parts (b) and (c) of the figure, as well as of the decision-making process noted in part (a). The production department was in charge of other implementation items. In comparison with the model (Fig. 9.2), each of the processes $A_3, A_4, \ldots, B_1,$ $B_2, \ldots,$ and $C_1, C_2, \ldots$ corresponds to the two research centers, the manufacturing department, and the engineering department activities. The three parts of the figure show how the PDPC is successively modified in accordance with the project's progress, adding new steps where new types of problems are revealed. The strengths of all four departments were concentrated on one point and the goal was achieved despite the short timeframe.

Establishing a new plan after consolidating complicated processes (an application for accident prevention)

A serious accident occurred at a company three years ago, but emergency measures were applied and production was continued. There was, however, a minor failure in terms of quality. Various studies in different areas during the last three years have attempted to promote stable production by introducing a permanent policy. Finally, all other plans were narrowed down to one permanent plan. It was discovered that the plan required too many intricate processes for implementation. The engineering department determined that in order to implement the plan, it was important for all persons within

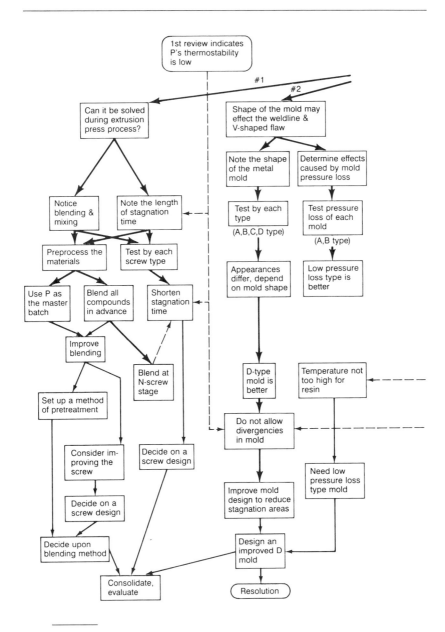

FIGURE 9.9 (a)
PDPC charts for technique review (pattern I)

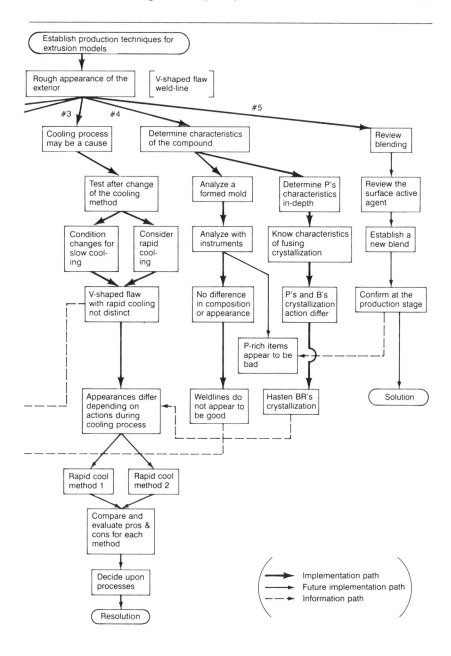

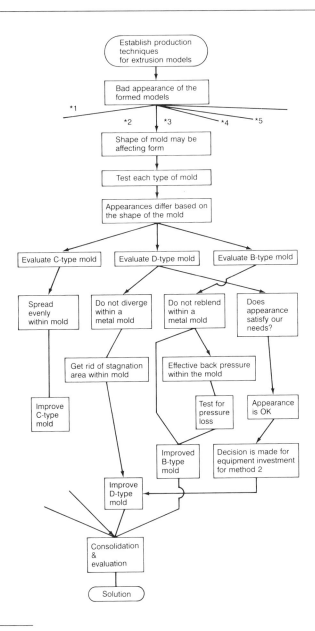

FIGURE 9.9 (b)
PDPC charts for technique review (pattern II)

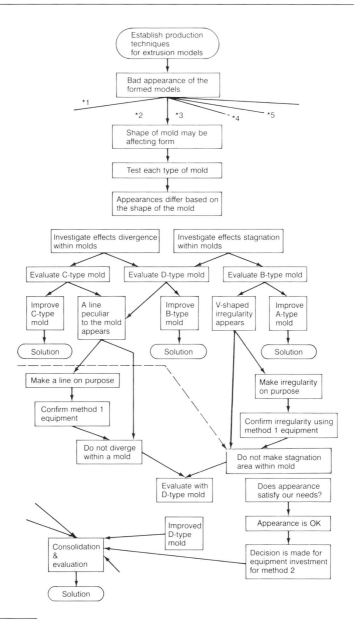

FIGURE 9.9 (c)
PDPC charts for technique review (pattern III)

the departments, including superiors, to have a good understanding of the group's past study processes.

The staff could quite easily understand past problems when the study processes were arranged in a process decision program chart. As a result of discussions, a plan that was initially rejected during the early stages now appeared to be more applicable because of technology and data developments and more economic than the current permanent plan. After three months of reexamination, the new plan became the new permanent plan (see Fig. 9.10).

When the model in Fig. 9.10 is compared with the model in Fig. 9.2, the processes follow $A_3, A_4, \ldots, B_2, \ldots, C_1, C_2, C_3, D_1, D_2, \ldots$, but during the investigation, all processes except A were terminated or abandoned. This left plan A_p as the only possible choice. When examination processes were consolidated in a PDPC chart, it became apparent that C_4, which had been discarded as impossible to implement, would, in fact, be the most effective in light of new data, cost, and operability. The last item for completion was a reevaluation. All these processes correspond with those noted in the model. As you can see, a plan that has been abandoned at an early stage can be easily forgotten as time passes. When the problems are complicated or the study requires a long period of time, a complete view of the processes, arranged according in a PDPC increases understanding and helps to prevent oversights.

Predicting critical accidents (an application for a safety study of a railroad car) (reference 9.3).

As an example of a system's safety examination, the process of designing countermeasures will show how to determine the possibility of danger to passengers if a train's brake system fails. The PDPC in this example corresponds to pattern II. Let us examine phenomena A_i ($i = 1, 2, \ldots, n$), which links A_0 with Z, presupposing that A_0 is an incident involving falling rocks and Z is the critical accident of aderailment and overturning of the train. Several different causes can be considered for the case of falling rocks leading to derailment and overturn. Here we prepared a process decision program chart by assuming that the derailment and overturn had occurred due to an air brake failure in the first and second carriage (see Fig. 9.11), which was caused by equipment failure. Physical phenomena, such as an operational failure or an engineer's error, are all considered in A_i. The process to reach Z and the process to stop the train are both considered in this PDPC.

When we study how an engineer would cope with an emergency situation in which the air brakes did not work because falling rocks damaged the brake system near the wheel unit between the first and second cars, we can consider two opposite cases: (1) derailment with overturn, and (2) a safe stop.

The objective is to learn from the PDPC how to increase the probability of obtaining a favorable state (stopping the train) and how to decrease the possibility of obtaining an unfavorable state. As shown in Fig. 9.11, we could develop countermeasures (1) and (2) for the first results and countermeasure (3) for the latter result.

Countermeasure (1) took into account the simplicity of inspecting the carriage and changing the location of part of the braking system. Countermeasure (2) considered the psychological difficulties accompanying shifting the air brake handle from the release position to the brake position as the engineer struggles to stop the train in an emergency situation. Thus it helped to develop the idea of an electrically controlled circuit that would perform the job just by pushing a button with the same effectiveness as moving the air brake handle by hand from the release to the brake position. Countermeasure (3) is a security brake to be used if countermeasures (1) and (2) do not operate. With this, the engineer is able to perform the last action of the process (located on the right side of the figure), which would normally follow.

Conclusion

These are just a few of the practical applications of PDPC. We hope that the PDPC method (as well as FEMA and FTA) will be more widely used in the future in the area of product liability planning, where the safety of goods or systems must be closely monitored.

Furthermore, since it is necessary to understand problem and design solutions at each step, it is important to utilize not only the conventional QC methods, but also value engineering, operations

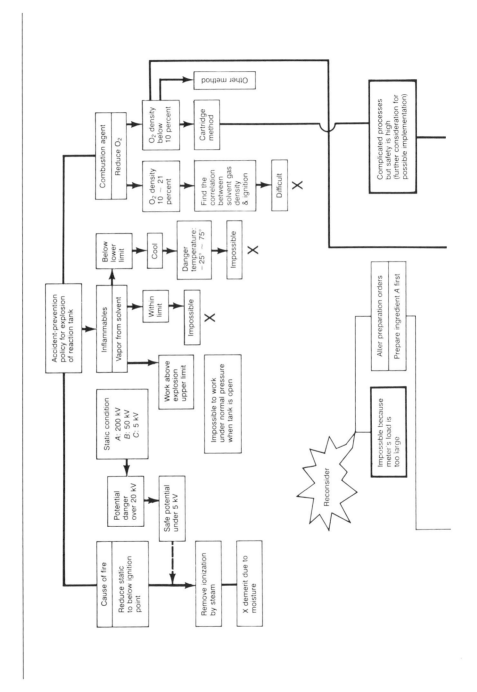

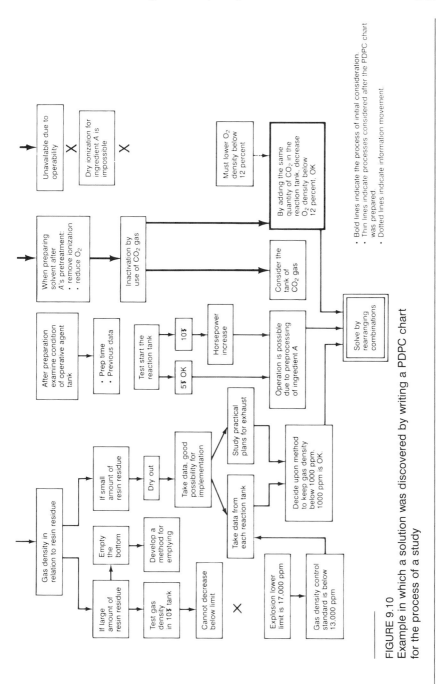

FIGURE 9.10
Example in which a solution was discovered by writing a PDPC chart for the process of a study

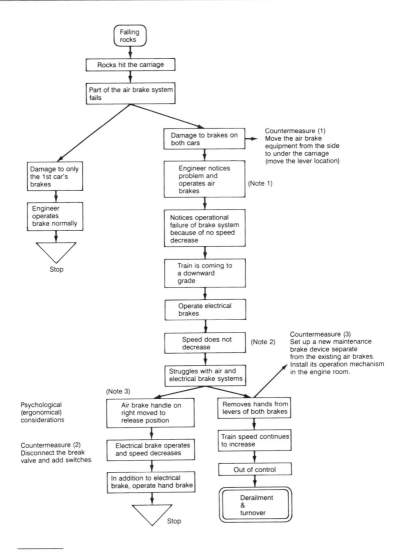

FIGURE 9.11
Application of PDPC to system's safety (derailment & overturn due to falling rocks and loss of control)

Note 1: There are two types of systems to stop trains: the air brake and the electrical brake. There is a separate handle to operate each.

Note 2: There is an order of priority set up for these systems because of peculiar technical reasons. When both handles are operated, the electrical brake does not work because the air brake has priority. In this type of emergency situation, the train cannot be stopped unless a system is developed where the electrical brake automatically works first.

Note 3: As stated in note 2, the air brake has priority when both systems are in operation; however, there is no braking action because of a failure in the air brake system. If the air brake handle were in the release (nonoperating) position, then the electrical brake would be effective for stopping the train.

research, and the seven new QC tools. The range of application for the PDPC method has been widened to include critical accident forecast charts, and it is now ready to be used in other areas of quality control. We hope that this method, as well as others, will be applied in many new areas.

Our thanks to Dr. Kondo and other experts advocating and promoting the application of the PDPC method for allowing us to refer to their works.

Notes

1. Kondo Jiro, *Introduction to Mathematics for the Social Sciences* (Tokyo: Toyo Keizai Shimposha, 1973).

2. Kondo Jiro, *Operations Research* (Tokyo: JUSE Press, Ltd., 1973).

3. Division of Machine Reliability (Eds.), *FMEA and FTA Explained* (Tokyo: JUSE Press, Ltd., 1978).

4. Mizuno Shigeru, (Ed.), *Prevention Plan for Product Responsibility* (Tokyo: JUSE Press, Ltd., 1975).

5. Yagi Juichi and Naya Yoshinobu, "Application of PDPC in Quality Control Systems," Japan Quality Control Academy, 10th Research Presentation Conference, 1976; — — — —, "PDPC Method," in *The Seven New QC Tools Summary for Managers and Staff* (Tokyo: JUSE Press, Ltd., 1978).

6. Eguchi, Kagoyama, and Kishimoto, "Nitrate Oxide Reduction Operations for LPG Boiler," from *Seven New QC Tools: Case Study Presentation Meeting* (Tokyo: JUSE Press, Ltd., 1978).

Additional references

Sano Motohiko, "PDPC Method and Technology Development," from *Hinjitsu Kanri* (Quality Control), vol. 29 (November 1978), special issue, pp. 167–171.

10

The Arrow Diagram Method

The arrow diagram method establishes the most suitable daily plan
for a project and monitors its progress efficiently.

What is an arrow diagram?

In addition to quality, timing is a vital management consideration in
QC activities. Planning schedules and controlling their progress are
very important to such management activities as planning and production of quantities of items within a designated schedule. Such
concerns as new products, manufacturing startup dates, delivery
dates, and project promotion plans and their progress require scheduling management.

Gantt charts have often been used for planning schedules and
project management. The Gantt chart is an excellent method for
rough plans and simple work instruction, but it cannot indicate subordinate relationships. In addition, with Gantt charts it is difficult (1)

249

to make a thorough plan, (2) to review a plan at the planning stage, (3) to cope with changes in plans or situations after the initial plan has been implemented, (4) to obtain accurate information promptly concerning influences of a delay of one part of the process on the whole project, (5) when the project becomes larger, to gain an overview of the entire project, and (6) to judge the priorities of the control processes.

Methods such as the program evaluation and review technique (PERT) and the critical path method (CPM) are used to supplement the Gantt chart and control processes effectively by creating an optimum plan. The arrow diagram illustrates schedule planning when PERT or CPM are used. An arrow diagram displays every job necessary for promoting a project and its subordinate relationships through the use of an arrow network.

The Gantt chart is located at the top of Fig. 10.1, and the arrow diagram is at the bottom. When one job is delayed, it is difficult to evaluate with the Gantt chart whether or not the whole construction schedule will be affected or which jobs have time margin requirements and which ones do not. By contrast, we can see that the arrow diagram in Fig. 10.1 provides more information about these areas.

A wealth of literature is available on PERT and CPM generally.[1] In this section, schedule planning and management methods that use the arrow diagram for PERT and CPM will be referred to as the arrow diagram method. We encourage its application to QC activities and consider it one of the seven new QC tools.

How to prepare an arrow diagram

Rules on preparation

Symbols and terms

Elements used in the construction of an arrow diagram are shown in Fig. 10.2.

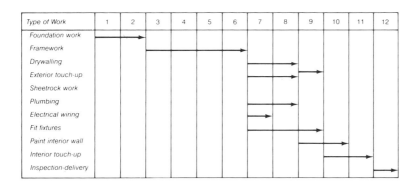

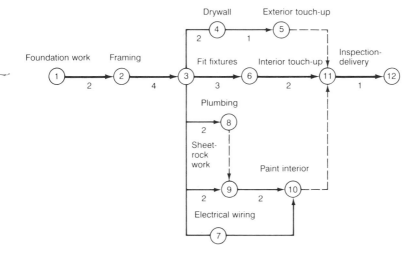

FIGURE 10.1
Gantt chart and arrow diagram

Preceding jobs and succeeding jobs

When there is a correlation between jobs A and B such that job A must be completed before commencing job B or job B can be started when job A is finished, A is B's preceding job and B is A's succeeding job. This relationship is illustrated in Fig. 10.3.

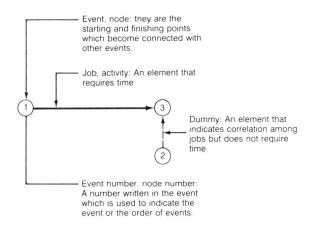

Event, node: they are the starting and finishing points which become connected with other events.

Job, activity: An element that requires time.

Dummy: An element that indicates correlation among jobs but does not require time.

Event number, node number: A number written in the event which is used to indicate the event or the order of events.

FIGURE 10.2
Symbols and their names

FIGURE 10.3
Preceding and succeeding jobs

Parallel jobs

When jobs A and B can be performed simultaneously, or when it is arranged so that jobs A and B are parallel, A and B are parallel jobs. This is illustrated in Fig. 10.4.

How to use a dummy (part 1)

No two events should be connected by more than one activity. For example, job A is described as job (1, 2). It is difficult to understand whether job (1, 2) is job A, B, or C, however, if an expression such as

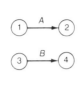

FIGURE 10.4
Parallel jobs

the one in Fig. 10.5 is used. We must use one of the expressions from Fig. 10.6.

How to use a dummy (part 2)

The use of dummy activities will be helpful when it is difficult to express the correlation between jobs by using the job elements only. For example, use a dummy if the four jobs, *A, B, C,* and *D* are correlated as follows: *C*'s preceding jobs are *A* and *B*, and *D*'s preceding job is *B*. This can be expressed with a dummy as shown in Fig. 10.7.

The same job cannot be used in more than one place in the diagram

The same job, a job performed at the same place and at the same time, should not appear more than once in an arrow diagram.

Do not use a loop

The loop shown in Fig. 10.8 should not be used for jobs *B, C,* and *D*.

Do not use unnecessary dummies

The use of a dummy in Fig. 10.9(a) is not a mistake; it only adds to the complexity of the arrow diagram. The diagram should be developed as shown in Fig. 10.9(b).

How to number a node

A number should be inserted at each node in the arrow diagram for identification purposes. The node number must be a positive whole

FIGURE 10.5
Example of graph that should not be used

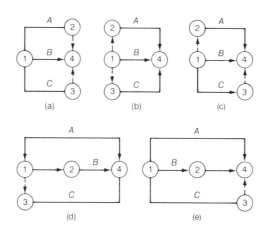

FIGURE 10.6.
How to use dummies (part 1)

number. A smaller number must be used at the job starting point
than at the completion point of a job. Thus $i < j$ in Fig. 10.10.

Preparing an arrow diagram using cards

When several people gather in groups or project teams to prepare
arrow diagrams, arrow diagram preparation cards and the procedures listed below should be used.

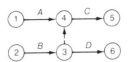

FIGURE 10.7
How to use dummies (part 2)

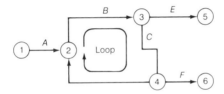

FIGURE 10.8
Arrow diagram with loop

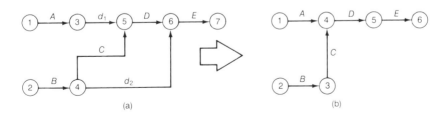

(a)   (b)

FIGURE 10.9
Arrow diagram with unnecessary dummy

_____
FIGURE 10.10
Node number

_____

To prepare, obtain five or so large pieces of construction paper, 50 to 100 cards (business-card size), and several marking pens.

Step 1: Abstract jobs.

By discussion, list the necessary jobs for project completion and then write them on the construction paper.

Step 2: Preparation of job cards.

After all the necessary jobs are listed, draw a straight line across the center of a card, as shown in Fig. 10.11, and write the type of work above the line. Do not write below the line, since this space will be used for noting the number of days required for the job. The cards or writing can be color coded to identify the person or department in charge of each job.

Step 3: Correlation of job cards.

When all the job cards are completed, arrange them on a large piece of construction paper according to whether they are preceding, succeeding, or parallel jobs. Remove all cards for unnecessary jobs and add the cards of necessary jobs that have been omitted.

Step 4: Determine the location of the cards.

Position the cards using the following criteria: (a) Find the process where the greatest number of job cards can be placed in a series. Position the job cards that have a preceding-succeeding relationship along this process with an interval large enough for a node to be placed between them (about 30 mm). (b) Job cards having parallel

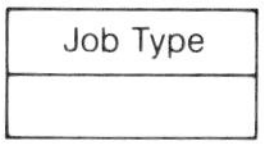

FIGURE 10.11
Job card

relationships must be positioned appropriately relative to the cards in step 4(a). Lightly pencil in the nodes and arrows. Decide on the final position for all cards and affix them to the paper.

Step 5: Preparation of the arrow diagram.

The arrow diagram is finished by connecting the final arrangement of nodes and job cards with arrows. An arrow should not branch off or join with other arrows. Branching and joining must occur only at a node.

Step 6: Survey to establish time requirements.

Make a survey of the amount of time required for each job in the arrow diagram, and place the information below the center line on the job cards.

Step 7: Calculation of node placement.

Calculate the earliest and latest node time for each of the nodes in the arrow diagram, and place them near the associated node. Calculating node times and expressing them will be explained in the next section.

The schedule of the project is completed by the use of an arrow diagram. (An example is given in Fig. 2.13.) If stricter time control is necessary, the work schedule and the number of marginal days must be calculated with the method that will be explained in the nextsection. It is, however, quite effective to perform steps 1 through 7.

Calculation of schedule

Node time and its calculation

Early and late node times are the two types of times for nodes. *Earliest node time* is the earliest possible time that the operation commencing at node i may be started and is expressed by t_i^E. *Latest node time* is the latest possible time that the operation ending at node i may be completed and is expressed as t_i^L. The expressions t_i^E and t_i^L must be indicated within the diagram frame near the node, as shown in Fig. 10.12.

The earliest node time is calculated as follows: In the arrow diagram, the earliest node time is at the starting point (node 1) and is equal to 0.

$$t_1^E = 0$$

When there is only one job followed by node j, the succeeding node, its earliest node time t_j^E can be found by using the following formula:

$$t_j^E = t_i^E + D_{ij} \tag{a}$$

In this formula, t_i^E represents the earliest node time for event i, which precedes event j. D_{ij} represents the number of days required for the job (i, j). When there are more than two jobs that have event j as a

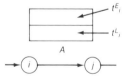

FIGURE 10.12
How to indicate node time

succeeding node, the earliest node time t_i^E can be found by using the following formula:

$$t_j^E = \max (t_i^E = D_{ij}) \tag{b}$$

The latest node time is calculated as follows: In the arrow diagram, the latest node time for the last event (node n) must be the same value as the earliest node time for that event. That is,

$$t_n^L = t_n^E \tag{c}$$

When there is only one job that has event i as its preceding node, its latest node time t_i^L is found using the following formula:

$$t_i^L = t_j^L - D_{ij} \tag{d}$$

In this formula, t_i^L represents the latest node time for node j, which succeeds node i, and D_{ij} represents the number of days required for job (i, j). When there are more than two jobs that follow preceding event i, the latest node time t_i^L is found by using the following formula:

$$t_i^L = \min (t_j^L \cdot D_{ij}) \tag{e}$$

The following correlation exists between the earliest node time t_i^E and the latest node time t_i^L of the same event:

$$t_i^E \leq t_i^L \tag{f}$$

The *critical path* is the longest process on the arrow diagram from the start to the final point and is a series of jobs that are vital for scheduling controls. In the critical path,

$$t_i^E = t_i^L \tag{g}$$

A bold, thick line is drawn in the arrow diagram for the process after calculating t_i^E and t_i^L.

Slack means the marginal time at node i and is expressed as SL_i by using the difference between the latest node time and the earliest node time:

$$SL_i = t_i^L - t_i^E \tag{h}$$

This slack is considered as a rough standard for marginal time when calculating the earliest and latest node times. When managing a more strict schedule, total float and free float, which are explained on page 263, also must be calculated.

An example of the calculations for earliest and latest node times is shown in Fig. 10.13. The bold line is the critical path.

Job schedule and float time

It is possible to control schedules with the use of node times; however, if more indepth schedule control is required, then it is essential to calculate the earliest and latest start times, the earliest and latest finish times, and the float time. Definitions for these terms and their calculation methods are given below.

Job schedule and calculation

The *earliest start time* indicates the earliest possible time when job (i, j) can be completed, and ES_{ij} is used to represent this. ES_{ij} is found

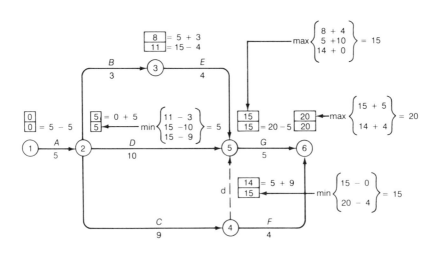

FIGURE 10.13
Calculation of Node Time

by using the following formula, since it is the same as the earliest node time t_i^E at even i:

$$ES_{ij} = t_i^E \tag{i}$$

The *earliest finish time* indicates the earliest possible time when job (i, j) can be completed, and EF_{ij} is used to represent this. EF_{ij} can be found by using the following formula, since job (i, j) is started at the earliest start time ES_{ij} and finished after D_{ij}:

$$EF_{ij} = ES_{ij} + D_{ij} \tag{j}$$

The *latest finish time* indicates the latest time by which job (i, j) must be completed, and LF_{ij} is used to represent this. LF_{ij} can be found by using the following formula, since it is the same as the latest node time, t_j^L:

$$LF_{ij} = t_j^L \tag{k}$$

The *latest start time* indicates the latest limit of time when job (i, j) must be commenced, and LS_{ij} is used to represent this. LS_{ij} can be found by using the following formula, since it is the latest possible time to commence job (i, j) so that it will be completed by the latest finish time LF_{ij}:

$$LS_{ij} = LF_{ij} - D_{ij} \tag{l}$$

Float time and critical path

Total Float is the total marginal time for job (i, j), represented by TF_{ij}. TF_{ij} is the difference between LF_{ij} and EF_{ij} (that is, $LF_{ij} - EF_{ij}$) when job (i, j) is started at ES_{ij} and finished at EF_{ij}. It is also the difference between LS_{ij} and ES_{ij} (that is, $LS_{ij} - ES_{ij}$) when job (i, j), scheduled to be finished by LF_{ij}, can be started at LS_{ij}. Thus TF_{ij} can be found by using the following formula:

$$TF_{ij} = LS_{ij} \cdot ES_{ij} = LF_{ij} \cdot EF_{ij} \tag{m}$$

Free float indicates the marginal time of job (i, j) independently; it is represented by FF_{ij}. FF_{ij} is the marginal time generated when the succeeding job (i, j) progresses to job (i, k). This starts at the earliest starting point ES_{jk} ($= t_j^E$) after job (i, j) at EF_{ij} is finished provided that ES_{jk} is later than EF_{ij}. Free float can be found by using the following formula:

$$FF_{ij} = ES_{jk} \cdot EF_{ij} \tag{n}$$

A job without any total float is called *critical work*. The process created by the critical work is called the *critical path* and is represented by *CP*; that is, *CP* is the sequence of work that satisfies the condition

$$TF_{ij} = 0 \tag{o}$$

The critical path is the longest process on the arrow diagram and is indicated by a thick, bold line. The jobs along the critical path influence the finish time of the whole project if the critical path jobs exceed the projected schedule period. Careful management of these jobs is essential.

If all the float time is used for one job that has total float, other succeeding jobs will not have any float time at all. Total float is the margin that must be carefully applied by the project manager throughout the entire schedule. If project members spend all the float time without any coordination, there could be a delay in completion of the entire project. On the other hand, free float is the marginal time that does not affect other succeeding jobs, even if all the float time is spent, as long as it is within a certain limit. It is considered to be the number of marginal days that can be used "freely" under the project members' control.

Correlation between float time and the work schedule

The correlation for the following float times is shown in Fig. 10.14: the earliest and latest start times, the earliest and latest finish times, total float, and free float.

The work schedule and float time for the arrow diagram in Fig. 10.13 are calculated and shown in Table 10.1.

Estimation of required number of days

The number of days (or time period) required for each job must be estimated to complete the schedule after the arrow diagram is prepared. The items noted below must be considered when estimating the required number of days.

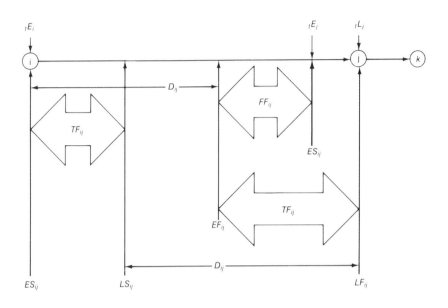

FIGURE 10.14
Correlation of each job schedule and float time

Tendency to overestimate number of days required

There is a tendency, in the interests of safety, to increase the number of days as the project becomes more long range. When estimating the number of days required, it is important to remember that "it can be done within this number of days" is the member's responsibility to the whole project.

Required number of days independently estimated for each job

When estimating the required number of days for each job, we must not relate the job to either preceding or succeeding jobs. Estimation

TABLE Table 10.1

Job i, j	Job type	Required Time D_{ij}	Earliest		Latest		Total Float TF_{ij}	Free Float FF_{ij}	Critical Path CP
			Start ES_{ij}	Finish EF_{ij}	Start LS_{ij}	Finish LF_{ij}			
(1.2)	A	5	0	5	0	5	0	0	·
(2.3)	B	3		8	8	11	3	0	
(2.4)	C	9	5	14	6	15	1	0	
(2.5)	D	10		15	5	15	0	0	·
(3.5)	E	4	8	12	11	15	3	3	
(4.5)	d	0		14	15	15	1	1	
(4.6)	F	4	14	18	16	20	2	2	
(5.6)	G	5	15	20	15	20	0	0	·
Calculation Sequence			①	③	④	②	⑤	⑥	⑦
Calculation Formula			t_i^E	$ES_{ij} - D_{ij}$	$LF_{ij} - D_{ij}$	t_j^L	$LS_{ij} - ES_{ij}$	$ES_{jk} - EF_{ij}$	$TF_{ij} = 0$

of the number of days it will take to execute that particular job must be done strictly independently.

Consideration of weekends and holidays

There are some types of work, such as aging and drying of paint, that can progress even on nonbusiness days. The duration of jobs can sometimes be drastically reduced by scheduling processes that can advance during the weekend throughout the entire project.

Remember to consider the weather

Every day may not be a sunny day. We must remember to take the weather into consideration if there is a type of work that can or cannot be done during inclement weather.

Application of average number of work days

The average number of work days is taken from past records of the actual number of work days required to complete a job. This average can be utilized in making estimates.

Applications of the arrow diagram method

How to shorten planned time

Process of shortening time

The possibility of shortening a project's time is one feature that is easy to examine when a schedule plan is prepared using an arrow diagram. A flowchart is used in Fig. 10.15 to summarize the methods for shortening planned schedules.

Examples of shortening time

Example 1. The entire schedule was shortened by decreasing the number of days required for jobs on the critical path. The early-plan's schedule is shown in Fig. 10.16. Right after the plan was prepared, the entire project had to be shortened by about a month. It was further shortened, beginning with the jobs on the critical path that required more days.

A total of 29 days was cut by reducing job (M_1, M_3) by 27 days, from 131 to 104 days, and by reducing job (M_5, M_8) by 2 days, from 10 to 8. The critical path, however, shifted to

$$1 \rightarrow E_1 \rightarrow E_2 \rightarrow 3 \rightarrow 4 \rightarrow 6 \rightarrow 7 \rightarrow 8 \rightarrow 9 \rightarrow 10 \rightarrow 11$$

so that the project was only shortened by 11 days after all.

Job $(4, 6)$ on the shifted critical path was cut five days, from 45 to 40 days, and job $(6, 7)$ was cut three days, from 10 to 7 days. A total of seven days was taken from the schedule, but the critical path shifted to

$$1 \rightarrow 2 \rightarrow M_1 \rightarrow M_4 \rightarrow M_6 \rightarrow M_7 \rightarrow 7 \rightarrow 8 \rightarrow 9 \rightarrow 10 \rightarrow 11$$

so that only 20 days were cut.

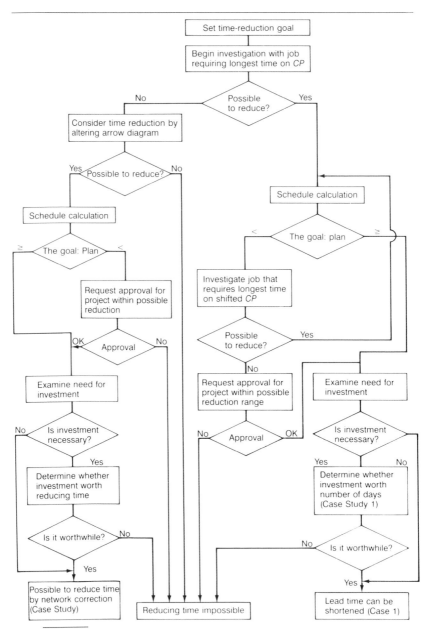

FIGURE 10.15
Examination procedures to shorten a project schedule

Finally, job (M_1, M_4) was cut nine days, from 123 to 114 days. The result, shown in Fig. 10.17, was that the completion schedule was reduced by about one month (29 days) by forming four critical paths.

As you can see in the example, the objective cannot be met when the critical path shifts, although the required number of days for the first plan was shortened to meet the reduction goal. The reduction goal can only be met by successively shortening each job of the newly formed critical path. Planning by arrow diagrams benefits the examination process in this manner.

Example 2. The entire schedule time was shortened by altering the arrow diagram. The initial plan is shown in Fig. 10.18. The requirement to shorten the entire schedule was identified shortly before the advance arrangement conference, event M_3. After studies were conducted, shortening the time required for a job on the critical path, as developed in Example 1, was found to be impossible. After many discussions and the use of an arrow diagram, a suggestion was made to use a handcrafted chassis for an engineering trial test in job (7, 8) and to use a metal mold from the mass production trial in job (10, 11). The arrow diagram was redesigned to accommodate this idea. The result was that the critical path shifted as shown in Fig. 10.19, for a reduction of 11 days. The new job (M_3, M_{17}) involved a trial of 70 handcrafted chassis units, at an additional expenditure of $350 ($5 × 70 units), thereby increasing overall expenses. This added expense averaged out to around $32 per reduction day. After the added expense was approved, the project progressed as shown in Fig. 10.19.

As you can tell from this example, when it is impossible to shorten the time required for a job on the critical path, it is easier to shorten the time by determining an alternative path using the arrow diagram.

Convenience of arrow diagrams

An arrow diagram can be used to express objectives in light of such considerations as size, type of project, management objectives, etc. The time-scale arrow diagram, which efficiently employs features of the Gantt chart is especially useful for small-scale projects or partial projects whose whole schedule period is relatively short.

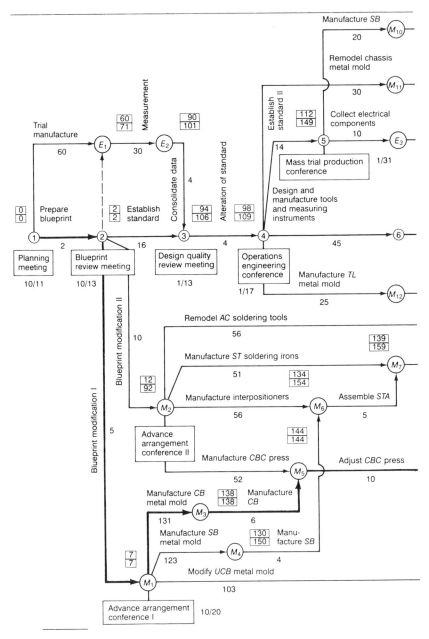

FIGURE 10.16
Electronic apparatus model 52 development plan (initial plan)

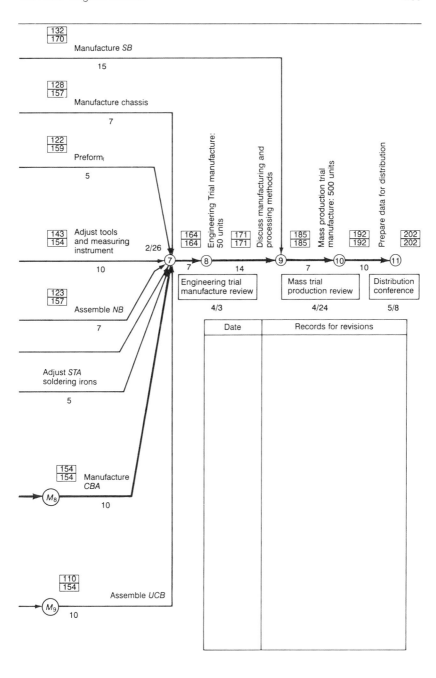

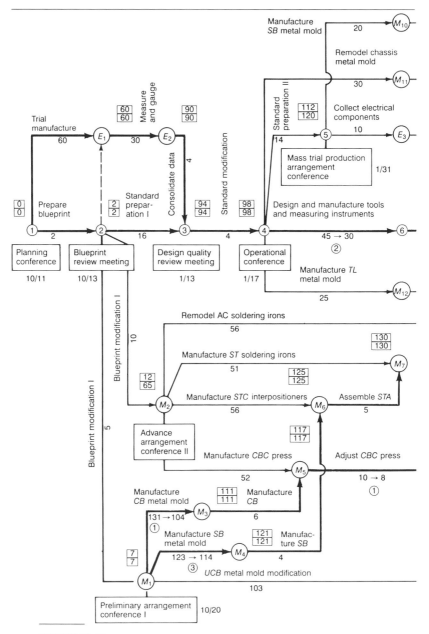

FIGURE 10.17
Electronic apparatus model 52 development plan (time-reduction plan)

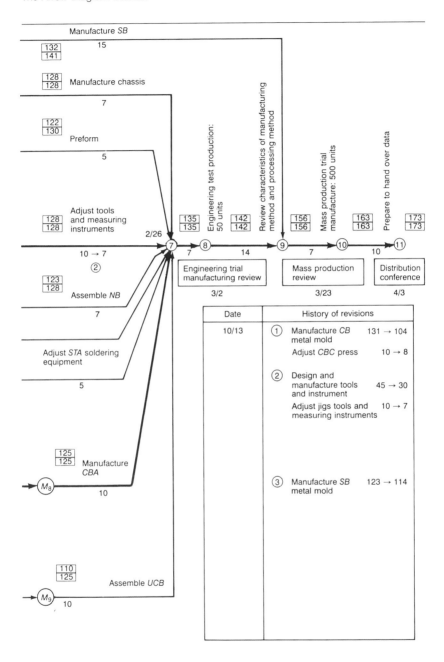

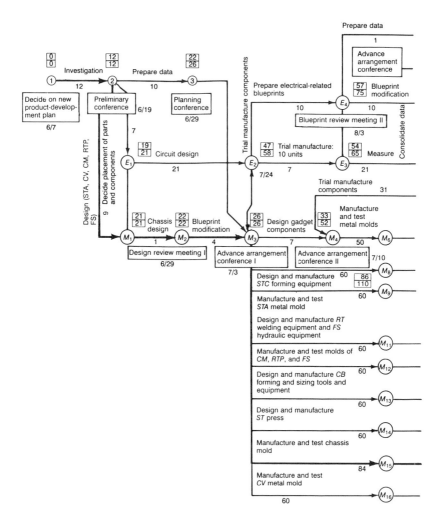

FIGURE 10.18
Electronic apparatus model 60 development plan (initial plan)

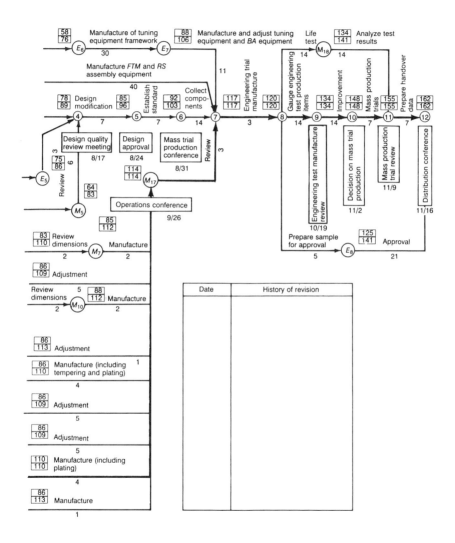

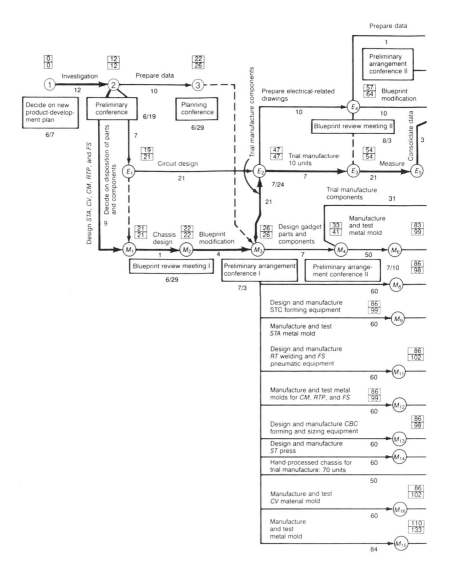

FIGURE 10.19
Electronic apparatus model 60 development plan (time-reduction plan)

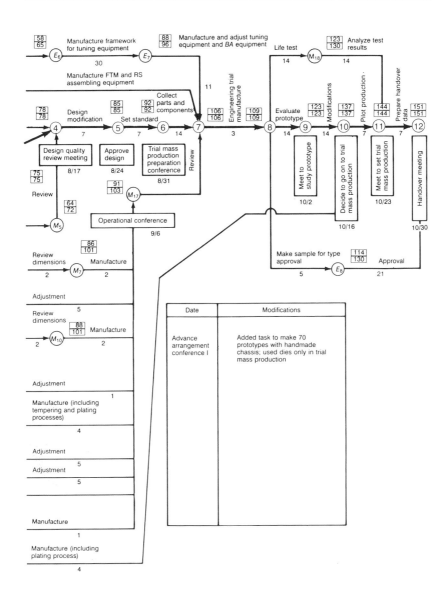

In the time-scale arrow diagram correlations of jobs are described by nodes and arrows in reference to precedence, succession, and parallels, as in the arrow diagram. In addition, arrow length corresponds to the time required for a job, as in the Gantt chart. It is simple to use and there is no need for calculation of time.

The time-scale arrow diagram can be used to prepare a plan that does not need a full-scale arrow diagram to calculate its schedule and when the Gantt chart cannot be used because it does not satisfy requirements. An example of a plan that was prepared with a time-scale arrow diagram is given in Figs. 10.20 and 10.21.

How to express a plan with uncertain elements

It is difficult to develop jobs uniformly at the planning stage when there are uncertain elements involved, e.g., new product development. In this case, it is impossible to express all items with the node-sand arrows of an arrow diagram as was described earlier. An arrow diagram cannot be used if we do not have all the details. As the job progresses, however, the plan can be prepared by using alternative judgment nodes — decision boxes (represented by a) — when one process can be chosen from among several alternative processes that are considered in advance.

The decision box shown in Fig. 10.22 can be used to express a choice to go to jobs R or S or to go to jobs T or U after job Q's completion point.

Synchronization of time and quality control

Methods to manage schedule control, in conjunction with non-time-related factors, were developed by the U.S. Navy in 1960 and have been put to practical use in PERT/cost and PERT/reliability. A relationship to quality control was advocated in 1963 in an article entitled "PERT and QC," by Professors Mizuno and Furukawa.[2] This theory has been successfully applied at Toyota Motor Company, Mitsubishi Heavy Industries, Inc., and Suzuki Motors Corporation under the guidance of Professors Mizuno and Furukawa.[3]

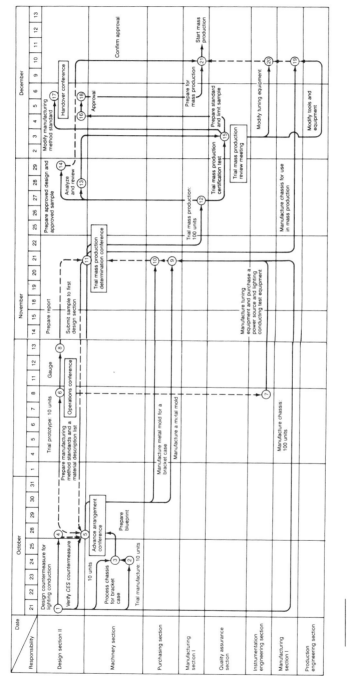

FIGURE 10.20
Model T-827 improvement plan (an example of a time-scale arrow diagram)

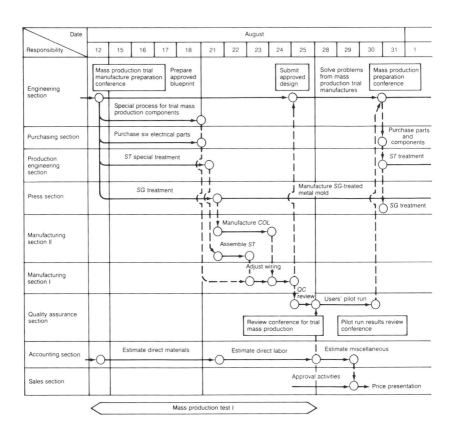

FIGURE 10.21
Model 62Q mass production promoting plan (an example of a
time-scale arrow diagram)

Because the schedule and delivery date are also considered as
points of quality, in a broad sense, they are essential for QC activities
related to schedule control. Moreover, the relationship between syn-
chronization of schedules and quality control is very important.

The critical path is used to identify schedule bottlenecks. It has
also been used to surface problems in the implementation of quality
improvements. Furthermore, the use of PERT/QC (quality and cost)
to monitor the progress of new product development is also gaining

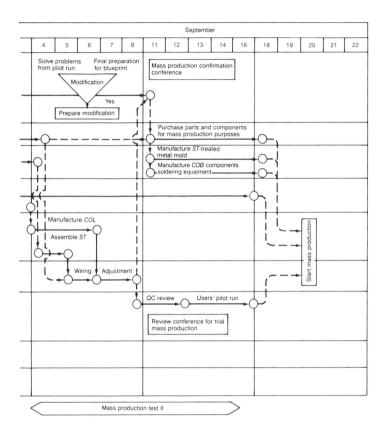

recognition. The PERT/QC not only monitors progress against schedules, but also helps in timing the building of quality into products, in the preparation of quality standards charts, and in controlling developmental and manufacturing costs.

In conclusion, we acknowledge our gratitude to Matsushita Electronic Components, Inc. and Yasukawa Electrical Manufacturing Company, Inc. for allowing us to publish their figures.

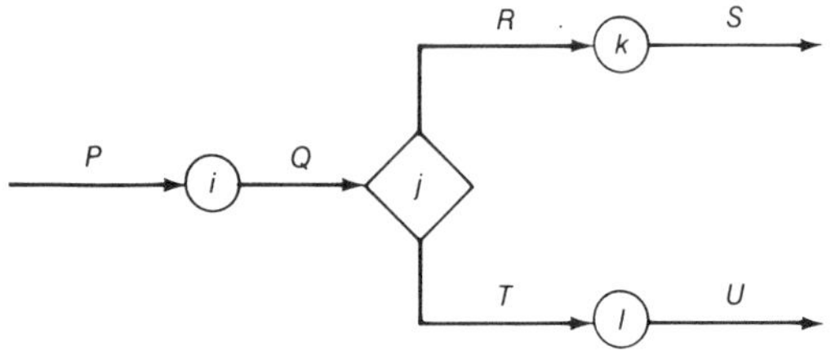

FIGURE 10.22
An arrow diagram used with a decision node

Notes

1. *See*, for example, Mori Tatsuo, *PERT — The New Way to Consolidate Jobs* (Tokyo: Japan Management Association, 1964); ———, *PERT II — Effective Application* (Tokyo: Japan Management Association, 1965); Sekine Tomoaki, *PERT/CPM Introduction* (Tokyo: JUSE Press, Ltd., 1965); Tone Kaoru (Ed.), *PERT Lecture I: Basics* (Tokyo: Toyo Keizai Shimposha, 1966); Kato Shokichi, *New Techniques for Planning and Management — Theory of PERT/CPM and Its Application* (Tokyo: Industrial Engineering Association, 1964).

2. Mizuno Shigeru and Furukawa Yasushi, "PERT and QC," *Hinshitsu Kanri* (Quality Control) (special issue), vol. 14 (November 1963).

3. Tone Kaoru (Ed.), *PERT Lecture IV: Applications* (Tokyo: Toyo Keizai Shimposha, 1967); Mizuno and Furukawa (Tokyo Engineering University) and Suzuki, Numano, Takimura, and Sato (Toyota Motor Company), "PERT and QC — Practical Examples in the Automobile Industry (2nd Report)," *Hinshitsu Kanri* (Quality Control), vol. 15 (fall, 1964), special issue, pp. 198–201; Mizuno and Furukawa (Tokyo Engineering University) and Mitsubishi Heavy Industries, Inc. and Mihara Manufacturing Corporation, "PERT and QC — Practical Examples in the Field of Industrial Machinery (2nd Report)," *Hinshitsu Kanri* (Quality Control), vol. 15 (fall 1964), pp. 201–206; Mizuno, Furukawa,

and Oba (Tokyo Engineering University) and Watase (Suzuki Motor Corporation), "PERT and QC — Quality Evaluation in the Development of New Automobile Models," *Hinshitsu Kanri* (Quality Control), vol. 15 (fall 1964), special issue, pp. 207–211.

11

Education to Introduce the Seven New QC Tools

The seven new QC tools like other QC methods, have proven effective from the first as we have applied them to solve problems. Therefore, we hope that you will freely use each of the techniques illustrated in this book. The new tools are more effective however, if users are first given adequate education about and practice in their use. In this chapter we discuss three examples of education about and introduction of the seven new QC tools. Frst, we introduce the approach to education and training in classes held by the Japanese Union of Scientists and Engineers. Second, we discuss the popularization and implementation of the seven new QC tools by QC personnel from each factory in a class hosted by the central QC department of Company M. Finally, we discuss the progress toward universal use of the seven new QC tools in the TQC process at Company S. You will be headed in the right direction if you begin your education and training with one of the methods described in the first two sections and afterwards if your whole company or whole branch cooperates in their actual use, as described in the last section.

Education and training classes

Education methods

In this section, we introduce a method for educating participants to use the seven new QC tools more effectively. For corporations, day-to-day operations may require that the plan be flexible.

A comprehensive schedule is shown in Fig. 11.1. Classes are held once a month, over a period of nine months. Overall, 10 days are scheduled:

> *Practice:*   Participants divide into groups to solve a given problem using the method taught in the morning. Each group works together and presents its solution.
>
> *Homework:*   Participants apply the method taught that day to actual company problems and present their work during the next class.
>
> *Study project with company examples:*   Participants continue to work on departmental problems during the period of study. They prepare both interim and final reports.
>
> *Symposium:*   This is held on the final day of class and is open to nonparticipants. Examples of solutions found are introduced.

Each meeting's timetable is to be set up according to the daily schedule (see Fig. 11.2). Information discussed will differ according to the theme.

Recommended methods

Training site: Typically the number of participants range between 30 and 50. The meeting place can be either on or off company premises. Some care should be taken in considering location since the KJ method is presented on an overnight. Although group size can vary,

	A.M.	P.M.	
	Lecture and explanation of method	Study and practice	Notes
1st Month Date:	What are the new seven QC tools?	Tree charts, orientation: Projects, homework, etc.	Homework 1. Tree charts and graphs
2nd month Date:	Relations diagram	Practice with relations diagrams	Homework 2. Practice with relations diagrams; submit project topics.
3rd month Date:	PDPC	Practice with PDPC, direction on projects	Homework 3. PDPC
4th month Date:	Matrix diagram	Presentation of homework and discussion; first project interim report	Homework 4. Matrix diagram
5th month Date:	Interpretation of matrix diagram data; implementation of policies	Direction on projects; interim report 2	Homework 5. Policy implementation
6th month Date:	KJ method	Practice with KJ method	One night for study
7th month Date:	Arrow diagram method	Practice with arrow diagram method; direction on projects	Homework 6. Arrow diagram method
8th month Date:	Presentation of projects; questions and answers General discussion		
9th month Date:	Symposium: 1. Explanation of the seven new QC tools 2. Presentation of examples; debate 3. Special lecture	Symposium is open to nonclass members.	

FIGURE 11.1
Program (example)

if the training room is large enough, there is no need for small rooms for each group. Generally, it is sufficient that the place chosen be quiet and not subject to outside noise. Make certain that adequate supplies for the training are available, for example, poster paper, cards, and markers.

Time	Subject	Number of Data	Instructor
9:30–11:00 a.m.	Matrix diagram		
11:10–12:15 p.m.	Homework examples • Introduction and discussion		
	—Lunch break—		
1:15–4:35 p.m.	Presentation of homework • Project interim report— 25 minutes per person (presentation: 10 minutes; discussion: 15 minutes)		
4:45–5:30 p.m.	Class projects • General discussion		

FIGURE 11.2
Example of timetable

Note concerning the training period: Outside distractions should be avoided as much as possible during this period. In addition, to create a friendly atmosphere and to promote better communication among students belonging to the same company, participants should have time to relax at scheduled breaks. This increases the effectiveness of their work.

Lecturer: At JUSE-sponsored trainings either an experienced member of the company or an outside consultant serves as the lecturer. Each case has its own advantages and disadvantages. In some cases, however, it is more effective if outside people present the material. Depending on the size of the group several instructors are needed during practice sessions, to make the rounds and work with each group.

Extensive use of the seven new QC tools in company M

Company M has already begun to promote the extensive use of the seven new QC tools inside the company. The content of its initiative is not particularly outstanding; it serves as a simple example.

Staff participation in a seminar held outside the company

The QC department of the main office informed the QC department of each factory that seminars regarding the seven new QC tools would be held outside their company, and that at larger meetings the results of their use would be presented.

Starting the class inside the company

A class of volunteers was gathered, hosted by the QC department of the main office. The purpose of this regular meeting was to give lectures and practical training about the seven new QC tools to QC personnel at each factory so they could put the training into actual use at each factory. The agendas of these meetings follow:

First meeting

>   Overview of the seven new QC tools: If a lecturer is invited from outside, then the top executives will attend the meeting.
>
>   Lecture and practice: Practice with relations diagram and PDPC charts.
>
>   Homework: Study of a practical problem in which each participant is involved until the next meeting.

Second meeting

>   Lecture and practice: Tree diagram and matrix diagram.
>
>   Presentation of examples: Introduction of good examples inside or outside the company.
>
>   Homework: Study of a practical problem in which each participant is involved until the next meeting.

Third meeting

>   Presentation and critique of homework: Reports on homework; questions and answers, discussions, critique of participants' applications of the tools.
>
>   Report of representatives of each factory concerning their applications of the tools.

Fourth and succeeding meetings

Plan and adjust lectures, practices, reports, etc. at each meeting.

On the basis of Company M's experience the following observations can be made:

- One full day is needed for the initial lecture and practice of a single method.
- One half day is needed for further practice, including the presentation of results.
- A lecturer from outside is more effective with the participants than one from inside the company.
- The topics for practice should be chosen from among common and relatively simple problems known to the participants.
- Practice exercises should be carried out by groups of four to five members.
- The practice should not be dominated by particular members (participation should be relatively equal).
- The interval between meetings should be two to three months.

Other activities

The lectures about the seven new QC tools were promoted as activities during "Quality Month." The results of the establishment of the new tools were announced to the whole company through regular communication systems within the company. The seven QC tools were also promoted within the QC circles. The staff from the main office publicized the positive results achieved through use of the system and encouraged its use in each factory. The company backed the presentation outside the company of outstanding results achieved through use of the seven new QC tools. In doing so, it increased the participants' consciousness of quality control.

Introduction of the system to Factory A of Company S

General details

The activities of total quality control at Company S started when Factory T was awarded the Deming Prize in 1975. At the same time, Factory A started reviewing quality control. At that time, Factory A had several problems in the process of implementation. Among these were how to select critical points within the production processes of higher-level activities and how to coordinate production processes generally. These problems were solved by using relations diagrams and systematic diagrams from the seven new QC tools.

In addition to these steps, the factory used an arrow diagram for schedule control and a matrix diagram to grasp the relationships among processes during actual production. In research and development involving many uncertain factors and comparatively complex work, the PDPC method was used and produced several remarkable results.

The relations diagram, systematic diagram, and the arrow diagram were included in the QC manual, as shown in Fig. 11.3, and were put into actual use. In the area of technological research, program decision process charts were developed on all subjects and reviewed by engineering committees assigned to solve the problems.

Important points for implementation

The following points where found to be important during implementation. First, top management must have a thorough understanding of the method. At Factory A, the factory manager himself proposed the policy, provided guidance on how to use the method, and was eager to lead other members. Second, these methods must be used consistently during the development and establishment of process control. These methods should not be used in isolation. Third, through regular study meetings, all participants have become very conscious of the methods.

There was no definite procedure for the introduction. The steps taken at Factory A were as follows:

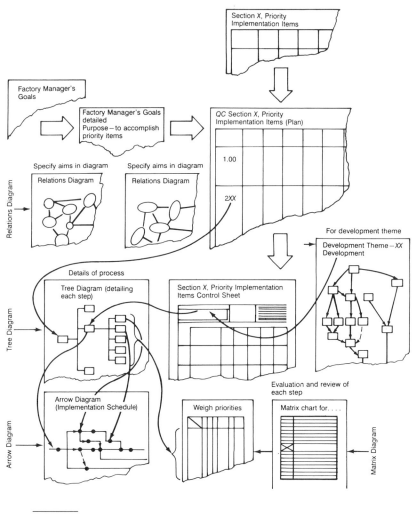

FIGURE 11.3
Process control and the seven tools for quality control

1. Introductory procedures. The introductory study and practice in the company was provided through on-the-job training. The presentation of examples was made at monthly meetings. The director of each department or division reported the problems of day-to-day operation and the process of their solution. Then discussions followed. After this meeting, a review meeting was scheduled. At the review meeting, participants pursued the improvement of matters pointed out at the monthly meeting and reviewed any new topics. The membership consisted of directors of divisions and higher staff. Then group study meetings were set up. Small groups of four to five people discussed how to apply the matrix diagram method and PDPC method to actual operations. This was mainly for staff members.

2. *Seminars outside the company.*   Factory A staff participated in the following seminars (participants included section managers, chiefs, and staff members): Seven New QC Tools Symposium, sponsored by JUSE; Multiple Variable Analysis Lecture, by JUSE.; and the Seven New QC Tools for QC Study Meeting.

———————

Conclusion

———————

Future of the seven new QC tools

We have tried to introduce simply the ideas, methods, and examples of actual use of the seven new QC tools. Since the first meeting of the QC Methods Research Division at the Osaka office of the Japanese Union of Scientists and Engineers, study and use of the seven new QC tools has been considerable. We hope to see this trend continue. Here are some of our hopes for the future of the seven new QC tools:

1. To supply more case studies of the seven new QC tools. In order for more people to understand and use the seven new QC tools we need to provide many examples of their application in different fields. Over the years JUSE has promoted this goal by sponsoring symposia and conferences to present case studies prepared by members as well as nonmembers in many different fields. Since many examples involve proprietary information, it is unfortunate that more case studies cannot be made available. For the future, however, we are content to hope that we will see more examples that effectively combine both the old and new QC methods.

2. *To incorporate the seven new QC tools into the QC system.* In the second section of Chap. 3, we reported the results of the application of the seven new tools in process control. We hope to see similar efforts made in each system of quality assurance, new product research, product liability, and so on. These efforts, combined with a union of new and traditional QC methods should facilitate more efficient establishment of corporate quality control systems.

3. *To use the seven new QC tools more comprehensively.* We have observed over the years that isolated use of individual QC tools does not produce significant results. Like the seven traditional tools, the seven new tools will become essential parts of quality control as the time and effort is taken to apply them companywide and to apply them consistently and in effective combinations with other tools.

4. *To promote the seven new QC tools to top management.* Top management understanding of the new tools and leadership is very important. To realize the first three goals, the chief executive officer of each corporation or division and the person in charge of corporate quality control must firmly direct the application of the seven new tools along with the traditional tools in the development of their processes and in every new product developed.

5. *To see more use of the relations diagram method and the PDPC method.* Some Japanese observers have commented that drawing up these charts is particularly difficult, because there is no formalized procedure for their preparation. Because of the very freedom with which they can be drawn, however, we anticipate wide and successful application. We are promoting this goal through our continuing course offerings and research.

6. *To discover and add new, effective methods to the seven new QC tools.* Our current concept of seven new tools does not preclude the development of additional tools. This means that we will continue to seek new methods applicable to the various control techniques, such as operations research, value engineering, creative techniques, management, and economics. In addition, we will initiate their application to quality control. The Osaka office of the Japanese Union of Scientists and Engineers has established the N Seminar, which grew from the QC Methods Research Seminar in April of 1978. We are

studying in the techniques (as described above) and their systematic use (as shown in item 2).

7. *To introduce the QC circle to the seven new QC tools.* The relations diagram, systematic diagram, matrix diagram, and program decision process chart (PDPC) do not have complicated rules; hence, they are not difficult to use. We promote the introduction of these methods specifically to QC circles as industrial problem-solving tools.

Index

BOOKS AVAILABLE FROM PRODUCTIVITY PRESS

Productivity Press publishes and distributes materials on productivity, quality improvement, and employee involvement for business and industry, academia, and the general market. Many products are direct source materials from Japan that have been translated into English for the first time and are available exclusively from Productivity. Supplemental services include conferences, seminars, in-house training programs, and industrial study missions. Send for free book catalog.

TQC Wisdom of Japan:
Managing for Total Quality Control
by Hajime Karatsu, translated by David J. Lu

As productivity goes up, the cost of quality comes down. And as quality improves, the cost to produce comes down. Karatsu, winner of a Deming Prize who has been involved with the quality movement in Japan since its inception, discusses the purpose and techniques of Total Quality Control (TQC), how it differs from QC, and why it is so effective. There is no better introduction to TQC than this book; essential reading for all American managers.
ISBN 0-915299-18-6 / 136 pages / $34.95

Poka-Yoke
Improving Product Quality by Preventing Defects
compiled by Nikkan Kogyo Shimbun, Ltd./Factory Magazine (ed.)
preface by Shigeo Shingo

If your goal is 100% zero defects, here is the book for you — a completely illustrated guide to poka-yoke (mistake-proofing) for supervisors and shop-floor workers. Many poka-yoke devices come from line workers and are implemented with the help of engineering staff. The result is better product quality — and greater participation by workers in efforts to improve your processes, your products, and your company as a whole.
ISBN 0-915299-31-1 / 288 pages / $59.95

Zero Quality Control
Source Inspection and the Poka-yoke System
by Shigeo Shingo, translated by Andrew P. Dillon

A remarkable combination of source inspection (to detect errors before they become defects) and mistake-proofing devices (to weed out defects before they can be passed down the production line) eliminates the need for statistical quality control. Shingo shows how this proven system for reducing defects to zero turns out the highest quality products in the shortest period of time. With over 100 specific examples illustrated. (Audio-visual training program also available.)
ISBN 0-915299-07-0 / 305 pages / $65.00

Productivity Press, Inc., Dept. BK, P.O. Box 3007, Cambridge, MA 02140 1-800-274-9911

Non-Stock Production
The Shingo System for Continuous Improvement
by Shigeo Shingo

Shingo, whose work at Toyota provided the foundation for JIT, teaches how to implement non-stock production in your JIT manufacturing operations. The culmination of his extensive writings on efficient production management and continuous improvement, his latest book is an essential companion volume to his other books on other key elements of JIT, including SMED and Poka-Yoke.
ISBN 0-915299-30-5 / 480 pages / $75.00

Managerial Engineering
Techniques for Improving Quality and Productivity in the Workplace
by Ryuji Fukuda

A proven path to managerial success, based on reliable methods developed by one of Japan's leading productivity experts and winner of the coveted Deming Prize for quality. Dr. W. Edwards Deming, world-famous consultant on quality, says that the book "provides an excellent and clear description of the devotion and methods of Japanese management to continual improvement of quality." (CEDAC training programs also available.)
ISBN 0-915299-09-7 / 206 pages / $34.95

Canon Production System
Creative Involvement of the Total Workforce
compiled by the Japan Management Association

A fantastic success story! Canon set a goal to increase productivity by three percent per month — and achieved it! The first book-length case study to show how to combine the most effective Japanese management principles and quality improvement techniques into one overall strategy that improves every area of the company on a continual basis. Shows how the major QC tools are applied in a matrix management model.
ISBN 0-915299-06-2 / 232 pages / $36.95

Productivity Press, Inc., Dept. BK, P.O. Box 3007, Cambridge, MA 02140 1-800-274-9911

BOOKS AVAILABLE FROM PRODUCTIVITY PRESS

Christopher, William F. **Productivity Measurement Handbook**
ISBN 0-915299-05-4 / 1983 / 680 pages / looseleaf / $137.95

Ford, Henry. **Today and Tomorrow** (originally published 1926)
ISBN 0-915299-36-4 / 1988 / 302 pages / hardcover / $24.95

Fukuda, Ryuji. **Managerial Engineering: Techniques for Improving Quality and Productivity in the Workplace**
ISBN 0-915299-09-7 / 1984 / 206 pages / hardcover / $34.95

Hatakeyama, Yoshio. **Manager Revolution! A Guide to Survival in Today's Changing Workplace**
ISBN 0-915299-10-0 / 1984 / 198 pages / hardcover / $24.95

Japan Human Resources Association. **The Idea Book: Improvement Through Total Employee Involvement**
ISBN 0-915299-22-4 / 1988 / 218 pages / $49.95

Japan Management Association and Constance E. Dyer. **Canon Production System: Creative Involvement of the Total Workforce**
ISBN 0-915299-06-2 / 1987 / 251 pages / hardcover / $36.95

Japan Management Association. **Kanban and Just-In-Time at Toyota: Management Begins at the Workplace, Revised Edition,** translated by David J. Lu
ISBN 0-915299-08-9 / 1986 / 224 pages / hardcover / $29.95

Karatsu, Hajime. **Tough Words for American Industry**
ISBN 0-915299-25-9 / 1988 / 179 pages / hardcover / $24.95

Karatsu, Hajime. **TQC Wisdom of Japan: Managing for Total Quality Control**
ISBN 0-915299-18-6 / 1988 / 138 pages / hardcover / $29.95

Lu, David J. **Inside Corporate Japan: The Art of Fumble-Free Management**
ISBN 0-915299-16-X / 1987 / 278 pages / hardcover / $24.95

Mizuno, Shigeru (ed.) **Management for Quality Improvement: The 7 New QC Tools**
ISBN 0-915299-29-1 / 1988 / 326 pages / hardcover / $59.95

Nakajima, Seiichi. **Introduction to Total Productive Maintenance**
ISBN 0-915299-23-2 / 1988 / 129 pages / $39.95

Nikkan Kogyo Shimbun. **Poka-yoke: Improving Product Quality by Preventing Defects**
ISBN 0-915299-31-3 / 1988 / 288 pages / $49.95

Ohno, Taiichi. **Toyota Production System: Beyond Large-Scale Production**
ISBN 0-915299-14-3 / 1988 / 176 pages / hardcover / $39.95

Ohno, Taiichi. **Workplace Management**
ISBN 0-915299-19-4 / 1988 / 176 pages / hardcover / $34.95

Ohno, Taiichi and Setsuo Mito. **Just-In-Time for Today and Tomorrow: A Total Management System**
ISBN 0-915299-20-8 / 1988 / 176 pages / hardcover / $34.95

Productivity Press, Inc., Dept. BK, P.O. Box 3007, Cambridge, MA 02140 1-800-274-9911

Shingo, Shigeo. **Non-Stock Production: The Shingo System for Continuous Improvement**
ISBN 0-915299-30-5 / 1988 / 480 pages / hardcover / $75.00

Shingo, Shigeo. **A Revolution in Manufacturing: The SMED System,** translated by Andrew P. Dillon
ISBN 0-915299-03-8 / 1985 / 383 pages / hardcover / $65.00

Shingo, Shigeo. **Zero Quality Control: Source Inspection and the Poka-yoke System,** translated by Andrew P. Dillon
ISBN 0-915299-07-0 / 1986 / 328 pages / hardcover / $65.00

Shingo, Shigeo. **The Sayings of Shigeo Shingo: Key Strategies for Plant Improvement,** translated by Andrew P. Dillon
ISBN 0-915299-15-1 / 1987 / 207 pages / hardcover / $36.95

Shinohara, Isao (ed.) **New Production System: JIT Crossing Industry Boundaries**
ISBN 0-915299-21-6 / 1988 / 218 pages / hardcover / $34.95

AUDIO-VISUAL PROGRAMS

Shingo, Shigeo. **The SMED System,** translated by Andrew P. Dillon
ISBN 0-915299-11-9 / 181 slides / 40 minutes / $749.00
ISBN 0-915299-27-5 / 2 videos / 40 minutes / $749.00

Shingo, Shigeo, **The Poka-yoke System**, translated by Andrew P. Dillon
ISBN 0-915299-13-5 / 224 slides / 45 minutes / $749.00
ISBN 0-915299-28-3 / 2 videos / 45 minutes / $749.00

TO ORDER: Write, phone or fax Productivity Press, Dept. BK, P.O. Box 3007, Cambridge, MA 02140, phone 1-800-274-9911, fax 617-868-3524.
Send check or charge to your credit card (American Express, Visa, MasterCard accepted).

U.S. ORDERS: Add $3 shipping for first book, $1 each additional. CT residents add 7.5% and MA residents 5% sales tax.

FOREIGN ORDERS: Payment must be made in U.S. dollars. For Canadian orders, add $8 shipping for first book, $1 each additional. Orders to other countries are on a pro forma basis; please indicate shipping method desired.

NOTE: Prices subject to change without notice.

UTAH STATE UNIVERSITY PARTNERS PROGRAM

Shigeo Shingo Medallion

Shigeo Shingo Prize for Manufacturing Excellence

announces the

Shigeo Shingo Prizes for Manufacturing Excellence

Awarded for Manufacturing Excellence Based on the Work of Shigeo Shingo

for North American Businesses, Students and Faculty

ELIGIBILITY

Businesses: Applications are due in late January. They should detail the quality and productivity improvements achieved through Shingo's manufacturing methods and similar techniques. Letters of intent are required by mid-November of the previous year.

Students: Applicants from accredited schools must apply by letter before November 15, indicating what research is planned. Papers must be received by early March.

Faculty: Applicants from accredited schools must apply by letter before November 15, indicating the scope of papers planned, and submit papers by the following March.

CRITERIA

Businesses: Quality and productivity improvements achieved by using Shingo's Scientific Thinking Mechanism (STM) and his methods, such as Single-Minute-Exchange of Die (SMED), Poka-yoke (defect prevention), Just-In-Time (JIT), and Non-Stock Production (NSP), or similar techniques.

Students: Creative research on quality and productivity improvements through the use and extension of Shingo's STM and his manufacturing methods: SMED, NSP, and Poka-yoke.

Faculty: Papers publishable in professional journals based on empirical, conceptual or theoretical applications and extensions of Shingo's manufacturing methods for quality and productivity improvements: SMED, Poka-yoke, JIT, and NSP.

PRIZES

Awards will be presented by Shigeo Shingo at Utah State University's annual Partners Productivity Seminar, held in April in Logan, Utah.

Five graduate and five undergraduate student awards of $2,000, $1,500, and $1,000 to first, second, and third place winners, respectively, and $500 to fourth and fifth place winners.

Three faculty awards of $3,000, $2,000 and $1,000, respectively.

Six Shigeo Shingo Medallions to the top three large and small business winners.

SHINGO PRIZE COMMITTEE

Committee members representing prestigious business, professional, academic and governmental organizations worldwide will evaluate the applications and select winners, assisted by a technical examining board.

Application forms and contest information may be obtained from the Shingo Prize Committee, College of Business, UMC 3521, Utah State University, Logan, UT, 84322, 801-750-2281. All English language books by Dr. Shingo can be purchased from the publisher, Productivity Press, P.O. Box 3007, Cambridge, MA 02140: call 1-800-274-9911 or 617-497-5146.

Japan's "Dean of Quality Consultants"

Dr. Shigeo Shingo is, quite simply, the world's leading expert on improving the manufacturing process. Known as "Dr. Improvement" in Japan, he is the originator of the Single-Minute Exchange of Die (SMED) concept and the Poka-yoke defect prevention system and one of the developers of the Just-In-Time production system that helped make Toyota the most productive automobile manufacturer in the world. His work now helps hundreds of other companies worldwide save billions of dollars in manufacturing costs annually.

The most sought-after consultant in Japan, Dr. Shingo has trained more than 10,000 people in 100 companies. He established and is President of Japan's highly-regarded Institute of Management Improvement and is the author of numerous books, including *Revolution in Manufacturing: The SMED System* and *Zero Quality Control: Source Inspection and the Poka-yoke System*. His newest book, *Non-Stock Production*, concentrates on expanding U.S. manufacturers' understanding of stockless production.

Dr. Shingo's genius is his understanding of exactly why products are manufactured the way they are, and then transforming that understanding into a workable system for low-cost, high-quality production. In the history of international manufacturing, Shingo stands alongside such pioneers as Robert Fulton, Henry Ford, Frederick Taylor, and Douglas McGregor as one of the key figures in the quest for improvement.

His world-famous SMED system is known as "The Heart of Just-In-Time Manufacturing" for (1) reducing set-up time from hours to minutes; (2) cutting lead time from months to days; (3) slashing work-in-progress inventory by up to 90%; (4) involving employees in team problem solving; (5) 99% improvement in quality; and (6) 70% reduction in floor space.

Shigeo Shingo has been called the father of the second great revolution in manufacturing.
— Quality Control Digest

The money-saving, profit-making ideas... set forth by Shingo could do much to help U.S. manufacturers reduce set-up time, improve quality and boost productivity ... all for very little cash.
Tooling & Production Magazine

When Americans think about quality today, they often think of Japan. But when the Japanese think of quality, they are likely to think of Shigeo Shingo, ... architect of Toyota's now famous production system.
Boardroom Report

Shingo's visit to our plant was significant in making breakthroughs in productivity we previously thought impossible. The benefits... are more far-reaching than I ever anticipated.
Gifford M. Brown, Plant Mgr.
Ford Motor Company